drink·ol·o·gy

drink·ol·o·gy

THE ART AND SCIENCE
OF THE COCKTAIL

REVISED AND UPDATED EDITION

JAMES WALLER

with contributions by
ANDREW MILLER

Illustrations by

stewart, tabori & chang

NEW YORK

Published in 2010 by Stewart, Tabori & Chang
An imprint of ABRAMS

Text copyright © 2010 Thumb Print New York, Inc.
Illustrations © 2010 Glenn Wolff

Library of Congress Cataloging-in-Publication Data

Waller, James.
  Drinkology : the art and science of the cocktail / James Waller with contributions by Andrew Miller ; illustrations by Glenn Wolff. — Rev. and updated ed.
      p. cm.
  Includes bibliographical references and index.
  ISBN 978-1-58479-828-6 (alk. paper)
  1. Cocktails. 2. Bartending. I. Miller, Andrew, 1964- II. Title.
  TX951.W28 2010
  641.8'74--dc22

                                    2009051838

Designed by Jay Anning, Thumb Print

The text of this book was composed in Adobe Caslon.

Printed and bound in China
10 9 8 7 6 5 4 3 2 1

Stewart, Tabori & Chang books are available at special discounts when purchased in quantity for premiums and promotions as well as fundraising or educational use. Special editions can also be created to specification. For details, contact special-sales@abramsbooks.com or the address below.

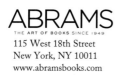

THE ART OF BOOKS SINCE 1949
115 West 18th Street
New York, NY 10011
www.abramsbooks.com

For Nina Cassian

"Highballs and cocktails—
the long and the short of it."

—William Powell, as Nick Charles,

The Thin Man

ACKNOWLEDGMENTS

M ANY PEOPLE DESERVE TO BE HEARTILY TOASTED FOR THEIR contributions to this volume. First and foremost, my thanks go to Andrew Miller, whose introductions to several of *Drinkology*'s recipe chapters remain as witty and informative as ever.

A special debt of gratitude is again owed to *Drinkology*'s superlative illustrator, Glenn Wolff, whose new drawings for the revised edition make it all the lovelier.

Next in line to receive my thanks—a little slurred after so many cocktails, but certainly heartfelt—are the core members of *Drinkology*'s tasting crew: my business partner (and the ingenious designer of this book), Jay Anning; my life partner, Jim O'Connor; and my great friends Betsy Keller and Michael Ross—both of whom participated in creating many of the revised edition's new recipes. Thanks go, too, to my *Drinkology Eats* coauthor Ramona Ponce, her husband Eric Mueller, and her sister Rachel Ponce, for organizing a sake-cocktail-tasting evening that was the inspiration for this edition's new chapter on sake.

Two of my grad students in the Technical Communications program at NYU-Poly provided notable help: Nicole Martindale and Fabricio Silva. Fabricio's knowledge of Brazilian culture—and his research foray to Newark, New Jersey's Ironbound district—provided essential background for the sidebar on cachaça. The ongoing interest and enthusiasm of a few other friends and colleagues—Joseph Aguiar,

Mary O'Connor, Paul DeSandre, Elisa Linsky, Jack Lamplough, Susan Sully, and Chris Andersson (who never met a typo he could overlook)—merit my deep appreciation.

Several food- and cocktail-world friends deserve special mention on general principles: Martha Hopkins, Christine Sismondo, Debra Argen, and Ed Nesta have graciously offered support and assistance through long stretches of the Drinkology series' long, strange trip. I thank them. I also thank the organizers of the annual Tales of the Cocktail festival in New Orleans, not just for the opportunities they've given me, but also for the enormous part they've played and are playing in inspiring interest in cocktails nationally and internationally.

A number of people who contributed to the original edition—and whose contributions continue to inform the new book—must be thanked again: Denell Downum, Holly Jennings, Randy Sonderman, Saed Ibrhim, and Marija Vukovic. The years have separated me from some of them, but they are not forgotten.

Finally, I raise my glass to the past and present staff at Stewart, Tabori & Chang who've played the critical role in *Drinkology*'s success. To STC publisher Leslie Stoker: Thanks for your belief in this book and for your shepherding of the entire Drinkology series into print. To my former editor, Marisa Bulzone: It could not have happened without you. To my current editor, Kate Norment: I couldn't be happier that you, with whom I've worked so often and so well, took over this project. Without STC's dedication, *Drinkology* would be nothing but a pink elephant in my bloodshot eye.

Cheers to one and all. A round of drinks for the house.

—JAMES WALLER

Preface to the Revised Edition

ALL TOO OFTEN, WHEN THINGS CHANGE, THEY CHANGE FOR THE worse. Fortunately, in the world of cocktails, that's not been the case. Over the seven years since the first edition of *Drinkology* was released, cocktail culture has changed enormously—and, for the most part, enormously for the better.

Seven years ago, it was difficult (even in New York City, where *Drinkology* was then based) to find any brand or type of bitters except good old Angostura. Now, numerous specialty shops carry a range of these essential elixirs. Seven years ago, you'd be hard pressed to find a single bottle of rye whiskey or absinthe in most American liquor stores; today, ryes and absinthes—some created by small, startup distillers dedicated to making top-quality products—are available in better liquor shops almost everywhere. Seven years ago, it was the rare bar or restaurant that *truly* cared about the proper mixing and serving of cocktails. Today, such establishments, while not quite thick on the ground, have opened their doors in cities nationwide. Back then, few newspapers and magazines had cocktail columns; now, many do—a trend complemented by a veritable explosion in the number of cocktail-themed websites. And *Drinkology* is willing to bet that, back in 2003, few younger drinkers (and few bartenders!) would have known what a Negroni is, or a Corpse Reviver, or a Ramos Fizz. That, too, has wonderfully changed.

This new edition of *Drinkology* celebrates these and other developments, while, we hope, retaining its jaundiced eye when observing certain aspects of cocktail culture—for instance, the metastasis of a class of cocktail "experts" whose main, self-imposed duty, it appears, is to scold those who prefer to make a given drink in any manner that strays, however minutely, from the purported "original" recipe. Fie, we say, to such fundamentalists. The important thing is that a cocktail should *taste good*.

That's the standard *Drinkology* means to keep on raising. When we prepared the book's first edition, we were assiduous about taste-testing all the recipes; we've carried that tradition forward, subjecting all the new recipes in the book—there are about forty, many of them original—to thoroughgoing evaluation. We've also learned a lot—about cocktail lore, history, ingredients, and so forth—in the interim since the first edition's publication. That increased knowledge is, we hope, reflected in this new book's pages: Mistakes have been corrected, nuances adjusted. Recipes for several important drinks that, through inexcusable oversight, did not make it into the first edition have been added here.

But we've also saved a great deal from the original—not just most recipes but also an irreverent attitude and a sensibility that emphasizes the practical. We see little worth, for instance, in including recipes calling for exotic ingredients that even world travelers have difficulty finding, and, while admiring their creativity, we have limited patience for enthusiasts who insist that you *simply must* make your own bitters, infuse your own flavored vodkas, and marinate you own maraschinos. In short: *Drinkology* always keeps the home bartender (your resources and your time) in mind—and *Drinkology*'s "art" of the cocktail is *always* the art of the possible.

—James Waller

Contents

Your Bar

THERE ARE A LOT OF PEOPLE WHO, WHEN THEY FIRST PAY A VISIT to a new friend's house, head directly for the bookshelf. And there are those who, when they're just getting to know you, insist that you tell them what's on your iPod. Such people tend to justify their snoopiness by saying, "Your taste in books [or music] gives me insight into your personality." They have a point: everyone is, to some extent, defined by his or her tastes.

But why limit one's nosiness to an investigation of the bookshelves or the MP3 player's contents? To find out what someone is really like, it makes just as much sense to explore his or her bar. If the person you're getting to know has lots of poetry on the shelf and an interesting selection of pop, jazz, and classical music on the iPod— but the liquor cabinet contains only an unopened bottle of grenadine and a liter of cheap vodka with three fingers' worth of hooch left at the bottom—is this a friendship you want seriously to pursue?

Those who drink are, at least in part, defined by *what they drink*: the keg-emptying frat boy, the encyclopedically pretentious oenophile—these are familiar types. And, just as important, people are defined by the kinds of hospitality they offer their friends and acquaintances. If, when you come to my place, I head for the fridge, crack open a couple of discount-priced brewskies, hand one to you, and start chugging my own, that marks me as, let's say, a specific sort of individual. If, after you've entered my apartment, I ask you what you'd like to drink—but quickly add that your choices are limited to bourbon, Diet Coke, orange juice, or, yeah, I think there's an open bottle of white wine around here somewhere—that defines me as another (perhaps equally objectionable) sort of person.

You don't want to be either of these people. (That's why you're reading this book.) You want to be the sort of person who, when asking friends, "What can I get you to drink?" *means* "What can I get you to drink? (I'll try my best to make something you'll like.)" In other words, while you *can* think of *Drinkology* as just another bartending book (with a bunch of recipes you mostly won't try), it might be wiser to think of it as a course in self-improvement.

COCKTAIL ART AND SCIENCE

Drinkology's subtitle—"The Art and Science of the Cocktail"—is meant to be taken seriously. Anyone who has ever watched a great bartender in action knows that crafting a superior cocktail requires considerable artistry. (This book, however, can't teach you the sophisticated choreography that great bartenders are capable of; for that, you may need a stint in bartending school and some sizable on-the-job experience, as well as innate talent.)

But the art of a cocktail or mixed drink extends beyond the making. It has to do with the thing itself. There are few sights more aesthetically pleasing than a well-crafted, well-presented Manhattan: the comforting reddish-amber glow, the shimmering (and daunting!) meniscus, the subtle aroma rendered just a bit tangy by the dash of bitters. (Why, *Drinkology* would whip up a batch right now if we didn't have to keep on writing.)

That a well-made cocktail is, in its way, a work of art is easy to grasp. But *science*? Where does the science come in?

Well, science, first and foremost, is about experimentation. If you look in a dozen different bartending guides, you're likely to find a dozen different methods for preparing, say, an Old Fashioned. To find the recipe that best suits your taste, you're probably going to have to do some experimenting. This book won't save you *all* that trouble—though "trouble" is an odd word for what might turn out to be a very pleasurable endeavor—but it does intend to give you some basic assistance.

In deciding which recipes to include, *Drinkology*'s stalwart, self-sacrificing taste-testers have made (and dutifully sipped) hundreds upon hundreds of mixed drinks. The recipes contained here are the ones we like best, or—since no one likes *every* kind of mixed drink—dislike least. In many cases, the comments that accompany the recipes give you guidance on which drinks you might like to try—and which you might avoid, depending on your preferences. (For example, if you don't enjoy sour tastes, you might do yourself the favor of eschewing the French 75, page 121, whose combination of gin, lemon juice, and champagne makes for a pretty mouth-puckering brew.)

TOOLS OF THE TRADE

So now you've donned your lab coat and are ready to start experimenting. But wait. First, you need the materials to work with—including not just the liquor and other ingredients but also the equipment and glassware necessary for pursuing this artistic-scientific enterprise.

Most other bartending guides pretend that each of us has infinite resources to devote to setting up a bar. That's not this book's point of view. It's probably not the case that you're immediately going to go out and buy a dozen each of 20 different kinds of glassware, 30 or more different bartending tools, and every kind of liquor ever distilled on this alcohol-friendly planet. Even if you've got the cash, where the hell would you *put* all that stuff? Even real saloons put a limit on the kinds of liquor they stock and the kinds of glassware and equipment they use. Unless you've got space (including *storage* space) galore, an inexhaustible budget, and time enough to do all that shopping, you'll have to do the same.

For that reason, *Drinkology* gives you advice (and lists of necessities) for setting up three kinds, or "levels," of bars: the Basic Bar, the Better Bar, and the (Almost) Professional Bar. We introduce you, of course, to the many kinds of glassware and equipment that exist, but we don't make the mistake of assuming that you'll want—or need—all these things. A good, well-functioning bar actually requires very little: a few different kinds of glasses, a number of essential pieces of equipment, and a limited array of spirits, other alcoholic beverages, and mixers and condiments. Let's start, though, by showing you the full range of glassware and bartending equipment that you have to choose from.

GLASSWARE

Walk into any good home-furnishings store and you'll be dazzled by the array of glasses available for purchase. If you're just setting up a home bar, you may be awestruck by the variety: What are all these glasses *for,* anyway, and which do you *need* to buy?

We're here to help. The drawings that accompany this section illustrate the basic shapes and sizes of 21 of the glasses commonly used for serving mixed drinks and other alcoholic beverages. (In addition, each of *Drinkology's* recipes is accompanied by a drawing showing the glass or glasses most appropriate for serving that particular drink.) The ways to use the various glasses are described below, but first some words of caution are in order.

The drawings show *extremely* generic versions of the glasses—sort of the Platonic Form of each type. And they're scaled to illustrate the glasses' relative sizes, though here, too, our renderings represent an "ideal" that may or may not closely resemble what you actually encounter in a real-world store. The truth is, glassware designers play around with these basic shapes and sizes all the time—reshaping them, distorting them, decorating them, making them distinctive-looking in uncountable ways. There's also been a tendency, in recent years, to "supersize" glassware. A set of martini glasses you might find in an antiques store will probably look absurdly small to you—as if they were fashioned for a cocktail party in Munchkin City.

Why is this important? For the simple reason that in most cases you want a drink to fill—or nearly fill—the glass it's served in. Recipe-makers (including *Drinkology's* crew) like to be *precise* about measurements, but the near-infinite variety of glasses available today wreaks havoc with that intention. We simply have no way of knowing whether the amounts we specify will suit the glasses you're using. That's not just a disclaimer; it's also another invitation to experiment. If our measurements turn out to be too small for your cocktail or highball glasses, adjust the recipes accordingly—always trying to keep the proportions of ingredients more or less the same. (By the way, you should know that *Drinkology*'s taste-testers used an eight-ounce cocktail glass—large, but hardly gigantic by today's glassware standards—and tried to make sure that each cocktail recipe filled the glass at least half to two-thirds full.)

Something else you need to know is that some kinds of glasses seem to be nearing extinction. Mixed drinks go in and out of fashion, and so do the glasses in which they're meant to be served. Walk into a glassware store today, and you'll be confronted with an immense range of margarita and cocktail glasses, but you'll have difficulty finding even a single sour glass. Hunting down a set of pousse-café glasses could well turn out to be a lifetime's endeavor.

With those warnings out of the way, here's the list of basic bar glasses—including the endangered species—and what they're used for:

BEER
MUG

BRANDY
SNIFTER

Beer mug: The name says all you need to know.

Brandy snifter: The balloon shape of a snifter's bowl is specially designed to capture the aroma of brandy and aromatic liqueurs.

Champagne flute: Because it so tightly restricts the liquid's surface area—preventing too many bubbles from escaping too quickly—this tall, narrow, stemmed glass will keep champagne effervescing longer than the more traditional champagne saucer. (The champagne saucer is not illustrated; saucers are so inferior as vehicles for champagne that virtually no one uses them any longer.)

CHAMPAGNE
FLUTE

Cocktail glass: A.k.a. the martini glass, this stemmed glass with its conical bowl is *the* glass for serving shaken and stirred cocktails.

Collins glass: Sometimes called an iced-tea glass, this tall and narrow glass is an elegantly streamlined vehicle not only for collinses but for a wide range of summertime refreshers.

COCKTAIL
GLASS

COLLINS
GLASS

Cordial glass: This little glass is designed for sipping liqueurs (especially the sweeter, not-so-aromatic kinds). Cordial glasses come in a very wide variety of shapes; not all are stemmed.

CORDIAL
GLASS

Double old-fashioned glass: This glass, often called a double rocks glass, is suitable for larger lowballs.

DOUBLE OLD-
FASHIONED
GLASS

Highball glass: Also called a tumbler, it's the glass of choice for large iced drinks.

HIGHBALL
GLASS

HURRICANE
GLASS

IRISH
COFFEE
GLASS

MARGARITA
GLASS

OLD-FASHIONED
GLASS

PARFAIT
GLASS

PILSNER
GLASS

POUSSE-
CAFÉ GLASS

Hurricane glass: A relatively recent invention, the hurricane glass was designed to hold the popular New Orleans libation after which it's named, though it's also serviceable for a range of frozen and tropical drinks.

Irish coffee glass: This heatproof, stemmed, and handled glass is the best choice for serving a wide range of hot drinks.

Margarita glass: Designed specifically for the tequila-based cocktail after which it's named, the margarita glass is also perfect for serving a wide range of frozen drinks.

Old-fashioned glass: The classic "rocks" glass is made-to-order for smaller lowballs, including (as the name denotes) Old Fashioneds.

Parfait glass: These elegant little glasses are used for some dessertlike, liqueur-based drinks.

Pilsner glass: This large and dramatic beer glass was created for the Czech lager known as Pilsner, though it's suitable for almost any beer.

Pousse-café glass: The straight-sided pousse-café glass is meant for layered drinks in which a variety of liqueurs are floated one atop the other.

Punch cup: Resembling miniature teacups (without saucers), punch cups are often made of crystal and usually come in sets accompanying a matching punchbowl.

PUNCH
CUP

Red wine glass: As the name indicates, this larger of the two standard wine glasses is used for serving red wine, but it's also appropriate for some large tropical drinks and for wine-based concoctions such as sangarees.

Sherry glass: This delicate, stemmed glass was created, of course, for sipping sherry, but it doubles nicely as a cordial glass.

RED WINE
GLASS

Shot glass: Some bartenders employ the shot glass for measuring (it holds about one and a half ounces, full), but today shot glasses are primarily used for shooters—shots of liquor downed in a single gulp.

SHERRY
GLASS

SHOT
GLASS

Sour glass: Looking like a stumpy champagne flute, the sour glass is the preferred vehicle not just for sours but also for the lemon-spiral-garnished drinks known as crustas.

SOUR
GLASS

White wine glass: Slightly smaller (and often narrower-mouthed) than its red-wine sibling, the white wine glass is recommended for a few iced mixed drinks.

WHITE WINE
GLASS

This basic list of common glassware types is, needless to say, a pretty long one. But don't let that overwhelm or depress you. *Drinkology* doesn't own all these glasses, and neither does any bar we've ever gone to. You can, without embarrassment, serve almost any of the cocktails and other mixed drinks in this book if you have just a few types of glasses. The most essential are these:

Wine glasses (red wine glasses are probably the more versatile)
Highball glasses
Double old-fashioned glasses
Old-fashioned glasses
Champagne flutes
Cocktail glasses

Unless you're in the habit of frequently hosting large gatherings, you can certainly get away with having eight or ten of each (or just half a dozen if storage space is at a premium in your cramped digs). And unless you've got money to burn, you'll be wise to choose glassware that's moderately priced and easy to replace. Glasses, as you may recall, break.

BAR EQUIPMENT

When deciding which of the multitude of kinds of bartending equipment to illustrate, *Drinkology* elected only to show those pieces that you might be unfamiliar with. Even the most basic bar requires a fair amount of other stuff: a good, sharp paring knife; a cutting board; a churchkey or other bottle and can opener; measuring spoons and a measuring cup; an ice bucket and (if you're the persnickety type) ice tongs; sponges and bar towels; beverage napkins; and toothpicks (or, if you want to get all fancy, those little, plastic, sword-shaped skewers known as *cocktail spears*). If you're serving frozen drinks, you'll need a blender—preferably of the professional caliber that's capable of grinding ice. And if you're mixing a batch of Bloody Marys or Martinis, you'll need a glass pitcher and, probably, a stirring rod. But we figure you already know what this stuff looks like, and what it's for.

Here, then, are some of the more specialized kinds of equipment used by bartenders. Only a relative few of these pieces are must-haves: a jigger-pony measure, a mixing glass (though you can make do with any large, heavyweight glass), a barspoon, a cocktail shaker (if you choose a Boston shaker, you'll need a strainer, as well), some sort of corkscrew, and some sort of device for juicing lemons and limes. Whether to invest in any of the rest of this is entirely your call.

ABSINTHE SPOON

BAR SPOON

BOSTON SHAKER

Absinthe spoon: Resembling a pie server with holes, this unusual tool has a single use: to hold the sugar cubes over which the liquor is poured in an Absinthe Drip (recipe, page 158).

Bar spoon: A long-handled spoon is an essential tool; a professional bar spoon has a spiraled handle that (supposedly) makes it easier to pour layered drinks.

Boston shaker: This kind of shaker, consisting only of a larger metal cup and a smaller glass, is the type preferred by most bartenders. *Drinkology* recommends the slightly different, British version of this shaker (see page 50).

CHAMPAGNE
STOPPER

CITRUS
REAMER

CITRUS
SQUEEZER

CITRUS STRIPPER

GRATER

If you use a Boston shaker, you'll also need a cocktail strainer—the julep or the Hawthorne variety—to pour the drink.

Champagne stopper: The illustration shows just one of many available kinds of champagne stoppers; *Drinkology* believes that keeping champagne bubbly is a losing proposition, but if you want to try one of these devices, be our guest.

Citrus reamer: This handy wooden tool is perfect for making small amounts of lemon or lime juice. But it's tiring on the wrist, so invest in an electric juicer if you're intending to throw a Daiquiri or Margarita party.

Citrus squeezer: Heavy, enameled, two-handled citrus squeezers like the one pictured make quick work of juicing lemons and limes. (But they work only for smaller-size fruit.)

Citrus stripper (channel knife): This little knife with a weirdly shaped blade enables you to make lemon twists lickety-split; the technique is explained on page 30.

Grater: You'll need a grater for the freshly grated nutmeg that many creamy drinks require as a garnish. (You may, of course, affront your guests by using ground nutmeg instead.) A variety of spice graters are available, but *Drinkology* is infatuated with the Microplane grater pictured here. It's an astonishingly effective tool.

Hawthorne strainer: You've undoubtedly noticed professional bartenders using this tool; the side with the wire coil fits snugly inside the shaker cup (or mixing glass), and the metal prongs hold the strainer securely to the cup's lip.

Jigger-pony measure: This is your absolutely essential measuring tool; its use is discussed in detail on page 41.

Julep strainer: *Drinkology* prefers this oval-shaped strainer to the Hawthorne strainer, only because we find it requires less dexterity to use. Feel free to differ with us on this score.

Mixing glass: Stirring cocktails requires a mixing glass. The glass component of a Boston shaker can double as a mixing glass, but the best mixing glasses, like the one shown here, are spouted for easy pouring.

Muddlers: Muddlers are pestles used to smash up fruit or mint leaves in a shaker cup, glass, or julep cup. (Muddling technique is discussed on pages 44 and 45.) Muddler #1 is the traditional, baseball bat–shaped variety. Muddler #2 is a newfangled type, with a stainless-steel handle and plastic tip; it's easier to use and more effective at pulverizing.

HAWTHORNE
STRAINER

JIGGER-
PONY

JULEP
STRAINER

MIXING
GLASS

MUDDLER
#1

MUDDLER
#2

SPEED
POURER

STANDARD
SHAKER

WAITER'S
FRIEND

Speed pourer: Professional bartenders use speed pourers, which fit tightly inside a liquor bottle's mouth, to make the job of pouring a drink easier. One problem: if a speed pourer is left in a bottle, the liquor inside will evaporate, so make sure to remove the pourer and recap the bottle once the party's over.

Standard shaker: This three-piece shaker (cup, strainer top, and lid) is easier to use than a Boston shaker, and we definitely recommend it for large mixed drinks (those with more than four or five ounces of liquid ingredients). But it can be difficult to pry the top from the cup for cleaning once the cocktail's been poured.

Waiter's friend: This ingenious device incorporates a bottle opener, a corkscrew, and a little foldaway knife for removing the foil that surrounds the top of a wine bottle.

YOUR LIQUOR CABINET AND PANTRY

Now we come to the most challenging aspect of setting up a bar: which liquors and other ingredients should you buy—and in what quantities? These are difficult calls, since the answers depend entirely on the kinds of mixed drinks you and your friends most enjoy. The best that *Drinkology* can do is to offer some educated suggestions. An important principle to keep in mind is that your bar, no matter what its scope, should enable you to create a fairly wide range of cocktails while also accommodating your beer-drinking, wine-drinking, straight liquor–drinking, and *non*drinking friends. (Beers and still wines don't appear on our checklists; suffice it to say that a decently stocked, company-ready bar should include, at the least, twelve or more bottles of good domestic or imported beer—chilled—as well as two or more bottles of dry red wine and two or more of dry white wine.) In the checklists that follow, we mostly shy away from recommending specific brands, since this is a matter of personal taste (and, often, of personal budget). Note that wines—still and sparkling—should be kept in a dark, cool place, with the bottles lying on their sides. Champagne should not be kept in the refrigerator for more than a few hours before serving.

THE BASIC BAR

Having on hand all the liquors, condiments and garnishes, and mixers on the lists that immediately follow will permit you to whip up a goodly number of the mixed drinks that appear in this book—including most of the classic concoctions. These lists don't represent an absolute minimum—you might, for example, decide that you'll prepare rum- or tequila-based drinks so seldom that there's no need to keep those liquors on hand. But this basic bar is a good starting point. (In fact, if you don't have much storage space, it's also a good *stopping* point.) A couple of notes: When stocking up on mixers, it's more economical in the long run to buy twelve-ounce cans of soda and six-ounce cans of canned juices. (If you buy larger bottles or cans, you may end up simply wasting the soda or juice that goes undrunk.) In all the lists that follow, "1 bottle" of liquor, unless otherwise noted, means one 750-milliliter bottle (the size that, ever-nostalgic for pre-metric days, *Drinkology* still insists on calling a "fifth").

Liquor

1 bottle of bourbon (preferably small-batch bourbon)

1 bottle of French brandy or cognac

1 bottle of Canadian blended whiskey

2 bottles of brut champagne or other dry sparkling wine

1 bottle of coffee liqueur

1 bottle of Cointreau, triple sec, or white curaçao

1 bottle of dry gin

1 bottle of Pernod, anisette, or other anise-flavored liqueur

1 bottle of ruby port

1 bottle of light rum

1 bottle of dark rum

1 bottle of blended scotch

1 bottle of dry sherry

1 bottle of white tequila

1 bottle of dry vermouth

1 bottle of sweet vermouth

1 bottle of imported vodka

1 375-ml ("pint") bottle of dark crème de cacao

1 375-ml bottle of white crème de cacao

1 375-ml bottle of white crème de menthe

1 375-ml bottle of green crème de menthe

2 or 3 bottles of other liqueurs or flavored brandies (your choice)

Condiments and Garnishes

Angostura bitters

grenadine

Rose's lime juice

Tabasco sauce

Worcestershire sauce

powdered (confectioners') sugar

simple syrup

superfine sugar

kosher salt

black pepper

whole nutmeg

eggs

lemons

limes

oranges

maraschino cherries

green (Spanish) olives (unpitted or pitted, with or without pimientos)

Mixers
club soda or seltzer
cola
ginger ale
tonic water
cranberry juice
grapefruit juice
orange juice
pineapple juice
tomato juice
cream (heavy or light) or half-
    and-half
whole milk

THE BETTER BAR

Expanding your liquor cabinet and pantry will greatly amplify the range of mixed drinks you can create. For a better bar—a bar that will no doubt be the envy of your friends (that may even threaten to become your drinking friends' home away from home)—add the following liquors, condiments and garnishes, and mixers to the basic lists above. One of the chief advantages of having these ingredients on hand is that they will allow you to create a wide variety of fruity, rum-based tropical concoctions.

Liquor
1 bottle of amaretto
1 bottle of applejack or apple
    brandy
1 bottle of cachaça or pisco
1 bottle of crème de cassis
1 bottle of Dubonnet Rouge
1 bottle of Irish whiskey
1 bottle of Lillet Blanc
1 bottle of maraschino liqueur
1 bottle of gold rum
1 bottle of single-malt scotch
1 bottle of gold tequila
1 bottle of lemon-flavored vodka
1 375-ml ("pint") bottle of
    apricot brandy
1 375-ml bottle of cherry
    brandy
1 375-ml bottle of peach
    schnapps or peach brandy
1 375-ml bottle of Southern
    Comfort

5 or 6 bottles (375 ml or 750 ml) of other liqueurs and fruit-flavored brandies chosen from the following list: B&B, Bailey's Irish Cream, Bénédictine, blackberry brandy, blue curaçao, Campari, Chambord, green Chartreuse, crème de banane, Frangelico, Galliano, Grand Marnier, melon liqueur, orange curaçao, Sambuca, sloe gin, strawberry liqueur

Condiments and Garnishes

almond syrup or orgeat syrup
orange bitters
Peychaud's bitters
ripe bananas
selection of fresh fruit (berries, kiwi, melon, pineapple, etc.)
vanilla ice cream
whipped cream (canned, or heavy cream for whipping)
cocktail onions

Mixers

cream of coconut
lemon-lime soda
selection of fruit nectars and juices (papaya, passion fruit, peach, etc.)

THE (ALMOST) PROFESSIONAL BAR

There is no end to the kinds of liquor, beer, and wine you might have on hand. An almost professional-level home bar might include a number of different kinds of beer (domestic and imported) and a selection of, at a minimum, two or three dry red wines and two or three dry whites, as well as a sweeter white (an off-dry Riesling, say). Compiling a superior bar isn't just a matter of adding different *kinds* of liquor to the basic lists above; it also—and just as importantly—involves *deepening* your collection of the "standards"—especially aperitifs (aromatized wines), bourbon, brandy, gin, rum, scotch, and vodka. It's a great pleasure to be able to offer your guests options: several kinds of small-batch bourbons or single-malt scotches, say, or a variety of different gins.

That's a long way of saying that the lists below are by no means complete. But, if you were to possess all the ingredients given here and in the other lists above, you'd be able to make virtually any of the mixed drinks in *Drinkology*. More than that, you'd also be able to satisfy any guest—even the most demanding—with a more-than-acceptable selection of aperitifs, hard liquors, and after-dinner libations.

Liquor

2 or 3 additional bottles of aperitifs (Byrrh, Cynar, Dubonnet Blanc, Lillet Rouge, etc.)

1 bottle of apple schnapps

1 bottle of armagnac

1 or 2 additional bottles of small-batch bourbon

1 bottle of butterscotch schnapps

1 bottle of V.S.O.P. cognac

1 bottle of Fernet Branca

1 bottle of grappa or other *eau de vie*

1 bottle of Madeira

1 bottle of Pimm's Cup No. 1

1 bottle of tawny port

1 bottle of *añejo* rum

1 bottle of Jamaican rum

1 bottle of Myers's Rum

2 or 3 additional bottles of single-malt scotch

1 bottle Plymouth Gin

1 bottle of cream sherry

2 or 3 additional bottles of flavored vodka (orange, pepper, vanilla, etc.)

1 bottle St-Germain elder-flower liqueur

1 bottle Liqueur Créole Clément Créole Shrubb

1 375-ml ("pint") bottle of Drambuie

1 375-ml bottle of peppermint schnapps

1 375-ml bottle of 151-proof
    rum
5 or 6 additional bottles (375
    ml or 750 ml) of assorted
    liqueurs

Condiments and Garnishes
apples
ground allspice
chocolate chips
ground cinnamon

cocoa powder
fresh horseradish
fresh mint leaves
orange blossom water
orange bitters
vanilla extract

Mixers
canned beef broth
Clamato juice
ginger beer

SWEET NEWS ON BITTERS

Those of you who think booze is medicine have history on your side. Numerous kinds of liquors and mixed drinks (e.g., juleps, the gin and tonic) originally had medicinal uses, and, of course, a goodly gulp of any potent potable was de-riguaur patient prep for surgery in the days before anesthesia. But the concoctions known as *bitters* underscore the age-old connection between medicine and alcohol.

Bitters—high-alcohol distillations of various kinds of flowers, herbs, barks, roots, citrus-fruit peels, and other botanicals—were the over-the-counter medications of an earlier era. The apothecaries who created these tonics claimed they offered relief from upset stomach and a host of other maladies. (French and Italian bitters are referred to as *digestifs* and *digestivos,* respectively; both terms mean "aids to digestion.")

One famous bitter-brewing chemist was the early nineteenth-century Creole druggist Antoine Peychaud, who, according to dubious legend, invented the cocktail when he stirred together brandy, sugar, and his own gentian-infused bitters and presented this concatenation to his New Orleans pharmacy's clientele in egg cups called *coquetiers.* According to the story, our word *cocktail* derives from *coquetier.*

Parts of the legend are verifiable enough: Peychaud *was* a New Orleans chemist; he *did* invent the bitters known as Peychaud's bitters (an essential ingredient in several cocktails associated with the Crescent City); and he was, apparently, the creator of a brandy-sugar-and-bitters beverage that's an ancestor of the Sazerac (see page 306). But that's as far as the truth extends. The etymology linking *coquetier* and *cocktail* is, to use another French expression, *faux*; no one really knows where the weird word *cocktail* comes from. Moreover, the practice of mixing bitters and booze was widespread bartending practice during Peychaud's

Sweet News on Bitters

lifetime. What *is* notable is that bitters were, during the early nineteenth century, an essential component of a bona fide cocktail. Although the word *cocktail* is now used loosely to mean any mixed alcoholic drink, back then, only a mixed drink containing bitters was a cocktail proper. (Other categories of mixed alcoholic drinks went by other names.)

Star bartenders of the nineteenth century typically made their own bitters from their own proprietary recipes, but the trade in commercially produced bitters also flourished. In the late 1800s and early 1900s, the market supported dozens of brands (in dozens of flavors) from bitters-makers in America, Great Britain, and elsewhere. But that market gradually dwindled—makers went out of business, foreign bitters were no longer imported—and, by the late twentieth century, only one brand of bitters was widely available in the United States: Angostura.

Manufactured in Trinidad since the 1850s, Angostura bitters had first been invented in 1820 by a German doctor and named after the Venezuelan town where he practiced. Without any meaningful competition, the Angostura Company's product became nearly synonymous with the word *bitters*. As excellent as the Angostura aromatic bitters is, the disappearance of other brands and kinds of bitters was a great loss to the cocktaildom.

There were a few other survivors of the American bitters shakeout: Peychaud's bitters, for one, which continued to be made by the New Orleans–based Sazerac Company, and the line of bitters produced by Fee Brothers, a family-owned firm based in Rochester, New York, that has produced bitters and other cocktail ingredients since the 1880s. But these brands' retail distribution was extremely limited, to say the least. In 2003, when *Drinkology*'s first edition was being researched, a thoroughgoing search of specialty shops in Manhattan (New York City, *not* Kansas) turned up just one store selling any brand of bitters besides Angostura. (The brand was Peychaud's.)

This was consternating: Many traditional cocktail recipes call for orange bitters, which *Drinkology* simply could not find. So we decided not to include such drinks in the first edition of the book (or, where possible, to substitute Angostura for orange bitters in the recipes) because we wanted to create a *usable* cocktail handbook, not one filled with arcane recipes that few readers would actually be able to make.

In seven short years, the world has changed very much for the better. (Well, in at least this regard.) Although supermarkets still rarely stock anything but the Angostura brand, a fair number of specialty shops now carry a selection. Fee Brothers has expanded its line (which now includes exotica like grapefruit and rhubarb bitters, among others), improved its distribution, and established a website (www.feebrothers.com). And the Internet is chockablock with DIY cocktailians offering recipes for creating bitters on your own.

This time around, *Drinkology's* shopping expeditions were bitters-sweet. One Manhattan emporium we visited carried *six* different brands of orange bitters alone. We bought them and taste-tested. All were good, but—somewhat to our surprise—the best was the orange bitters that the redoubtable Angostura Company has recently taken to making.

To celebrate bitters' return, this new *Drinkology* includes a number of recipes employing different flavors of bitters. (One note: If a recipe specifies Angostura bitters, it means the traditional variety, in the familiar little bottle with the white label and yellow cap.)

Basic Bartending

(A CRASH COURSE)

LEARNING TO BARTEND IS A BIT LIKE TAKING A BASIC CHEMIS-TRY class—except that the compounds that you, in your wizardry, create aren't likely to blow up in your face. This connection, between mixology and chemistry, is an old one, and it isn't just a metaphor: the Renaissance-era monks who invented the liqueurs known as Bénédictine and Chartreuse were simultaneously engaged in alchemy, and they employed the same techniques they used in trying to turn lead into gold when they turned their attention to transmuting distilled spirits, fruits, flowers, and herbs into potent and delicious potables. (They were, it goes without saying, a lot more successful at the latter task than at the former.)

You won't need a Bunsen burner, flasks, retorts, or test tubes to conduct your drinkological experimentation, but you will need some specialized equipment (discussed in the previous chapter), a variety of "reagents" and "catalysts" (the booze itself, along with all the mixers and condiments your work requires), and a suitable laboratory environment. That lab can, of course, be as simple as your own kitchen counter or as specialized as a built-in home bar, but there are several features it's *got* to have: adequate clear space to work at, a sink, a refrigerator and freezer, and (if you're making hot drinks) a source of heat. Hmm. When it's described this way, a bar *does* begin to sound an awful lot like a lab, doesn't it?

You'll also need the kind of attitude that characterizes any successful science student—a mindset that's capsulized in the old saw, "If at first you don't succeed, try, try again." Some of your experiments are bound to fail: you'll spill things, break stuff, and (probably) produce at least a few potions that only a Dr. Jekyll would enjoy slugging down. You will make a mess. But don't worry: with practice, you'll get there.

Drinkology can't, of course, teach you *everything* that you, as a budding bartender, need to know. But we can reveal at least a few secrets—garnered from our own cocktail-testing experience—that will help you pass an introductory course in the mixological arts and sciences. Think of this chapter not as a textbook but as a kind of "cheat sheet."

PREPPING THE BAR

Ever notice that professional bartenders, before they come on duty, spend an awful lot of time setting up? Of course, the demands you'll face when entertaining a few friends at home are nothing compared to those a pro barkeep must deal with—chatting up the clientele while quickly mixing a wide variety of drinks, constantly making sure that supplies (everything from ice, to glasses, to lemon wedges, to the liquor itself) remain sufficient, toting up bills, swiping credit cards and making change, politely bouncing customers who've had one too many, and so on. It's to be hoped that your bosom buddies won't mind waiting for a few minutes while you create a drink—and that you won't be worrying about how much they'll tip you. But, even so, your job as a home bartender will be made much easier—and you'll be able to spend a lot more time enjoying your company—if you adequately prep the bar before your guests arrive.

Beyond clearing counter space to work at, prepping a bar involves common-sense stuff like setting out the glassware (or, if you're chilling some glasses, placing them in the fridge), making sure all the equipment you'll require is laid out or readily accessible, ensuring you have bar towels aplenty and a serviceable sponge to deal with spills, and seeing to it that the liquor bottles and condiment containers are lined up and ready for action. There are a few aspects of prepping a bar, however, that warrant detailed discussion.

ICE

Adequate ice is *the* essential component of a well-prepped bar. You will need *scads* of it—shocking amounts, really. Think about it: preparing a single highball—one that demands that some of the contents be shaken before being added to the glass—may require upwards of a dozen standard-size ice cubes (six or so for the shaker and just as many for the glass). Depending on the dimensions of your ice cube trays, that could be a whole tray's worth. Even if your refrigerator has an ice maker, you shouldn't feel secure: if you're hosting six friends, each of whom may have three mixed drinks, demand is likely to outstrip supply very quickly. You don't want to have to send someone out to the local convenience store to get ice during the middle of the party, so be sure to lay in a hefty supply beforehand. Do *not* trust your instincts on this: buy (or pre-make) at least *twice as much* ice as you think you could possibly need.

Which brings us to the second important point about ice: *make sure it's fresh.* Ice that's been taking a wintry vacation in your freezer for a couple of weeks probably subtly smells—and tastes—of whatever else it's been sharing that compartment with. Its flavor will affect the flavor of the drinks you make with it—so don't use it. For the same reason, don't use ice made with tap water if your municipality's bilge tastes too strongly of chlorine or minerals; make the ice you'll use in mixed drinks with (noncarbonated) bottled water, or—the easier alternative—buy it from a grocery or convenience store.

Since ice is used at some point in the preparation of all mixed drinks (except the hot ones), *Drinkology's* recipes don't usually list it as an ingredient. The exception is *crushed ice,* used in frozen drinks and a number of other concoctions (Mint Juleps, Swizzlers, etc.). For more on using crushed ice, see pages 327 to 329.

Chilling Glasses

Many—maybe most—of the recipes in this book call for chilled glasses. Now, don't freak out. You don't *have* to chill the glasses you'll be serving cocktails in. It's just a nice thing to do, since a chilled glass gives the drink an icier, more inviting look and—just as important—helps keep it cold for a longer time. Chilling glasses requires nothing more than some free space in the fridge; for the glasses to be properly chilled, put them in at least two hours before your gathering is to begin. For an even wintrier look and feel, you can *frost* the glasses by dipping them in water and setting them inside the freezer for half an hour or so before use. If you don't have enough refrigerator or freezer space to do this (or if you forget), there's a simple trick that many bartenders use to chill a glass quickly: fill it to the brim with ice and water (equal amounts) while you're making the drink in the cocktail shaker or mixing glass; when the drink's ready, just dump out the water and ice and pour in the cocktail.

Not all glasses should be chilled ahead of time. *Drinkology* frankly doesn't see much purpose in pre-chilling old-fashioned or highball glasses that will be used for on-the-rocks–type drinks. And champagne flutes—when they're being used for champagne-based cocktails, that is—shouldn't be chilled, since that might deaden the bubbly's bubbliness. Chilled beer glasses likewise kill the beer's head.

CHILLING THE LIQUOR?

Should you also chill the liquor you'll be using? The answer is both "yes" and "well, maybe." If you're serving vodka (plain or flavored) neat, you should definitely cool it *way* down by putting the bottle in the freezer for several hours beforehand. (In fact, if drinking vodka neat is a favorite pastime, why not just keep a bottle in the freezer? Because the freezing point of alcohol is so much lower than that of water, the vodka won't solidify, so there's no danger of the bottle cracking.)

But what if you're mixing some cocktails? There are Martini enthusiasts who always keep their gin (or vodka) and vermouth in the freezer, and doing so is O.K. by *Drinkology*—just as long as you don't forego adding ice to the mixing glass when stirring the drink. As we point out when discussing the classic Martini (pages 134–136), adding ice to the mixing glass, along with the liquor, is an absolute necessity. In short, pre-chilling the liquor isn't necessarily a bad idea, especially if the cocktails you're making are stirred as opposed to shaken. (Shaking a cocktail with ice will make it so cold that chilling the liquor's sort of superfluous.)

FRUIT AND FRUIT JUICES

Countless cocktails and other mixed drinks require fruit for flavoring and garnishing. You can't make a proper Old Fashioned without maraschino cherries and fresh orange slices, and tropical drinks that aren't festooned with fresh fruit look as naked as a clear-cut rain forest.

An even greater number of drink recipes call for fruit juices—*especially* lemon and lime juice, but also orange, cranberry, and so on. It stands to reason that, if you're intending to serve Piña Coladas, you'd better go to the store and get some pineapple juice and cream of coconut. But some of the other principles for prepping fruit and fruit juices may not be so obvious.

Beyond making sure that you have enough ice, laying in an adequate supply of fresh limes, lemons, and (possibly) oranges—and readying these citrus fruits for use at the bar—is the second most important aspect of your prep work. Before your cocktail party, brunch, or other gathering, consult the recipes for the drinks you're likely to serve. Do they call for lemon or lime wedges? Orange slices? Lemon twists or orange peels? Fresh lemon or lime juice? No matter what the drinks' citrus requirements, you'll save yourself an enormous amount of time and trouble while bartending if these components are prepared beforehand. Do note, though, that once cut, citrus fruits begin to lose their juiciness, aroma, and flavor, so save these preparatory steps until the last hour or so before the guests arrive.

Wedges and slices are simple. Lemon and lime wedges need not be very large: a good-size lemon or lime should yield about 16 perfectly adequate wedges. Similarly, lemons and limes—and even oranges—can be sliced fairly thin (about one-eighth of an inch) without losing their sturdiness. You definitely want a citrus slice to look crisp and neat when perched on the lip of a glass, so make sure you slice the fruit evenly. And *Drinkology* recommends that when you're choosing oranges for garnishing cocktails, you select smaller oranges with relatively thin rinds. (Navel oranges, for example, have thick, leathery skins and lots of that white, inner-rind stuff—it's called the *albedo,* in case you'd like to know—and are therefore a not-so-good choice for garnishing drinks.)

Twists and peels are more challenging. (A twist, by the way, is nothing other than a longish, narrow slice of the lemon's skin; it's called a twist—or so we guess—because you twist it, releasing a tiny spray of essential oils from the rind, before dropping it into the drink.) There are three basic methods for creating a lemon twist. The first, and probably the least satisfactory, is to carefully slice off a strip of the lemon's skin with an ordinary, sharp paring knife. This is somewhat difficult, since, as you cut, you want to remain near the surface of the skin without breaking the twist.

A far easier method involves the use of a handy little tool called a *citrus stripper,* or *channel knife* (see the equipment list, page 12).

The drawing here illustrates the technique. Cut the ends off the lemon, and, holding the lemon firmly in one hand, apply the notched blade to the rind at one end of the fruit. Gradually pull the knife toward you, keeping a steady amount of pressure on the blade as you

USING A CITRUS STRIPPER

go. (Do this slowly and deliberately, so as not to cut yourself.) You can also use a citrus stripper to create a long, looping lemon twist by cutting a spiral strip around the surface of the fruit (the Brandy Crusta, page 73, calls for just such a twist), though in this case *Drinkology* recommends the more arduous paring knife method; if the lemon isn't absolutely fresh, the thin, long strip of rind you'll produce by using a citrus stripper may be too flaccid to work well in a crusta or other similar drink.

Yet a third method for creating a lemon twist—one employing a paring knife and spoon—allows you to create a number of twists at once. It's illustrated below and is performed in several steps: (1) Cut off both ends of the lemon. (2) Score the surface of the fruit from end to end, gradually working around the whole lemon. (When scoring the fruit, be careful to pierce the skin completely without letting the blade sink too deeply into the rind.) (3) Now, using the bowl of a teaspoon, carefully lift the strips of skin from the rind below. (This works best if the concave side of the spoon is turned toward the fruit, so that its shape follows the lemon's curvature.)

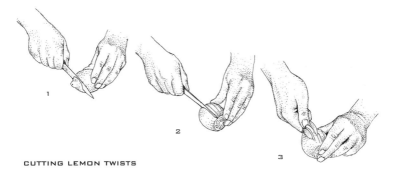

CUTTING LEMON TWISTS

Drinkology thinks that orange peels ought to be big and dramatic-looking. To cut an orange peel, use a paring knife and work around the orange, slicing off the rind in a spiral fashion. (Do we have to say that you should be very careful when doing this? You don't want your orange to inadvertently become a *blood* orange, now do you?)

About juices, let us talk out of both sides of our mouth. First: almost any mixed drink requiring fruit juice will be better if prepared with fresh-squeezed juice. (Well, we don't really expect you to make your own cranberry or pineapple juice, but certainly Screwdrivers, Greyhounds, or Mimosas made with freshly squeezed juice are markedly superior to those made with the stuff you buy in the grocery store.)

Having said this, however, allow us to immediately retreat from our position: even if you have an electric juicer, squeezing a bunch of oranges or grapefruits is *a lot* of work, and we do not upbraid you for not wanting to do it. We will only insist that, if you're using store-bought orange or grapefruit juice, you choose the expensive, nonreconstituted kind.

Drinkology is much more adamant, however, when it comes to lemon and lime juice. We beg you, please do *not* use bottled lemon or lime juice for your cocktails. (and, for God's sake, don't use sour mix instead of juice). There are a few—*very* few—cocktails for which *Drinkology,* almost against its will, prefers Rose's lime juice cocktail to fresh-squeezed lime juice (the Gimlet, page 122, is one of these rare exceptions). Now, we realize that you may balk when instructed to use only fresh lemon and lime juice, but we're convinced that once you've gotten into the habit of doing so, you'll thank us for being so persnickety on this score. If you're just fixing a couple of cocktails, a citrus reamer or squeezer will do you fine—and you can squeeze the lemons and limes as you need them—but if you're preparing for a sizable gathering, or even if you're just making a few drinks that call for a relatively great amount of lemon or lime juice (Margaritas, say), you'll definitely want to make use of an electric juicer.

And, though we're loath to add to your workload, we're going to make one more recommendation regarding lemon and lime juice: you should *strain* the fresh juice through a kitchen strainer or sieve before using it. This step is more important for lemon than for lime juice—lemons usually have seeds, and their juice is pulpier. But clear lime-juice cocktails—Daiquiris, for instance—will look much crisper and more inviting if the juice has been strained before being added to the drink.

A note on presentation: you could probably think of this by yourself, but let us mention the fact that a brunch or cocktail party bar will look all the handsomer if the juices—tomato, orange, pineapple, whatever—are set out in glass or ceramic pitchers rather than the containers they came in.

BEVERAGE NAPKINS

And while we're on the subject of presentation, let us clue you in on a little trick that will make your bar more interesting to look at—and that serves a practical purpose, as well. You've no doubt noticed that, at many bars, the paper beverage napkins are arranged in a spiral-shaped pile. You might've thought that such bars employ a flunky whose sole duty it is to painstakingly create these piles by carefully laying one napkin upon another, each at a slight angle to the one below.

But no. It's actually a snap to create such an engineering wonder, which has the benefit of allowing you to take an individual napkin

CREATING A NAPKIN SPIRAL

from the pile without inadvertently grabbing several and destroying the pile's architectural integrity in the process. As the drawing above shows, you begin with an ordinary, rectilinear pile of bevnaps (1). Setting a straight-sided tumbler diagonally across the top of the pile, exert moderate pressure on the tumbler and begin to twist it so that the top napkins fan out from those below (2). Continue doing this, working in a clockwise direction, until the spiral is complete (3).

SWEETENERS

The recipes for a large number of mixed drinks call for sweeteners: some form of sugar or (much more rarely) honey, agave syrup, or maple syrup. This may seem a simple subject, but it's not, so let us apprise you of a couple of things.

If you can avoid it, do *not* use plain old granulated sugar in mixed drinks. It simply doesn't dissolve quickly enough in cold liquids, and you'll be left with a sugar residue at the bottom of your cocktail shaker or highball glass. (And, because some of the sugar remains undissolved, the drink won't be as sweet as it's supposed to be.) When it comes to sweetening a drink with sugar, you have several options—sugar cubes, superfine granulated sugar, powdered sugar, simple syrup, and brown sugar. Each of these is best for a specific purpose, so let's outline briefly what those uses are.

- *Sugar cubes* are used for sweetening champagne-based cocktails—and for intensifying the little drama that transpires inside the flute once the champagne is poured in (the bubbles will seem to emanate from the dissolving cube as it rests at the bottom of the flute). Sugar cubes are also used for the Absinthe Drip (page 158) and a few other drinks. *Drinkology,* however, does not recommend that you use a sugar cube for muddling with fruit in an Old Fashioned or with mint leaves in a Mint Julep. Sugar cubes, after all, are *hard and crunchy,* and using a cube of sugar rather than a spoonful of superfine sugar simply adds work to an already energetic task.

- *Superfine sugar* is just granulated sugar whose crystals have been milled smaller and finer than usual. Almost all supermarkets carry it (it typically comes in one-pound boxes), and you should definitely have some on hand for drinks that require muddling or that call for a sugar-rimmed glass. (For more on muddling and rimming, see pages 44 to 46.) Despite superfine sugar's superiority to the ordinary granulated kind, however, *Drinkology* doesn't recommend it for use in stirred or shaken drinks, or for those lowballs and highballs that are "built" directly in the glass. Superfine sugar does dissolve more quickly than ordinary granulated sugar, but, if you ask us, it's still not quick enough. For most mixed drinks that require sugar sweetening, you'll need either powdered sugar or the sugar-and-water solution called simple syrup.

- *Powdered sugar* (a.k.a. confectioners' sugar) is just dandy for sweetening many shaken drinks—which are often meant to be cloudy and frothy-looking. Because powdered sugar is less dense—less concentratedly sweet, if you will—than granulated sugar, we recommend that it be measured out in generously *heaping* teaspoons or half-teaspoons, depending on the recipe.

- *Simple syrup* provides a way of getting the sweetness into the drink without having to worry about the sugar dissolving—because the sugar is *already* dissolved. You can buy prepared sugar syrup in some grocery stores, but it's so easy to make that you'll be better off cooking some up yourself. Here's the formula: Combine two cups of granulated sugar and one cup of water in a saucepan. Stir, and bring the mixture to a boil. Once it's started boiling, reduce the heat and allow it to simmer for five minutes. Remove the pan from the heat, and allow the syrup to cool before using. See? Nothing to it. Once it's cooled, you can bottle the syrup and refrigerate it. (It will keep for a week or longer, though it will eventually ferment and sour, so make sure to test simple syrup that's more than a week old before using it in cocktails.)

- *Brown sugar,* which is more robustly flavored than refined white sugar, is used only in a few hot drinks.

In general, you should use the form of sugar that's called for in a particular recipe. If you must make a substitution, remember the following rule: measure by measure, powdered sugar is less intensely sweet than superfine sugar, which in turn is less sweet than simple syrup. So if you're substituting powdered or superfine sugar for simple syrup, use a little *more* than the amount the recipe calls for; if you're using simple syrup rather than granulated or powdered sugar, slightly decrease the amount specified in the recipe. If a recipe calls for an unusual sweetener (e.g., agave syrup), make no substitution.

SUBSTITUTIONS

That's the perfect segue to our next topic: substituting one ingredient for another. When can you do it, and when can't you? What's acceptable and what's not?

As a home bartender, you're almost sure to face this sort of quandary. You want to make something but just don't have the exact ingredients the recipe demands. The crummy liquor store you frequent doesn't carry everything you want. Or you've miscalculated, and you've run out of an essential ingredient before the party's over. What do you do?

The bad news first: you should be extremely wary of making substitutions. Some of this is common sense: a maraschino cherry is small and round and comes in a jar crowded with its fellow fruits, but, beyond that, it's nothing like an olive, so you can't use a cherry instead of an olive in a Martini (or an olive instead of a cherry in a Manhattan). But some of it isn't so transparently obvious: you can make a Martini with either gin or vodka, but most gin-based cocktails do not lend themselves to being made with vodka instead; their flavor—their whole reason for being—depends on gin's distinctive taste. Despite their similarity, lemon juice and lime juice are *not* interchangeable. Light rum and white tequila are both colorless liquids, but, you know, they just don't taste the same.

In some cases, making a substitution—using scotch instead of Canadian whiskey when making a Manhattan, say—won't produce a disastrous result. What it *will* produce is a swell-tasting cocktail that's so significantly different from the one you intended to make that it rates a different name (a Manhattan made with scotch is a Rob Roy). In some cases, though, true disappointment may ensue: for example, you just *can't* substitute light rum for dark in a recipe that specifically calls for dark rum, or vice versa. You'll wind up with a drink that's insipid or—if you use dark instead of the required light rum—a concoction that's inappropriately muddy-looking and unpleasantly strong.

We hope all this negative talk isn't making it sound as if *Drinkology* is contradicting one of our basic principles—that of encouraging experimentation. We *do*, in fact, want you to feel free to play around with combinations of ingredients. Just never forget one of science's—and mixology's—elementary truths: that experiments don't necessarily produce the desired, or a desirable, result.

Having rendered that harsh and stern caution, we can move on to the good news: there are a number of perfectly acceptable substitutions you can make (and even a few cases in which omitting an ingredient won't do terrible damage to the resulting drink). The substitutions first:

• The orange-flavored liqueurs known as *curaçaos* are (except for their colors) more or less interchangeable. Feel free to substitute triple sec (a kind of curaçao) for white curaçao, and white curaçao for orange. Blue curaçao doesn't taste appreciably different from the others—though using it will, of course, produce a bright blue drink. Of all the curaçaos, *Drinkology* prefers Cointreau, and recommends its use in many recipes—but triple sec or even white curaçao will do almost as well. The delicious orange-flavored liqueur known as Créole Shrubb can also substitute for Cointreau, triple sec, or curaçao in many drinks.

- *Rye* whiskey can be successfully substituted for bourbon in many bourbon-based recipes (and vice versa). And though we're partial to Canadian blended whiskey and recommend it in our recipes for many whiskey-based cocktails, we're forced to admit that either bourbon or rye makes a drinkable Manhattan (many people, in fact, prefer bourbon or rye Manhattans).

- *Lemon-flavored vodka* is an acceptable substitute for orange-flavored vodka, but not vice versa. (By the way, you should be aware that *citron* is the French word for "lemon," not "citrus.") And you can use plain vodka and just a drop of vanilla extract in any recipe that calls for vanilla-flavored vodka.

- *Orgeat syrup*, a constituent of some tropical drinks, can be difficult to find—so if you can't find it, *Drinkology* recommends using the slightly-easier-to-find *almond syrup* instead. And, while we're on the subject of hard-to-find ingredients, let us mention that we gave up on trying to locate a bottle of crème de noyaux after fruitlessly inquiring at *five* New York City liquor stores, and decided to substitute amaretto in recipes that traditionally call for the other liqueur.

- *Drinkology*, ever-sybaritic, calls for *heavy cream* in most (not all) cream-based drinks. If you're worried about consuming all that butterfat, do feel free to use light cream or half-and-half in those recipes—but do *not* substitute whole or (heavens!) skim milk for cream. Drink something else instead.

- *Fruit garnishes* are wide open to experimentation. In many cases, the garnish called for in a particular recipe is just a matter of tradition; there's no reason on God's palm-fronded earth that you shouldn't decorate your Piña Colada with a strawberry rather than a maraschino cherry–and–pineapple "flag." (*Flag* is the term for several different fruits skewered together, shish-kabob style, on a cocktail spear.) So be fruity, and multiply the garnishes however you wish.

And, as we indicated at the start of this section, it *is* occasionally acceptable to leave out certain ingredients without greatly damaging the resulting drink. Thirsting for a Bloody Mary (page 253) but fresh out of fresh horseradish? Just skip it. Desperately in need of a Brandy Alexander (page 71) but unable to locate the nutmeg? Forget the nutmeg. Let your common sense be your guide in this— if a recipe calls for only a tiny amount of something (a quarter-teaspoon or less) or if the ingredient is just a garnish, you might well be able to skip that ingredient and still make a successful drink. (Do note, though, that this is seldom true of bitters; a dash of bitters is often an essential ingredient, despite the infinitesimal amount.)

The best example of something that can often be omitted without harm is an egg white, whose sole purpose, usually, is to make a drink frothy. If a recipe calls for an egg yolk or whole egg, however, you *can't* leave it out without significantly altering the drink's taste. If your immune system is compromised or you're simply worried about salmonella poisoning, avoid any drinks that require raw eggs.

MAKING DRINKS

If you've never done it before, making a drink for someone can be almost as intimidating as cooking a four-course meal for a houseful of guests. *Drinkology* isn't exaggerating: we know some excellent cooks who go all aquiver if asked to make a Martini. Well, be calm. We're going to approach this step by step.

MEASURING

Ever noticed how expert bartenders—unless they're asked to make something really unusual or complex—rarely seem to measure anything? Well, believe it or not, that ability to merely "eyeball" the amounts is a skill that, with practice, you'll develop relatively quickly. To begin with, however, you'll have to measure everything, and do so rather painstakingly. But—and this is the scary part—even when you're just starting out, a bit of eyeballing is necessary.

Your chief tools for measuring mixed-drink ingredients are a *jigger-pony measure* (see the equipment list on page 13) and a standard set of kitchen measuring spoons. How to use the measuring spoons is, we hope, self-evident, but using the jigger-pony measure—or "jigger," for short—is a bit trickier. The jigger, you'll notice, has two cups: a larger cup (the jigger per se, which holds 1½ ounces) and a smaller (the pony, which holds 1 ounce). To measure out an ounce or an ounce and a half, you simply fill the appropriate cup and pour the contents into the mix.

So far, so good. Now comes the hard part. You should also use the jigger to measure *fractional* amounts: ¼ ounce, ½ ounce, ¾ ounce, and so on. (You can, of course, get yourself a little shot glass with fractions of an ounce marked on the side, but this looks *dumb*, and will foster

the impression that you are an inexperienced and inept bartender.)
The keys to doing this right are (1) to always make sure you're using
the appropriate cup (jigger or pony), and (2) to remember that these
little cups are *conical* (narrower at the bottom than at the top, which
means that the volume of the cup increases as you approach the lip).
To measure ¼ ounce, use the pony cup, and fill it *a little more* than
one-quarter full; to measure ½ ounce, fill it a bit more than half full.
To measure ¾ ounce, use the jigger cup, and—you're getting it!—fill
a little past halfway.

POURING A "STRAIGHT" DRINK

What is it that makes pouring a "straight" drink—a bourbon on
the rocks, say—so frightening? *Drinkology* thinks it's the fact that
people who drink their liquor straight (or with water or soda) are
so goddamned *particular* about how their drinks are poured. One
scotch-and-soda drinker will prefer his drink made in a highball
glass, with lots of ice and club soda; another will like her drink in
an old-fashioned glass (that is, a "rocks" glass) with just a few cubes
and the merest splash of soda. As a bartender, you fear—and your
fear may not be unfounded—that you'll completely alienate the
drinker if you pour the drink "wrong."

The surest way to avoid this faux pas, of course, is to *ask* the
drinker how she or he likes the drink made. But suppose the person
who's requesting the drink is getting it for someone else? Or suppose you're just too shy to ask?

Well, here's our suggestion—one based on long, close-hand
observation of the drinking preferences of straight-liquor drinkers.
Those who drink their booze straight—or adulterated only with

water or seltzer—generally *really like* the taste of liquor, so don't overdo the other stuff. By the same token, don't make the mistake of filling the glass to the brim with hooch, since part of the pleasure of having a scotch, bourbon, or Campari on the rocks has to do with swirling it around in the glass, inhaling its aroma as it's sipped, etc. To strike the delicate balance between too little and too much, try the following "recipe" for any on-the-rocks drink:

ANY ON-THE-ROCKS DRINK

  2 to 2½ ounces liquor
4 or 5 standard-size ice cubes

Place the ice cubes in an old-fashioned or double old-fashioned glass, and pour the liquor over them. Stir very briefly. (Note: Some like their on-the-rocks drinks garnished with a lemon twist, but you should add a twist only if specifically requested to do so.)

If the request is for a bourbon and water or a scotch and soda, it is likelier than not that the drinker wants only a minimal amount of the mixer, so you'll be relatively safe adding about an ounce or so of water or soda to the drink as described above. If the drinker wants more, it won't be any problem to add some. (People who like just a tiny amount of water or soda generally say, " . . . with just a splash of [fill in the blank].")

When pouring brandy (or a liqueur that you're presenting in a brandy snifter), it's a good rule of thumb to pour only as much as the snifter would hold, without spilling, if set on its side (see illustration on page 44). Snifters differ in size, so test yours ahead of time to determine the proper fill level. Because the pleasure of brandy (or of an aromatic liqueur) resides partly in its aroma—and because a

BARTENDING

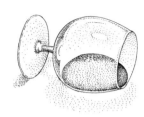

MEASURING BRANDY

snifter is designed to capture that bouquet in its distended bowl—it's a *real* mistake to overpour a brandy. So control your generous impulses.

MUDDLING

Some drink-making instructions—those for the Mint Julep, Mojito, and Old Fashioned, among others—involve a preliminary step called *muddling*. (No, muddling isn't what you find yourself doing the day after a drinking binge; that's called *muddling through*.) The muddling procedure is as unglamorous as its name— what you're doing, basically, is mashing and mixing together some of the ingredients, creating a little mess of blended gook at the bottom of the glass or cup. (In the case of the Mint Julep, for example, you muddle mint leaves, sugar, and a splash of water before adding the crushed ice and bourbon.)

Many bartending guides will tell you that muddling requires an instrument called—wouldn't you know?—a *muddler,* which is nothing more than a long wooden or plastic-tipped metal pestle. (See the equipment list on page 13 for pictures of both kinds.) In fact, using a muddler *is* helpful, since the length of the stick allows you to get a good grip—and prevents you from bruising your knuckles on the rim of the glass in what can be a fairly energetic process. If you don't have a muddler, however, you need not despair: you can muddle with a metal spoon (the convex side of the bowl, please), the handle of a wooden spoon, or—*Drinkology*'s recommended trick—the handle of a wooden citrus reamer.

When muddling fruit or, say, mint leaves, it's really important that you *pulverize* the stuff, and that you mix it well with the sugar and whatever liquid you're muddling it with. The aim is to produce a gloppy substance whose flavor will easily infuse the rest of the drink. If it's a maraschino cherry you're muddling, remove the stem first. If it's a slice of orange or other citrus fruit, remove the rind from the glass and discard it after you've thoroughly mashed up the pulp.

RIMMING A COCKTAIL GLASS

A number of cocktail and mixed-drink recipes require you to *rim* the glass beforehand. Often, rimming is a very simple matter: when a recipe calls for garnishing the drink with a lemon twist or orange peel or a lemon or lime wedge, it's always a good idea to prepare the glass by gently pinching the twist or wedge between your thumb and index finger and dragging it around the glass's rim. This will ensure you get a subtle hint of the citrus flavor with every sip.

Sometimes, though, rimming a glass involves a slightly more complicated procedure. A few cocktails and mixed drinks are traditionally served in glasses that have been rimmed with salt (for example, the Margarita) or sugar (the Lemon Drop). Not only does the salt or sugar intensify the drink's flavor, but it gives the chilled cocktail glass an even frostier, icier look.

No matter whether you're using salt or sugar, the method is the same. You need to prepare by pouring a decent helping of salt or superfine sugar onto a small plate. (A salad or dessert plate will do, but make sure its diameter is greater than that of the mouth of the glass you'll be rimming.) Distribute the salt or sugar evenly across the surface of the plate (yes, you may use your fingers). Then follow

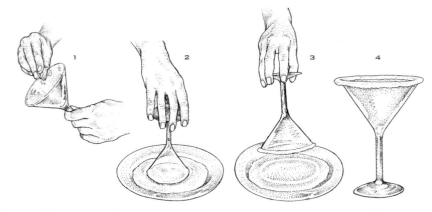

RIMMING A GLASS

these steps, illustrated in the drawings above. (1) Wet the rim of the chilled glass by dragging a citrus wedge—whichever kind the recipe calls for—along it, squeezing the wedge gently as you move it around the edge; don't miss any spots, and try to make sure the rim is evenly wetted. (2) Immediately turn the glass upside-down onto the salt- or sugar-coated plate. Gripping the foot, turn the glass gently—about one full revolution—until the entire rim is coated. (3) Shake off any excess salt or sugar, and—if you're lucky—you'll wind up with a glass that looks like this (4).

Note: For salt-rimmed glasses, ordinary table salt will do, though *Drinkology* prefers a rougher-grained salt (kosher salt, for instance), which makes for an even icier, more crystalline look. When rimming with sugar, the outcome's likely to be a lot more successful if you use superfine sugar rather than the ordinary granulated kind. It sticks better.

STIRRING COCKTAILS

There are three basic ways of concocting a mixed drink: *stirring* it in a mixing glass and then straining it into the serving glass; *shaking* it in a cocktail shaker before straining it into the serving glass; and *building* it directly in the glass in which it's served. The last of these is self-explanatory—though the exact way in which a highball or lowball is built will differ from recipe to recipe. Stirring and shaking, though, require some explanation.

As a general rule, *clear* cocktails are stirred, and *opaque, creamy,* or *cloudy* cocktails are shaken. (This traditional distinction is really a matter of preference, though: James Bond wasn't breaking any laws when he ordered his Martinis "shaken, not stirred." He simply wanted a *colder* drink than mere stirring can produce.)

To stir a drink, fill a mixing glass about two-thirds full with ice cubes, add the called-for ingredients, and—using a bar spoon or other long-handled spoon—stir. For how long should you stir? Well, just long enough—*Drinkology* thinks that about ten revolutions of the spoon should do it. To strain the drink into the cocktail glass, position a Hawthorne or julep strainer (see the equipment list on page 13) just inside the mixing glass at its lip, and carefully pour. (The drawing for step 7 of shaking a cocktail, page 51, illustrates the technique.)

SHAKING COCKTAILS

Let's get this much straight: a shaken cocktail should be *shaken.* Shaken hard. The goal isn't merely to chill the drink—though a drink that's shaken vigorously will be colder than one that's given a couple of limp-wristed flicks—but also to erode the ice cubes slightly (the bit of water they release is essential to the drink's taste) and to thoroughly meld the ingredients' flavors. Shaking well also

BARTENDING

froths up a drink—especially important if it contains an egg white or yolk (or both), cream, or a thickish, opaque fruit juice (pineapple juice, say). So, please, apply a little elbow grease.

That said, it's usually equally important that you *not* shake a drink too long. A couple of seconds of shaking—ten or twelve back-

---

THE NON-STIR "STIR"

At the suggestion (one might even say the insistence) of *Drinkology*'s bartender friend Joseph Aguiar, we offer this alternative method for "stirring" a drink—a method that involves no stirring whatsoever. Instead, you chill and dilute the drink by *chopping* at the ice in the mixing glass. Joseph much prefers this method when making a Martini, because it produces a very thin layer of tiny ice-particles across the drink's surface. That icy cap—a pretty effect—persists long enough to produce an intensely cold sensation on the drinker's lips and tongue when the cocktail is first sipped.

The procedure is simple: Pour the drink's ingredients into the glass and add the ice. Place a bar spoon in the glass, bowl-end down. Cover the mouth of the glass with the fingers and palm of one hand, positioning the bar spoon's handle between the index and middle fingers. (You're covering the glass only to prevent the liquid from splashing out.) Now, using your other hand, rapidly and energetically move the spoon up and down, chopping away at the ice in the glass. Do this for about five seconds, then use a Hawthorne strainer to strain the drink into a chilled cocktail glass.

and-forths, maybe—is plenty. Keep shaking for too long a time and you'll end up with a concoction that's too watery. By the way, for any shaken drink, you should fill the shaker's cup about half to two-thirds full with ice.

Equipment-wise, you have two basic options: a *standard shaker* or what's called a *Boston shaker*. (Actually, there are three options, but we'll get to that in a minute; and don't ask us how the Boston shaker got its name, because we don't know. Nobody knows.)

If you're a beginning mixologist, you'll find the standard shaker much easier to use: the three pieces (cup, strainer top, and lid) fit together neatly, and, so long as you keep hold of the top, you don't have to worry about the thing flying apart while you're shaking it. A standard shaker is definitely the preferable option if you're making a drink whose liquid ingredients total more than four or five ounces—the chance of spillage is much reduced—but standard shakers have one *real* disadvantage compared to Boston shakers. If all the components of a standard shaker are made of metal, it can be difficult to pry the thing apart after the cocktail's been made. Metal shrinks when it gets cold, and this shrinkage may cause the strainer top to lock onto the cup as if you'd Krazy Glued it in place. Cursing, struggling, and tearing at the blasted thing with your fingernails won't help dislodge it; what *may* help is to run very hot water over the top—just the top—for a few seconds, hoping that this will expand the top sufficiently to release it.

A better idea might be to learn to use a Boston shaker—or, even better, the "modified" Boston shaker that is *Drinkology*'s preferred cocktail-shaking apparatus, and which we're just about to discuss.

Granted, using a Boston shaker—which usually consists of a large stainless steel cup and a smaller (but still large) mixing glass, and which requires a separate cocktail strainer—is more challenging than using a standard shaker. Daunting, even. It's especially difficult if you've got small hands, since grasping the cup and the glass in one hand requires about an octave's reach.

That's why *Drinkology* so prefers the *modified* Boston shaker, which is much easier to keep hold of. This version, shown in the drawing below, consists of two stainless-steel cups: one larger (32 ounces) and one smaller (16 ounces). (Preferred by bartenders in Great Britain, it is sometimes called a British shaker.)

As the drawings opposite show, you begin by placing ice in the larger of the cups, filling it about half full (1), and then adding the called-for ingredients to this cup (2). Next, insert the smaller cup upside-down into the larger, positioning it *at a slight angle* and pressing it so that it lodges tightly in the larger cup (3). Grasping the two-cup shaker in one hand, shake vigorously for a few seconds (4). When you're finished shaking, set the shaker down (with the larger cup on the bottom), and remove the smaller cup (5). (It may take a little bit of effort to do this.) Now, transfer the contents into the smaller cup (6), and strain into the serving glass (7). Drawing

MODIFIED BOSTON SHAKER

number 7 shows a julep strainer being used, but you may prefer a Hawthorne strainer, which will fit fairly tightly inside the mouth of the cup (the side of the strainer with the wire coil goes *inside* the cup.)

Sound difficult? It's really not, once you get the hang of it—which may take a couple of tries.

USING THE MODIFIED BOSTON SHAKER

KEEPING IT CLEAN AND NEAT

One of the hardest aspects of tending bar—far harder, really, than shaking cocktails—is keeping up with the housekeeping. You want to make sure that each cocktail is prepared with perfectly clean equipment, which means that you're constantly washing up. You want to be able to quickly find the implements and ingredients you need, which means you're constantly straightening up. Keeping things neat and clean is immensely time-consuming, which is why busy bars employ a person—he or she is called the *barback*—to help the bartender keep pace with all the housekeeping details. It's also why you, if you're having more than eight or ten friends over for cocktails, should definitely consider *hiring* a bartender for the evening. Otherwise, you'll stay so busy tending bar that you won't have any fun.

And *Drinkology* definitely wants you to enjoy yourself.

· ◆ ·

These are the basics—or some of them. Other bartending tips are scattered throughout the book. You'll find instructions on preparing frozen and blended drinks in the introduction to the Frozen and Blended Drinks chapter; tips on hot drinks in the Hot Drinks chapter intro. Special instructions for making champagne-based cocktails are contained in the opening pages of the Champagne chapter. The vicissitudes of pouring Pousse-Cafés and other layered drinks are painfully laid out on pages 177 through 179. And, of course, each recipe provides specific instructions for preparing that drink.

Cheers, and good luck. We're convinced you're headed for an A+ (at least for effort).

Beer

IN *DRINKOLOGY*'S HOUSE, BEER ISN'T MIXED WITH ANYTHING except pretzels, canasta, or heartache, so it was hard for us to accept the fact that there are mixed drinks—a fair number of them—that have beer as their major ingredient. In general, these are tough drinks for a non-beer-drinker (or even, we'd imagine, some true beer lovers) to like: they're uncompromising, and many of them are a bit he-mannish. But beer-based concoctions have a long and rich history—as does the brew itself.

Beer is a truly ancient beverage, having been around for upwards of 6,500 years. The making of beer may predate the baking of bread, and it was imbibed by—among other ancient peoples—the Egyptians. (Now you know how they relaxed after a hard day of pyramid-building and obelisk-erecting.) But the flavor of the beer brewed in antiquity wouldn't necessarily be recognized, or enjoyed, by beer drinkers today. How come? Because ancient beers contained no hops, which weren't added to the basic beer formula—malted grain (usually barley) fermented with yeast—until sometime during the Middle Ages. (Hops, by the way, are the flowers of the hop vine; their bitterness plays against the sweetness of the malted grain to give beer its tangy bite.)

Today, beer is brewed virtually everywhere in the world—an estimated twenty to thirty thousand varieties in all, and that's not counting the products of small craft-brewers nor, of course, do-it-yourself brewmeisters. A goodly selection of the world's beers is readily available almost everywhere in America, which unfortunately does not mean that American beer drinkers have given up on the watery, flat, insipid brews churned out by the big beer makers. Among many beer aficionados, the most-favored imported beers are those made in Britain and Ireland and in the countries of northwestern and central Europe (especially Holland, Belgium, and, of course, Germany), but we've found that we also like some of the exquisitely balanced lagers produced in Asian countries whose beer-making traditions are more recent: China, India, Japan, Thailand, and Turkey. If you've never had Thai or Indian beer, you're missing something.

Because *Drinkology*'s crew are Americans, we prefer our beer rather cold. The Brits differ on this question, as we've been reminded every time we've ordered a pint in a London pub. We guess that we have to agree, though, that beer or ale that's served at "room temperature" (granted, rooms in England are chillier than they are stateside) is more complexly flavorful.

If you're not partial to beer but like to keep some on hand for friends, do note that most kinds of beer do *not* improve with age. A bottle of beer that's been loitering in the fridge for a year is a *stale* bottle of beer. Note, too, that sunlight ruins beer—that's why it's so often bottled in brown or green glass. So make sure to store bottled beer in a dark or shaded place—and don't keep it around too long.

Ale versus Lager

All beers begin as *wort* (pronounced WERT)—a cooked, strained mixture of water, hops, and malted grain (grain that's been moistened and allowed to sprout, then dried or roasted). Although common American parlance makes a distinction between beer and ale, this distinction isn't really correct. The term *beer* more properly refers to all alcoholic beverages made from fermented malt and hops (ale included). A better way of broadly categorizing types of beer is to differentiate between *ales* and *lagers*. The difference between these two classes of beer has to do with the kind of yeast used to ferment the wort—and *where* in the tank that yeast likes to do its work of converting sugars to alcohol. Ale yeasts ferment on top of the brew, and ales are thus *top-fermented* beers. By contrast, lagers are *bottom-fermented,* meaning that lager yeasts sink to the bottom of the tank. In general, lagers are lighter in color and body than ales, but do note that there are many exceptions to this rule. The following list provides brief definitions of some specific styles of beer:

Barley wine: A powerfully malty, high-alcohol beer that, unlike most other beers, *improves* with age. Barley wines are aged in bottle for lengths of time ranging from several months to several years.

Bitter (a.k.a. amber ale): A medium-dark ale, favored by British pubgoers, whose bitter taste results from additional hops added to the brew.

Bock beer: A darker, sugary lager whose rich taste results from the especially potent malts used in its making.

Brown ale: A sweet, dark ale (though lighter in color than stout). The category includes **nut brown ale.**

BEER

India pale ale (IPA): A heavily hopped ale that is sometimes citrusy in flavor. A current favorite among American craft brewers, IPA was originally brewed in England for shipment to British troops serving in India (hence the name).

Lambic: A distinctive Belgian beer that is fermented with wild yeasts rather than cultivated brewer's yeasts. Many lambic beers are **fruit beers,** flavored with fruit syrups or whole fruits.

Pale ale: A light-colored, relatively sweet ale (compared, that is, to bitter or stout).

Pilsner: A dry, light lager. The original Pilsner, named for the town of Pilsen (now Plzeň), in the Czech Republic, was first brewed in 1842; today, the basic Pilsner method is used to make most American mass-produced beers.

Porter: A dark brown beer whose color results from the charred malts used in making it. Some describe porter's flavor as coffee-like.

Stout: A sharp-flavored ale with a very dark—almost black—color. Stout's distinctive flavor and color are due to the roasted barley used in brewing it.

Vienna: A malty, hoppy, reddish-colored lager named for the Austrian capital (where it was first made).

Wheat beer (a.k.a. Weiss beer): A sweet, pale, lagerlike ale (it's top-fermented) usually made from a combination of wheat and barley malts.

BEER BUSTER

This saucy brew ups the ante on beer's natural alcohol content.

1½ ounces ice-cold vodka
2 dashes Tabasco sauce
chilled beer or ale

Combine vodka and Tabasco in a beer mug or highball glass. Carefully pour in the beer (or ale).

BLACK AND TAN

Also known as a Half-and-Half, this mixture combines bitter and mild tastes as well as darker and lighter colors. This recipe is for a 16-ounce glass or mug; if you're using a smaller glass, reduce the amounts but keep them equally proportioned.

about 8 ounces lager or pale ale
about 8 ounces stout

Pour the lager (or pale ale) into a beer mug or 16-ounce glass; carefully add the stout. (If you like, you might try layering the stout on top of the lager. If the attempt fails, so what?)

BLACK VELVET

Let's face it: this is a strange drink. It was, by all accounts, invented as a beverage-of-mourning following the death of Queen Victoria's consort, Prince Albert, in 1861. But nobody explains the conceptual connection between the late German-born semi-monarch and this Irish-French combo.

about 8 ounces Irish stout
about 8 ounces champagne

Very carefully, pour the stout and champagne into a beer mug or 16-ounce glass.

BLACK VELVETEEN

If you're tired of grieving over Black Velvets (above), try crying into this variation.

about 8 ounces Irish stout
about 8 ounces hard cider

Very carefully, pour the stout and cider into a beer mug or 16-ounce glass.

BLOODY BREW

Try this earthier version of a Bloody Mary if, say, you're grilling hot dogs and hamburgers for Sunday brunch.

1½ ounces vodka
4 ounces tomato juice
4 ounces beer
dash Tabasco sauce, if desired
salt
↳ dill pickle spear

Pour the vodka and tomato juice into a highball glass filled with ice. Carefully pour in the beer. Stir gently, season to taste, and garnish with the pickle spear.

BOILERMAKER

This prelude-to-a-hangover qualifies as a mixed drink only in the sense that the ingredients mix it up in your gut.

shot glass of whiskey (bourbon, rye, sour mash, Irish, or blended Canadian)
mug or large glass of cold lager or pale ale

Down the shot of whiskey in one gulp. Immediately chase with the lager (or ale), drinking in large, continuous swallows. (And please don't have too many.)

BROADWAY

Virtually every cocktail website describes this yecchy-sounding combo as "very popular in Japan." If true, the Japanese are onto something: the Broadway is, in fact, much better tasting than you'd guess.

about 8 ounces lager
about 8 ounces *cold* Coca-Cola

Very carefully, pour the lager and Coca-Cola into a beer mug or 16-ounce glass.

SHANDY

Shandies have been drunk in Britain since the late 1800s (the name's a corruption of *shant*, or *shanter*, slang for a pub). This recipe and that for the Shandygaff (page 61) are for a 16-ounce glass or mug; if you're using a smaller glass, reduce the amounts but keep them equally proportioned.

about 8 ounces chilled lemonade or lemon-lime soda
about 8 ounces ice-cold lager or pale ale

Pour the lemonade or lemon-lime soda into a beer mug or 16-ounce glass; carefully add the lager (or ale).

SHANDYGAFF

This is a crisper, spicier version of the Shandy.

about 8 ounces chilled ginger beer
about 8 ounces ice-cold lager or pale ale

Pour the ginger beer into a beer mug or 16-ounce glass; carefully add the lager (or ale).

SHOOTER-CHASER COMBOS

It's hardly a sophisticated approach to drinking, but if you're determined to slake your thirst while rapidly achieving a fulsome level of inebriation, you can't do better than to down a shot of liquor and chase it immediately with a glass of ice-cold beer. The "classic" shooter-beer chaser combination, the Boilermaker, is covered on page 59, but you're free to name your poison. Hot pepper–flavored vodkas, cinnamon schnapps, and root beer schnapps make for suitable shooters.

shot glass of plain or flavored vodka, schnapps, or other
    liquor
mug or glass of ice-cold lager or pale ale

Down the shot of liquor in one gulp. Immediately chase with the lager (or ale), drinking in large, continuous swallows.

STOUT SANGAREE

This mixture is for the robust, strong-willed palate.

2 teaspoons simple syrup
10 ounces stout
2 ounces ruby port
pinch of freshly grated nutmeg
pinch of ground cinnamon

Pour the simple syrup into a beer mug or highball glass, then carefully add the stout. Float the port, and garnish with the nutmeg and cinnamon.

BEER

Brandy

D RINKOLOGY'S FAVORITE STORY ABOUT BRANDY INVOLVES THE late British actor David Niven. While on location in the Swiss Alps during the filming of the 1963 comedy classic *The Pink Panther,* Niven decided to go skiing all by himself. Temperatures were subzero, and Niven was unlucky enough to get frostbitten— not on his nose and not on his toes, but on his you-know-what. To rectify matters—or so he reported in his autobiography—he forced himself to dip his afflicted appendage in a glass of gently warmed brandy. His manhood, it seems, was soon restored.

Talk about a cocktail.

Sorry. Shall we begin again? Properly speaking—and to speak more properly—brandy is a spirit distilled from grapes and then aged, generally in wooden casks, before being bottled. Actually, there's always been some controversy about this definition, since distilled spirits made from a wide range of other fruits are also often termed brandies, at least in casual parlance. *Drinkology* isn't purist about this, and so we include recipes for drinks based on several sorts of "brandies" in this chapter. But let's return, for the while, to the widely accepted definition—and to the history of brandy per se.

No one really knows who invented brandy, or where, or when. The French—whose Cognac and Armagnac regions produce what are widely regarded as the world's finest brandies—claim credit, but so do the Italians, the Dutch, and others. In fact, it's possible that fruit brandies may date back thousands of years, originating in the Middle East or Egypt, and that brandy may first have made its way to Europe via the Moors—the Muslim North Africans who ruled Spain for hundreds of years. (Incidentally, today's Spanish brandies are quite good, if relatively unsubtle when compared with the French products.)

The etymology of the word *brandy* is clearer; it comes from the Dutch *brandewijn* ("burned [i.e., distilled] wine"). The name seems to date from the sixteenth century, when Dutch merchant ships transported cargoes of brandy far and wide and were instrumental in spreading its popularity.

THE STAR SYSTEM (AMONG OTHERS)

Just as with wine, the making and enjoyment of brandy have given rise to a sophisticated culture and a complex jargon that can be intimidating to the uninitiated. There's so much to know about brandy that *Drinkology* can't give you more than the most paltry of introductions.

One of the first puzzles that confronts the neophyte involves the words, symbols, and abbreviations that commonly appear on the labels of cognacs, armagnacs, and other French brandies. A cognac label will sometimes identify the specific subdivision of the Cognac region in which the grapes used to make that particular cognac were grown. In order of quality, these are *Grande Champagne, Petite Champagne, Borderies, Fins Bois, Bons Bois, Bois Ordinaires,* and *Bois à Terroir.* But it's more common to see a cognac identified on its label as *Fine Champagne,* which means that at least 60 percent of the grapes from which it was distilled grew within the borders of the Grande Champagne subdivision.

Armagnacs are similarly identified by the subregion from which they hail: *Bas-Armagnac, Ténarèze,* and *Haut-Armagnac* are the three designations (again, listed in order of quality; if the label simply says "Armagnac," it means the brandy inside is a blend).

Beyond these designations, some brandies are identified on their labels as *Extra, Napoléon, Réserve,* or *Vieille Réserve.* Unfortunately, these terms tell you little of a specific nature about what's in the bottle, except that it's reasonably well aged and (in some cases) that it's the best brandy produced by that particular house.

Then there are the stars. A cognac whose label has a single star was aged in oak at least three years before being bottled; two stars means it was allowed to age at least four years; and three stars, at least five years. This star system is regulated by the French government.

And *then* there are the initials: V.S., V.S.O.P., and V.V.S.O.P. These abbreviations—so frighteningly uncommunicative to the wannabe cognac connoisseur—simply mean "Very Special [or Superior]," "Very Special Old Pale," and "Very Very Special Old Pale." They, too, are indications of a cognac's age—but, beyond the fact that a V.V.S.O.P. is older than a V.S.O.P., which in turn is older than a V.S., the designations are irritatingly nonspecific. (Another abbreviation, X.O., means "Extra Old," and is also indicative of a superior product.)

All this terminology is very significant if you're intending to make brandy appreciation a life's pursuit. It's much less important if all you want to do is to whip up some good brandy-based cocktails. In fact, you should *not* employ superior cognacs or other brandies in mixed

BRANDY

drinks: that would be nothing short of throwing your money away. (And don't ever use armagnacs in mixed drinks; their flavors are much too distinctive.) To make any of the (grape) brandy-based drinks in this chapter, all you need is a good-enough, relatively inexpensive French cognac or other brandy. One, however, requires the South American brandy known as pisco.

BRANDING BRANDIES "BRANDY"

Which brings us, somewhat circuitously, back to the topic of those other "brandies"—the ones that are distilled from fruit other than grapes or that contain fruit flavorings (and sugar) added to a distilled-grape base. U.S. law prohibits a producer or distributor from calling a distilled spirit "brandy" *unless* it actually has a grape-brandy base, so a cherry, peach, or apricot brandy sold as such in America has at least some claim on legitimate brandy-ness, as technically defined.

Drinkology is indifferent to such issues. In fact, our taste-testers are so enthusiastic about the merits of one particular American-made distilled fruit spirit—applejack—that we dare to include applejack-based recipes right alongside those that use its distant, and much haughtier, French cousins. (One note: do *not* use the superb, dry French apple brandy called Calvados in any recipe calling for apple brandy; like armagnac, Calvados is simply too distinct in character for mixed drinks, and the result won't be pleasing.)

Drinkology would even go so far as to guess that Mr. Niven would have achieved just as satisfactory a cure had he used New Jersey apple-jack rather than whatever oh-so-fine champagne cognac was hanging around the chalet. For certain purposes, all brandies are equal.

AMERICAN BEAUTY

Presumably, this cocktail's named for the American Beauty rose, though the shocking-pink color resembles nothing found in nature. It weirdly (and enjoyably) looks and tastes something like Hawaiian Punch.

½ ounce brandy
½ ounce dry vermouth
¼ teaspoon white crème de menthe
1 tablespoon orange juice
1 tablespoon grenadine
dash ruby port

Combine all ingredients except port in a cocktail shaker, with ice. Shake well, and strain into a chilled cocktail glass. Dribble the dash of port on top.

APPLEJACK COBBLER

This is *Drinkology*'s favorite cobbler. (A cobbler, by the way, is just a drink in which liquor and a sweetener are poured over crushed ice.)

crushed ice
2½ ounces applejack
½ ounce simple syrup
♢ 2 or 3 thinly cut apple slices

Pack a large red wine glass with crushed ice. Pour in the applejack and simple syrup, and stir very briefly. Garnish with the apple slices.

APPLEJACK COCKTAIL

 Its rosy color, apple fragrance, and lightly fruity flavor make this an appealing cocktail.

2 ounces applejack
½ ounce fresh lemon juice
½ ounce grenadine

Combine ingredients in a cocktail shaker, with ice. Shake well, and strain into a chilled cocktail glass.

APPLEJACK COLLINS

 What an underrated liquor applejack is. *Drinkology* thinks this New Jersey–distilled spirit makes a *great* collins.

2 ounces applejack
½ ounce fresh lemon juice
½ ounce simple syrup
club soda or seltzer
♦ 2 or 3 thinly cut apple slices

Combine the applejack, lemon juice, and simple syrup in a cocktail shaker, with ice. Shake well, and strain into a collins or highball glass filled with ice cubes. Top with soda (or seltzer), and stir briefly. (If you're using a collins glass, stirring the drink can be slightly challenging because of the glass's narrowness; try using the long handle of a bar spoon.) Garnish with the apple slices.

APPLEJACK RICKEY

Our praise for the Applejack Collins (previous page) applies equally well to the Applejack Rickey.

🍸 lime wedge
2 ounces applejack
½ ounce fresh lime juice
club soda or seltzer

Rim a highball glass with the lime wedge, and fill the glass with ice cubes. Pour in the applejack and lime juice, and top with soda (or seltzer). Squeeze the lime wedge into the drink, and drop it in. Stir briefly.

APRICOT COCKTAIL

Even if you're not overly fond of apricot brandy, you may like this drink. The flavors complement one another very well.

1½ ounces apricot brandy
2 teaspoons vodka
¾ ounce fresh lemon juice
¾ ounce orange juice

Combine ingredients in a cocktail shaker, with ice. Shake well, and strain into a chilled cocktail glass.

BRANDY

BETWEEN THE SHEETS

This lasciviously named cocktail has been around since the 1920s. It nicely balances sour and sweet flavors.

¾ ounce brandy
¾ ounce white rum
¼ ounce Cointreau or triple sec
¾ ounce fresh lemon juice
¼ teaspoon simple syrup

Combine ingredients in a cocktail shaker, with ice. Shake well, and strain into a chilled cocktail glass.

BOMBAY COCKTAIL

This cocktail's color and taste are surprisingly reminiscent of a good sherry.

1 ounce brandy
½ ounce dry vermouth
½ ounce sweet vermouth
½ teaspoon Cointreau or triple sec
¼ teaspoon Pernod or other anise-flavored liquor

Combine ingredients in a mixing glass, with ice. Stir, and strain into a chilled cocktail glass.

BRANDY ALEXANDER

Is there *anyone* who doesn't like this scrumptious cocktail? A well-made Brandy Alexander will appeal even to those who disdain "sissy" drinks. Legend has it that the Brandy Alexander, like the gin-based Alexander (page 111) it resembles, made its debut during Prohibition: the cream smoothed and disguised the harsh and wretched taste of the swill purveyed by many speakeasies. Let's just be glad that someone was canny enough to notice how good the concoction is when made with decent liquor, and that the drink survived Prohibition's repeal.

This version ups the ante on the standard Brandy Alexander recipe by including whipped cream in the mix (it goes into the cocktail shaker along with the rest of the ingredients). If that's not creamy enough for you, try the Ice Cream Alexander on page 358. By the way, you can of course use pre-ground nutmeg instead of grating your own, but freshly grated nutmeg *does* add another level of ecstasy to the experience.

1 ounce brandy
¾ ounce dark crème de cacao
1 ounce heavy cream
2 heaping teaspoons whipped cream
freshly grated nutmeg

Combine ingredients—including whipped cream—in a cocktail shaker, with ice. Shake well, and strain into a chilled cocktail glass. Sprinkle nutmeg on top.

Brandy Cobbler

The cobbler's an old-fashioned drink that's making a comeback. That newly regained popularity is no surprise, given how enjoyable it is to drink almost any liquor over crushed ice, with just a bit of sugar syrup added to sweeten the mix.

crushed ice
2½ ounces brandy
½ ounce simple syrup
orange slice

Pack a large red wine glass with crushed ice. Pour in the brandy and syrup, and stir very briefly. Garnish with the orange slice.

Brandy Cooler (Brandy and Soda)

This combination's the very definition of simple chic.

lemon wedge
2 ounces brandy
club soda or seltzer

Rim a collins or highball glass with the lemon wedge, and fill it with ice. Pour in the brandy, and top with soda (or seltzer). Stir briefly. Squeeze the wedge into the drink, and drop it in.

BRANDY CRUSTA

This New Orleans–born cocktail has long been out of favor but deserves a revival. For a proper crusta, it's essential that the lemon peel be cut in a long spiral and looped around the interior of the glass.

lemon wedge
superfine sugar
✄ lemon peel cut into a long spiral
2 ounces brandy
½ ounce Cointreau or triple sec
½ ounce fresh lemon juice

Prepare a chilled sour glass by rimming it with the lemon wedge and sugar. (Discard the wedge.) Loop a long spiral of lemon peel around the glass's interior. Combine the other ingredients in a cocktail shaker, with ice. Shake well, and strain into the prepared glass.

BRANDY DAISY

The Daisy will appeal to those who like light, fruity drinks. If you find the taste too tart, increase the amount of simple syrup slightly.

2 ounces brandy
1 ounce lemon juice
½ teaspoon simple syrup
½ teaspoon grenadine
⚘ maraschino cherry
⚘ orange slice

Combine all ingredients except the fruit in a cocktail shaker, with ice. Shake well, and strain into a double old-fashioned glass filled with ice cubes. Garnish with the cherry and orange slice.

BRANDY FIZZ

Those who don't care for gin will appreciate this brandy-based variation on the classic summertime refresher.

2 ounces brandy
1 ounce fresh lemon juice
1 heaping teaspoon powdered sugar
club soda or seltzer

Combine all ingredients except club soda (or seltzer) in a cock-tail shaker, with ice. Shake well, and strain into a highball glass filled with ice cubes. Top with soda or seltzer, and stir briefly.

BRANDY RICKEY

This variation on the Gin Rickey (page 125) is for those who prefer a more flavorful refresher.

⌀ lime wedge
2 ounces brandy
½ ounce fresh lime juice
club soda or seltzer

Rim a highball glass with the lime wedge, and fill the glass with ice cubes. Pour in the brandy and lime juice, and top with soda (or seltzer). Squeeze the lime wedge into the drink, and drop it in. Stir briefly.

BRANDY SLING

Grand Marnier is an extremely sweet liqueur, so it's surprising just how beautifully balanced this classic highball is.

⌀ lemon wedge
2½ ounces brandy
½ ounce Grand Marnier
½ ounce fresh lemon juice
club soda or seltzer

Rim a highball or collins glass with the lemon wedge, and fill the glass with ice cubes. Combine the brandy, Grand Marnier, and lemon juice in a cocktail shaker. Shake well, and strain into the ice-filled glass. Top with club soda (or seltzer). Squeeze the lemon wedge into the drink before dropping it in. Stir briefly.

BRANDY SOUR

Those who like sweet-and-sour sensations but aren't enamored of whiskey will prefer the Brandy Sour to its better-known, whiskey-based relation.

2 ounces brandy
¾ ounce fresh orange juice
½ ounce simple syrup
♦ maraschino cherry
♦ orange slice

Combine liquid ingredients in a cocktail shaker, with ice. Shake well, and strain into a chilled sour glass. Garnish with the cherry and orange slice.

BULLDOG

The strong cherry flavor of this rich brown cocktail is cut, slightly, by the lime juice, but it still predominates.

1½ ounces cherry brandy
¾ ounce light rum
2 teaspoons fresh lime juice

Combine ingredients in a cocktail shaker, with ice. Shake well, and strain into a chilled cocktail glass.

BULL'S MILK

This frothy concoction looks and tastes like a malted milk.

1½ ounces brandy
1 ounce dark rum
8 ounces (1 cup) milk
1 teaspoon powdered sugar
freshly grated nutmeg

Combine liquid ingredients and sugar in a standard cocktail shaker, with ice. Shake well, and strain into a chilled highball glass. Sprinkle the nutmeg on top.

CHARLES COCKTAIL

The Charles is a brandy variation on the scotch-based Rob Roy.

2 ounces brandy
1 ounce sweet vermouth
dash Angostura bitters

Combine ingredients in a cocktail shaker, with ice. Shake well, and strain into a chilled cocktail glass.

BRANDY

CHARLIE CHAPLIN

This cocktail's coral color and sweet-and-sour mix of flavors make it as entertaining as the silent-film star after whom it's named.

♂ lime wedge
1 ounce apricot brandy
1 ounce sloe gin
1 ounce fresh lime juice

Rim a chilled cocktail glass with the lime wedge. Combine the other ingredients in a cocktail shaker, with ice. Shake well, and strain into the glass. Garnish with the lime wedge, squeezing it into the drink and dropping it in.

CHERRY BLOSSOM

Drinkology prefers this cocktail to most other drinks incorporating cherry brandy. Its color is decidedly *unlike* that of a blooming cherry tree (well, the bark, maybe), but the flavor's nicely balanced and not too sweet.

1½ ounces brandy
1 ounce cherry brandy
½ ounce Cointreau or triple sec
½ ounce fresh lemon juice

Combine ingredients in a cocktail shaker, with ice. Shake well, and strain into a chilled cocktail glass.

CLASSIC COCKTAIL

Some might accuse this drink of being "generic" rather than classic, but the lemony-rosy color and good sweet-sour balance are appealing.

lemon wedge
superfine sugar
1½ ounces brandy
½ ounce Cointreau or triple sec
½ ounce maraschino liqueur
½ ounce fresh lemon juice

Rim a chilled cocktail glass with the lemon wedge and sugar. (Discard the wedge.) Combine the other ingredients in a cocktail shaker, with ice. Shake well, and strain into the cocktail glass.

COLD DECK

Crème de menthe—even in minimal amounts—often lords it over the other flavors in a mixed drink. Here, it plays a supporting role, beautifully melding the brandy and vermouth.

1½ ounces brandy
¾ ounce sweet vermouth
2 teaspoons white crème de menthe

Combine ingredients in a cocktail shaker, with ice. Shake well, and strain into a chilled cocktail glass.

BRANDY

CORPSE REVIVERS

 Though certainly a colorful tag, *Corpse Reviver* is a fairly meaningless term, in that it refers to a whole class of drinks, popular during the Victorian era, that resemble one another only in that they combine equal measures of various liquors untainted by any mixer or garnish. One *Drinkology* taste-tester suggested that Corpse Revivers resemble nothing so much as what an inventive teenager, let loose in his or her parents' liquor cabinet, might concoct. Originally devised as hangover "cures," Corpse Revivers are not the *hair* of the dog that bit you—they're the rabid, growling, canine-baring beast itself. Here are two variations; neither is for the faint of heart (or tongue).

VARIATION #1

1 ounce brandy
1 ounce applejack
1 ounce sweet vermouth

Combine ingredients in a mixing glass, with ice. Stir well, and strain into a chilled cocktail glass.

VARIATION #2

1 ounce brandy
1 ounce Fernet Branca
1 ounce white crème de menthe

Combine ingredients in a mixing glass, with ice. Stir well, and strain into a chilled cocktail glass.

EAST INDIA

Brandy and pineapple juice make for a frothy, fruity, scrumptious cocktail.

1½ ounces brandy
1½ ounces pineapple juice
dash Angostura bitters

Combine ingredients in a cocktail shaker, with ice. Shake well, and strain into a chilled cocktail glass.

HARVARD COCKTAIL

This extremely aromatic cocktail's color isn't quite Harvard crimson (it's more a blood-orange hue).

1½ ounces brandy
¾ ounce sweet vermouth
2 teaspoons fresh lemon juice
1 teaspoon grenadine
dash Angostura bitters

Combine ingredients in a cocktail shaker, with ice. Shake well, and strain into a chilled cocktail glass.

BRANDY

HONEYMOON COCKTAIL

This butterscotch-yellow cocktail's lemon-drop flavor nicely balances tart and sweet.

1½ ounces applejack
¾ ounce Bénédictine
1 teaspoon Cointreau or triple sec
1 ounce fresh lemon juice
♂ maraschino cherry

Combine liquid ingredients in a cocktail shaker, with ice. Shake well, and strain into a chilled cocktail glass. Garnish with the cherry.

INTERNATIONAL COCKTAIL

The anisette acts as an assimilating agent in this melting pot of flavors.

2 ounces brandy
¼ ounce anisette
¼ ounce Cointreau
2 teaspoons vodka

Combine ingredients in a cocktail shaker, with ice. Shake well, and strain into a chilled cocktail glass.

Is Paris Burning?

Brandy and the black raspberry–flavored liqueur Chambord carry on a fiery love affair in this richly colored, richly flavored cocktail.

♣ lemon twist
2 ounces brandy
½ ounce Chambord

Rim a chilled cocktail glass with the lemon twist. Combine brandy and Chambord in a mixing glass, with ice. Stir, and strain into the glass. Garnish with the twist.

Jack-in-the-Box

Using a good-quality applejack brings out this tart, refreshing cocktail's virtues.

1½ ounces applejack
1½ ounces pineapple juice
½ teaspoon fresh lemon juice
dash Angostura bitters

Combine ingredients in a cocktail shaker, with ice. Shake well, and strain into a chilled cocktail glass.

JACK ROSE

The Jack Rose has been around a long time—it dates back to the 1910s, at least—but it doesn't have the status of other classic cocktails. That's a shame; it's a delicious, good-looking drink—well worth featuring at a cocktail party.

2½ ounces applejack
½ ounce fresh lemon juice
¼ ounce grenadine

Combine ingredients in a cocktail shaker, with ice. Shake well, and strain into a chilled cocktail glass.

JERSEY LIGHTNING

If you're of the opinion that applejack's a déclassé liquor, try this drink. Its appealing, cidery color and beautifully balanced, articulate flavor make it a *Drinkology* favorite. "Jersey Lightning," by the way, is a nickname for applejack, which was first distilled in the Garden State.

2 ounces applejack
1 ounce sweet vermouth
1 ounce fresh lime juice
¼ ounce simple syrup

Combine ingredients in a cocktail shaker, with ice. Shake well, and strain into a chilled cocktail glass.

METROPOLITAN

This sweet, mahogany-colored drink will appeal to those who like Manhattans.

1½ ounces brandy
1½ ounces sweet vermouth
½ teaspoon simple syrup
dash Angostura bitters
⚬ maraschino cherry

Combine liquid ingredients in a cocktail shaker, with ice. Shake well, and strain into a chilled cocktail glass. Garnish with the cherry.

MIDNIGHT COCKTAIL

The pretty lemonade color of this cocktail seems a bit perky for the midnight hour; the taste is dominated by the apricot brandy, so try it only if that's a taste you're especially fond of.

1½ ounce apricot brandy
¾ ounce Cointreau or triple sec
½ ounce fresh lemon juice

Combine ingredients in a cocktail shaker, with ice. Shake well, and strain into a chilled cocktail glass.

MIKADO

The Mikado is about as Japanese as the Gilbert and Sullivan operetta of the same name, but it's a very drinkable concoction all the same.

1½ ounces brandy
½ ounce Cointreau or triple sec
1 teaspoon amaretto
1 teaspoon grenadine
dash Angostura bitters

Combine ingredients in a cocktail shaker, with ice. Shake well, and strain into an ice-filled old-fashioned glass.

MOONLIGHT

Applejack fans who like sweet-and-sour tastes will love this ginger-colored cocktail.

2 ounces applejack
1 ounce fresh lemon juice
1 teaspoon simple syrup

Combine ingredients in a cocktail shaker, with ice. Shake well, and strain into a chilled cocktail glass.

MORNING COCKTAIL

 This complex mixture produces an amber-colored, clean-tasting drink.

1 ounce brandy
1 ounce dry vermouth
¼ teaspoon Cointreau or triple sec
¼ teaspoon Pernod or other anise-flavored liqueur
dash Angostura bitters
♂ maraschino cherry

Combine liquid ingredients in a cocktail shaker, with ice. Shake well, and strain into an old-fashioned glass filled with ice. Garnish with the cherry.

OLYMPIC

 Few brandy-based drinks really seem suitable for brunch or afternoon cocktails. This tangy concoction—with a clean and pleasant aftertaste—definitely does.

1½ ounces brandy
½ ounce Cointreau or triple sec
1 ounce orange juice

Combine ingredients in a cocktail shaker, with ice. Shake well, and strain into a chilled cocktail glass.

BRANDY

PARADISE

This cocktail's so gently aromatic that apricot-brandy lovers will find it hard to resist the urge to gulp it down.

1 ounce apricot brandy
¾ ounce gin
¾ ounce orange juice

Combine ingredients in a cocktail shaker, with ice. Shake well, and strain into a chilled cocktail glass.

PISCO SOUR

Peru and Chile both lay claim to being the original home of pisco—a powerful brandy whose taste resembles that of grappa. Both countries likewise claim ownership of the Pisco Sour. We'll let them fight it out while we relax with this iconic cocktail.

2 ounces pisco
1 ounce fresh lemon juice
1 ounce simple syrup
½ egg white
a few drops of Angostura bitters

Combine the pisco, lemon juice, simple syrup, and egg white in a cocktail shaker, with ice. Shake vigorously and strain into a chilled cocktail glass. Gently shake a few drops of bitters onto the frothy surface of the cocktail, and, using a toothpick, delicately swirl the bitters around to create a looping or feathery pattern. (This decoration is traditional.)

SHARKY PUNCH

The Sharky Punch is a light-textured but strong-flavored lowball.

1½ ounces applejack
½ ounce rye whiskey
1 teaspoon powdered sugar
club soda or seltzer

Combine applejack, rye, and sugar in a cocktail shaker, with ice. Shake well, and strain into an old-fashioned glass filled with ice cubes. Top with the soda (or seltzer), and stir briefly.

SIDECAR

This well-known, well-balanced cocktail, which dates from the early 1900s, was purportedly named to honor a Frenchman who always arrived at his favorite Paris bar in a motorcycle sidecar.

lemon wedge
superfine sugar
1½ ounces brandy
1½ ounces Cointreau or triple sec
½ ounce fresh lemon juice

Rim a chilled cocktail glass with the lemon wedge and sugar. (Discard the wedge.) Combine the other ingredients in a cocktail shaker, with ice. Shake well, and strain into the prepared glass.

BRANDY

STAR COCKTAIL

This stellar cocktail—a *Drinkology* favorite—is reminiscent of a Manhattan, but with a hint of apple flavor.

♂ lemon twist
1½ ounces applejack
1½ ounces sweet vermouth
2 dashes Angostura bitters

Rim a chilled cocktail glass with the lemon twist. Combine the other ingredients in a mixing glass, with ice. Stir, and strain into the glass. Garnish with the twist.

STINGER

The Stinger is traditionally drunk as a nightcap. (You might think of it as more potent soporific than peppermint tea.)

2 ounces brandy
1 ounce white crème de menthe
crushed ice

Combine ingredients in a cocktail shaker, with ice. Shake well, and strain into a chilled cocktail glass or a rocks glass packed with crushed ice.

Champagne and
Sparkling Wine

T HE WINE WE CALL CHAMPAGNE IS THE RESULT OF A VERY HAPPY
accident of geography, climate, and biology—though it wasn't
always considered so happy.

The Champagne region of France is among the most northerly of
the world's wine regions, meaning that its growing season is short and
its winters relatively cold. Well, back in the day—*way* back, centuries
before the process of fermentation was scientifically explained—
the winemakers of Champagne frequently encountered what they
thought of as a *big problem*. It wasn't bad enough that their wines,
made from grapes that often did not have the chance to ripen fully
before harvest, were generally considered subpar. Worse was the fact
that Champagne's wines sometimes *fizzed*—unpredictably, and for
reasons unknown. At the time, bubbly wines were decidedly unfash-
ionable, and the trait was viewed as a serious fault.

As we now understand, Champagne's wines were sometimes
fizzy because their fermentation was sometimes interrupted by

especially chilly autumns. The region's winemakers, unaware that the yeast in their fermenting vats had gone dormant—unaware, even, that fermentation is caused by yeast—would transfer their presumably "finished" wines into casks (the typical wine containers of that era), not realizing that fermentation would naturally recommence when warmer temperatures returned in spring. And that second fermentation, confined within the sealed casks, would, of course, produce carbon dioxide gas that was released as streams of bubbles when the casks were opened.

Much effort was devoted by the vintners of Champagne to solving this problem. In fact, the great Benedictine vintner-botanist Dom Pérignon (1638–1715), far from being the "inventor" of champagne (that was nature's doing), expended considerable energy trying to stop his region's wines' from bubbling. In vain.

A New Problem (And a Solution!)

The chronic *mal de tête* only began to be relieved, really, when wine fashion unaccountably changed. Round about the late seventeenth century, the roués of London cafés and the courtiers of Versailles (and their trendsetting mistresses) conceived an unquenchable thirst for the bizarrely bubbly wines of Champagne. Now, the region's winemakers were suddenly faced with a diametrically opposite problem—how to meet this new demand by making sure that their wines, whose fizziness had previously been a matter of chance, would *always* sparkle.

That necessity was the mother of the invention of the *méthode champenoise*—a several-step process for ensuring and controlling Champagne's second fermentation. The *méthode*, which was developed over decades of experimentation, involves the deliberate introduction of a mixture of yeast and sugar into still (i.e., nonbubbly) wine, the refermentation of the wine in bottle (bottles having replaced casks as the preferred wine containers), the disgorgement of the lees (the fermentation residue, consisting mostly of dead yeast cells) from the bottle, and, finally, the addition of sugar to achieve the desired level of sweetness.

The names of most of the winemakers responsible for perfecting the *méthode* are lost to us, but the last in that long line of experimenters was, notably, a woman. She was Nicole Barbe Clicquot-Ponsardin, better known as la Veuve Clicquot (the Widow Clicquot), who inherited her husband's champagne-making operation on his death in 1806. Some time thereafter, she created the ingenious contraption known as the riddling board—as legend has it, by drilling holes in her kitchen table. The board's holes hold bottles containing refermented wine; it is gradually repositioned so that the bottles are eventually turned upside down, allowing the lees to drift into the bottles' necks, where the residue can easily be disgorged. What a gal. Until Clicquot-Ponsardin's time, champagne was always cloudy; she transformed it into the brilliant, crystalline beverage we enjoy today.

A Few Bubbly Basics

The sparkling wines of France's Champagne region are the *only* sparkling wines that can legitimately be called *champagne*. Other sparkling wines—even those that are produced by a process replicating the *méthode champenoise*—are . . . well, they're *not* champagne. In the past two hundred years, two other ways of creating sparkling wines have been introduced: In one of these, the *tank method*, the second fermentation occurs in (you guessed it) a big tank rather than inside individual bottles. In the other, the wine is made to sparkle through a *carbonation* process like that used to make soda pop. (There is no second fermentation.) Both these methods produce wines that are inferior—in the complexity of their taste and the quality of their effervescence—to champagnes and the other sparkling wines created in the "classic" way. That doesn't mean they aren't drinkable: Italian Proseccos, for instance, are deliciously quaffable wines made using the tank method.

Most champagnes are *nonvintage* (NV) champagnes, which means that they are made from wines from several different years (vintages) that are meticulously blended before being bottled and refermented. When making NV champagne, each house (i.e., champagne maker) aims to produce a wine that is consistent from year to year and one whose "style" is readily identifiable as that house's own. By contrast, *vintage* champagnes are made from the grapes of a single harvest; the harvest has to be a very good one, in terms of the grapes' quality, for a house to "declare a vintage." Because of their relative rarity, vintage champagnes are costlier than NV champagnes—but note that their taste is not nearly so predictable. The costliest of all champagnes are the so-called *prestige cuvées*—vintage wines created by the top champagne houses from grapes grown in the region's very best vineyards.

Although sparkling wines can be—and are—made from all sorts of grapes, champagne proper is made from only three varieties: the white grape called Chardonnay and the black grapes Pinot Noir and Pinot Meunier. Pinot Noir dominates, being used in most champagnes. A champagne labeled *blanc de blancs* ("white of whites") is made entirely of Chardonnay; one labeled *blanc de noirs* ("white of blacks") is made entirely of black grapes. Though the vast majority of champagnes are white wines (white wines can be made from either white or black grapes), there are also rosé champagnes. (Nobody who knows anything about champagne ever calls such wine "pink champagne.")

Champagnes are also distinguished from one another by levels of sweetness. Champagne marked *extra brut* is exceptionally dry, containing less than 0.6 percent sugar; *brut* is just a bit less dry, with up to 1.5 percent sugar. Because American wine drinkers tend to prefer dry wines, the champagnes available stateside generally fall into the brut or extra-brut categories, although champagne makers produce bubblies in a spectrum of sweetnesses.

SERVING CHAMPAGNE

There are nearly half a billion bubbles in a bottle of sparkly, with enough internal pressure to keep a truck tire inflated, so watch where you point the thing when you open it. A big pop is festive, sure, but the idea is to keep the fizz in your glass. With a towel draped over your hand and the bottle at ten o'clock, hold the cork firmly while rotating the bottle with your other hand. Twist until the cork is loosened. It won't make as much noise as prying the cork off with your thumbs, but the golden liquid will dance across your palate.

The original champagne *coupe,* or saucer, was purportedly created by Louis XVI and based on an impression of Marie Antoinette's breast made by a French porcelain maker. As appealing as this legend may be, the modern champagne flute is much better at keeping the bubbles in your glass, and will yield more satisfying results.

Champagne should always be served cold, so refrigerate it for about two hours before serving. (Don't store champagne for too long in the fridge, however: it will lose its oomph.) If the bottle you want to open hasn't been refrigerated, you can chill it down in about twenty minutes by setting it in a champagne bucket that's half filled with equal amounts of ice and water. (To get the proper chilling effect, you've got to add water to the ice.) Once a bottle is opened, finish it. Forget what you've heard about a silver spoon preserving the wine's effervescence: it's nonsense. While a champagne stopper may keep it sparkling a little longer, why risk it? If you run out, you can always open another bottle.

Better yet, you can buy a bigger one. Champagne can be purchased by the magnum, equivalent to two bottles, the Methuselah (eight bottles) the Nebuchadnezzar (twenty bottles), and various sizes in between, all of which are, oddly, named for Old Testament personages. Experts declare that the bigger bottles have a salutary effect on the champagne's flavor; several of *Drinkology*'s taste-testers were lucky enough to have sampled a Nebuchadnezzar of Veuve Clicquot at a New Year's Eve party several years back, and we can vouch for . . . well, we frankly can't remember much about it. (If you're only in the mood for a glass or two, take heart: champagne also comes in half-bottles and in the very small bottles called splits, which hold about one and a half flutes' worth.)

SPARKLING-WINE COCKTAILS

Champagne is a fine mixer, enhancing the flavors of bitters, sugar, citrus, brandy, and fruity syrups and liqueurs. By the same token, you may not want to use—some would say *waste*—expensive

French champagne in sparkling-wine cocktails. Except when preparing the classic (and very simple) Champagne Cocktail (page 101), which truly benefits from a good NV champagne, you'll do better choosing a decent, dry California sparkling wine—preferably one made according to the classic method—for the recipes in this chapter. Actually, any good, dry sparkling wine—no matter where it hails from—will do. (If you're tempted to make sparkling-wine cocktails from a vintage champagne or—God help you—a prestige cuvée, you have too much money for your own good and should give it all to *Drinkology* instead.)

Do notice that there's a basic similarity among sparkling-wine mixed drinks: all are mostly wine and use only sparing amounts of the other ingredients. There's a good reason for that: the taste of champagne and other good sparkling wines is so delicate that it can easily be overwhelmed by other flavors. Since champagne flutes differ in size, the recipes in this chapter are necessarily inexact; a good principle for most sparkling-wine cocktails is that the ratio between the wine and the other ingredients should be roughly 5 to 1—and weighted even more heavily in the wine's favor for cocktails using strong-flavored liqueurs and syrups.

When making any champagne- or sparkling wine–based cocktail, be *very* careful. Always place the other ingredients—including the garnishes, if any—in the flute before topping with the wine. Sparkling wines, remember, are *fizzy,* and plopping a piece of fruit in after the wine's been added will cause it to froth up and overrun the glass. Pour the wine slowly, gently, and deliberately, tilting the glass slightly and letting the champagne run down its inside wall. You might have to pause a couple of times while pouring to prevent a spill.

CHAMPAGNE

BELLINI (BONA FIDE VERSION)

Drinkology thinks the Venetian painter Giovanni Bellini was a great artist—and that the sparkling-wine cocktail named for him is a great drink. Appropriately invented at Harry's Bar in Venice in the 1940s, it calls for just two ingredients: the Italian dry sparkling wine called Prosecco and a ripe white peach. Prosecco is easy enough to come by; ripe white peaches, not so easy. Lots of cocktail guides tell you to cheat on the peaches—advising you to use (ripe) yellow peaches instead or, in their absence, bottled peach nectar. And you can make a nice cocktail that way—it's just not a *real* Bellini. (See our "phony baloney" Bellini, opposite.)

Drinkology despaired of ever being able to make a real Bellini at home, but then we moved to New Jersey, a state that has fabulous farmers' markets, where, in late summer, one can readily procure heavenly white peaches. Hence the addition of the actual, bona fide Bellini to our canon.

Some notes: The amount of Prosecco to be used is not specified in the following recipe, since this will depend on the size of your champagne flutes. Make sure that the peach is absolutely ripe, and make sure, too, that you chill both the peach and the Prosecco before beginning. (Do *not*, however, chill the flute.) To peel the peach, fill a large saucepan with water and bring it to a boil over high heat. Cut a small, shallow *X* in the bottom of the peach (the end opposite the stem end). Using tongs, place the peach in the boiling water for about thirty seconds (or just until the skin begins to curl away from the slits forming the *X*). Use the tongs to remove the peach from the water and immediately plunge it into ice-cold water. The skin should come off very easily.

1 medium-size, extremely ripe fresh white peach, peeled
    and pitted
Prosecco
♺ thin, peeled slice of white peach

In a blender, purée the peach until liquefied. (This will take only a second or two.) Pour the purée into a champagne flute, filling the glass about one-third full. (You'll have peach purée left over—probably plenty enough to make a second or even a third Bellini.) Drop the peach slice into the flute. Now, pouring ever so gently, slowly, and carefully, *top with Prosecco. (It will foam up mightily, so take this caution seriously.)*

BELLINI (PHONY BALONEY VERSION)

As we indicate in the previous recipe, white peaches aren't always easy to find. And although Prosecco is widely available, not every wine shop carries it. So if you have a hankering for a Bellini but can't find the proper ingredients, try this phony baloney version. Consider it an oil-on-velvet copy of the Harry's Bar masterpiece.

1 ounce peach nectar
1 teaspoon peach schnapps
about 5 ounces dry or off-dry sparkling wine

Pour the peach nectar and schnapps into a champagne flute. Gently top with sparkling wine.

BRANDY CHAMPAGNE COCKTAIL

Brandy and sparkling wine make excellent flute-mates.

1 sugar cube
2 dashes Angostura bitters
½ ounce brandy
about 5 ounces dry sparkling wine

Drop the sugar cube into a champagne flute. Soak the cube with the bitters, and add the brandy. Gently top with sparkling wine.

CAMPARI CHAMPAGNE COCKTAIL

Campari has its detractors, but those who like its bitter fruitiness will relish this combination. The sugar cube helps buffer the aperitif's bite—but doesn't dispel it entirely.

♂ orange peel
1 sugar cube
1 ounce Campari
about 5 ounces dry sparkling wine

Rim a champagne flute with the orange peel. Drop the peel and sugar cube into the flute. Add the Campari. Gently top with sparkling wine.

CHAMPAGNE

CHAMPAGNE COCKTAIL (CLASSIC)

Why ruin good champagne by mixing it with other stuff? The answer is more complicated than you might imagine. Many sparkling wine–based cocktails are wonderfully refreshing drinks, but there's no sense in using expensive French champagne to make them. The classic Champagne Cocktail, however, is of a different order. Its simplicity very nearly demands that it be prepared with a superior bubbly. The other flavors—sugar, bitters, lemon—will enhance, not degrade, the champagne experience . . . .

Or so insist friends who are Champagne Cocktail enthusiasts. If you remain doubtful, choose a cheaper California (or Italian, or Spanish) sparkling wine instead (do make sure it's a *dry* one). If you don't already have a favorite, ask the proprietor of your local liquor store for advice, and specify that you want a robustly flavored bubbly. (Some sparkling wines are too delicately flavored and will be overpowered by the other ingredients.)

♂ lemon twist
1 sugar cube
2 or 3 dashes Angostura bitters
about 5 ounces champagne

Rim a champagne flute with the lemon twist. Drop the twist and the sugar cube into the glass. Add the bitters. Gently top with champagne.

CHAMPAGNE FIZZ

This tingling cocktail—a *Drinkology* favorite—is the perfect starter for a summertime brunch. (Your guests might just renounce Mimosas forever.) If this version proves too tart, try increasing the amount of simple syrup slightly.

1 ounce gin
1 ounce fresh lemon juice
½ teaspoon simple syrup
about 4 ounces dry sparkling wine

Combine gin, lemon juice, and simple syrup in a cocktail shaker, with ice. Shake well, and strain into a champagne flute. Gently top with sparkling wine.

CHICAGO

The mild and pleasant-tasting Chicago is just a bit more complicated than most other sparkling wine–based cocktails.

lemon wedge
superfine sugar
1½ ounces brandy
¼ teaspoon Cointreau
dash Angostura bitters
about 5 ounces dry sparkling wine

Rim a white wine glass with the lemon wedge and sugar. (Discard the wedge.) Combine the brandy, Cointreau, and bitters in a cocktail shaker, with ice. Shake well, and strain into the prepared glass. Top with sparkling wine, and stir very briefly.

FRENCH CHAMPAGNE COCKTAIL

Calling this cocktail "French" may be a bit of overkill. It's basically a sweeter, bolder version of the Kir Royale (page 104), which is already as French as you can get.

1 sugar cube
2 dashes Angostura bitters
½ ounce crème de cassis
about 5 ounces dry sparkling wine

Drop the sugar cube into a champagne flute. Soak the cube with the bitters, and add the cassis. Gently top with sparkling wine.

IRISH CHAMPAGNE COCKTAIL

This variation on the classic Champagne Cocktail has a discernable brogue.

♂ lemon twist
1 sugar cube
2 dashes Angostura bitters
1 ounce Irish whiskey
about 5 ounces dry sparkling wine

Rim a champagne flute with the lemon twist. Drop the twist and sugar cube into the flute. Add the bitters and whiskey. Gently top with sparkling wine.

CHAMPAGNE

KIR IMPERIALE

This is a raspberry-flavored sibling of the Kir Royale (below). The color's wonderful, and the taste is crisp and definite.

1 teaspoon Chambord
5 or 6 ounces dry sparkling wine
♻ lemon twist, if desired

Pour the Chambord into a champagne flute, and gently top with sparkling wine. (If using a twist, rim the flute beforehand and drop the twist into it before adding the Chambord.)

KIR ROYALE

The ordinary Kir (page 319) has a social-climbing sibling— the Kir Royale. When preparing this drink, obey the dictum "Less is more"; if you increase the amount of cassis, you'll end up with a gorgeously purple but cloying, syrupy concoction in which the currant flavor completely masks that of the sparkling wine.

½ teaspoon crème de cassis
5 or 6 ounces dry sparkling wine
♻ lemon twist, if desired

Pour the cassis into a champagne flute, and gently top with sparkling wine. (If using a twist, rim the flute beforehand and drop the twist into it before adding the cassis.)

MIMOSA

A brunchtime favorite, the Mimosa is undoubtedly the sparkling wine–based cocktail that's most familiar to Americans today. Unfortunately, most of the Mimosas served are drab, flat, half–orange juice, half-wine concoctions. *Drinkology* prefers the following recipe, which resembles the purported original, first poured at the Ritz Hotel in Paris in 1925. Fresh-squeezed orange juice isn't a must, but it improves the drink enormously.

1 ounce orange juice, preferably fresh-squeezed
¼ ounce Cointreau or triple sec
about 5 ounces dry sparkling wine

Pour the orange juice and Cointreau into a champagne flute. Gently top with sparkling wine. Stir very briefly.

STRAWBERRY-RHUBARB PIE

The herbal quality of the rhubarb bitters (available from Fee Brothers, www.feebrothers.com) tartly contends with the strawberry liqueur's sweetness in this far-from-rustic cocktail—a *Drinkology* original.

½ ounce strawberry liqueur
2 dashes rhubarb bitters
about 6 ounces dry sparkling wine

Rim a champagne flute with the lemon twist and drop it in. Pour in the liqueur, add the bitters, and gently top with sparkling wine.

THAMES CHAMPAGNE COCKTAIL

The wonderfully unique liqueur called Pimm's Cup complements sparkling wine beautifully. This amber-colored cocktail—a *Drinkology* favorite—is crisp and delicious.

⚘ lemon twist
1 sugar cube
½ ounce Pimm's Cup No. 1
about 5 ounces dry sparkling wine

Rim the champagne flute with the twist. Drop the twist and sugar cube into the flute. Add the Pimm's Cup. Gently top with sparkling wine.

TWIN SET

The highly perfumed French elderflower liqueur St-Germain does well combined with citrus, especially grapefruit, and sparkling wine.

1½ ounces St-Germain elderflower liqueur
2 ounces pink grapefruit juice
1 ounce vodka
2 dashes grapefruit bitters
dry sparkling wine
⚘ strawberry half

Place the strawberry half in a champagne flute. Combine St-Germain, grapefruit juice, vodka, and bitters in a cocktail shaker, with ice. Shake well and strain into the flute. Gently top with sparkling wine.

Gin

G IN IS A NEUTRAL GRAIN SPIRIT THAT, AT ONE OR ANOTHER STAGE in the distilling process, has been flavored with juniper berries and, in the case of most gins, other aromatic botanicals as well. (The word *gin* is probably derived from either the Dutch *jenever* or the French *genièvre,* both meaning "juniper.") Some younger drinkers today are apt to diss gin, considering it an older (and more besotted) generation's liquor of choice. It's ironic: the young urban pub-crawler who wouldn't think of having a "gin Martini"—preferring the bastardized, vodka version of the cocktail—probably has no idea that gin is basically nothing other than a specially flavored kind of vodka, that is, a neutral grain spirit to which water has been added. (To be fair, younger drinkers do remain partial to the Gin and Tonic: so much so that they've made this mixed drink, which used only to be served in the sweltering heat of summer—or India!—acceptable year round.)

NAUGHTY AND NICE

Gin's bad rap is nothing new. Famous tippler W. C. Fields once joked, "I never drink anything stronger than gin before breakfast," and among those who view a drinker's career as a sort of slippery-slope affair, developing a taste for gin represents the penultimate stage of degeneration—the one you hit just before you hit skid row. This is one-sided and unfair—gin, after all, is the essential ingredient in a host of classic cocktails and mixed drinks associated with a sophisticated and elegant style of living. But it also has a ring of truth about it. The history of gin is a checkered one, to say the least.

Gin was invented in Holland in the mid-seventeenth century by a physician-chemist who promoted it as a cure for kidney ailments. (Such was the state of medical science at the time.) It's the English, however, not the Dutch, who are most responsible for fostering the spirit's international popularity. England became a nation of gin drinkers as the result of a trade war. In 1689, the country's new (and Dutch) king, William III, imposed heavy tariffs on French wine and brandy—a minor, nonmilitary skirmish in an ongoing and otherwise bloody contretemps between England and France. The English turned for solace to the gin makers of King William's homeland, who were more than happy to pick up the slack.

It wasn't long before English distillers began making gin themselves—and gin began accruing a root-of-all-evil sort of reputation. Gin was cheap and plentiful. The poor drank it. British soldiers drank it before heading into battle (the boost of fearlessness gin provided them was dubbed "Dutch courage"). Pregnant women who didn't want to be pregnant drank it, (mistakenly) believing it would cause them to miscarry. The eighteenth century saw a proliferation of "gin palaces" and a rise in unseemly public drunkenness—and, unsurprisingly, the start of the modern temperance movement.

GIN

Interestingly, gin, which was invented as a medicine (though one of dubious value), had its reputation salvaged by a genuinely medicinal purpose to which it was put in the nineteenth century. British colonials in the more tropical reaches of the Empire (especially South Asia) developed the habit of mixing their gin with quinine water in hopes of staving off malaria. This mixture, ancestor of today's Gin and Tonic, can't prevent or cure malaria, but it actually does have some worth in controlling the symptoms of the disease—due, of course, to the quinine, not the gin (which merely helps the medicine go down).

And gin got a further leg-up out of the gutter in the mid- to late nineteenth century, as bartenders in England and elsewhere began employing it as the basis for a range of high-toned cocktails, especially the Martini. Today, gin serves as the foundation for a wider variety of cocktails than any other liquor.

TYPES OF GIN

Most gins commonly available in American liquor stores are of the "dry" variety. (Dry gins made in England are often labeled "London Dry.") Don't let this apparent conformity fool you, however: though they're all distilled primarily from corn, different dry gins taste very different from one another because of the distinctive combinations of juniper and other spices and herbs used to flavor them. If you don't believe *Drinkology,* just try sipping a shot of a mild dry gin like Beefeater or Gordon's and comparing it with a more highly "perfumed" gin—Bombay, say. Most of the gin-based recipes presented here will work best with a relatively nonaromatic dry gin. For the Martini and a few other drinks in which the taste of gin predominates, however, it's really taster's choice.

GIN

More and more liquor stores are carrying a range of gins beyond the standard "dry" gins. Distilled in Plymouth, England, *Plymouth Gin* (a brand name as well as a distinctive type) is less aromatic and slightly lower in alcohol than many dry gins. Its flavor is subtly candylike, and it makes a great mixer—especially for Martinis (many Martini drinkers prefer it) and for any of the sweeter gin-based drinks. Even sweeter is *Old Tom gin*—perhaps the original basis for the Tom Collins (see page 151). Old Tom, which used to be next to impossible to find in the U.S., is now fairly widely available. The sweet and malty-flavored *Dutch gin* (also known as *Genever*) is also showing up on more liquor stores' shelves, as are a variety of flavored gins. One flavored gin—infused with saffron—is the basis for our Saffron Sunset cocktail (page 145). Finally, note that *sloe gin* isn't gin at all; it's a liqueur flavored with sloe berries.

ABBEY COCKTAIL

This pleasant cocktail resembles a gin Screwdriver; the Lillet smoothes and balances the taste.

2 ounces dry or Plymouth gin
1 ounce Lillet Blanc
1 ounce orange juice
2 dashes orange bitters
♴ maraschino cherry

Combine liquid ingredients in a cocktail shaker, with ice. Shake well, and strain into a chilled cocktail glass. Garnish with the cherry.

ALEXANDER

The gin-based Alexander is the ancestor of the more famous Brandy Alexander (page 71). *Drinkology* has reversed the lineage, basing our (gin) Alexander recipe on our pumped-up version of the brandy drink.

1 ounce dry or Plymouth gin
¾ ounce white crème de cacao
1 ounce heavy cream
2 heaping teaspoons whipped cream
pinch freshly grated nutmeg

Combine ingredients—including whipped cream—in a cocktail shaker, with ice. Shake well, and strain into a chilled cocktail glass. Sprinkle nutmeg on top.

ARTILLERY

If you like your Martinis sweet, you might really go for the Artillery, which is basically a shaken Martini that uses sweet vermouth instead of dry.

2 ounces dry or Plymouth gin
1 ounce sweet vermouth

Combine ingredients in a cocktail shaker, with ice. Shake well, and strain into a chilled cocktail glass.

GIN

AVIATION

The Aviation looks (and tastes) like lemonade. It's a mouth-puckering refreshment for a sultry summer evening.

2 ounces dry or Plymouth gin
¾ ounce fresh lemon juice
1 heaping teaspoon powdered sugar
2 dashes maraschino liqueur

Combine ingredients in a cocktail shaker, with ice. Shake well, and strain into a chilled cocktail glass.

BEAUTY SPOT

Its delicately chocolatey flavor and pale complexion ("blemished" by a drop of garnet-red grenadine) make this cocktail a pageant winner.

2 ounces dry or Plymouth gin
¾ ounce white crème de cacao
1 egg white
½ teaspoon grenadine

Combine gin, crème de cacao, and egg white in a cocktail shaker, with ice. Shake well, and strain into a cocktail glass. Carefully drip the grenadine into the center of the cocktail.

GIN

BLUE BOY

A *Drinkology* original, the Blue Boy is a more masculine (well, sort of) variation on the Pink Lady (recipe on page 143).

2 ounces dry or Plymouth gin
1 teaspoon blue curaçao
½ ounce heavy cream
2 teaspoons fresh lemon juice
1 egg white

Combine ingredients in a cocktail shaker, with ice. Shake well, and strain into a chilled cocktail glass.

BOSTON COCKTAIL

This tart, peachy-colored cocktail has a deep apricot flavor— so try it only if you're a fan of the fruit.

1½ ounces dry or Plymouth gin
1½ ounces apricot brandy
¼ ounce fresh lemon juice
2 or 3 dashes grenadine

Combine ingredients in a cocktail shaker, with ice. Shake well, and strain into a cocktail glass.

GIN

BRONX COCKTAIL

The Bronx Cocktail—basically a sweet, shaken Martini—
was invented by a Waldorf Astoria barman just after he'd
paid a visit to the Bronx Zoo, though it's hard to see the
connection between this sophisticated brew and a bunch of
caged wild animals.

2 ounces dry gin
½ ounce dry vermouth
½ ounce sweet vermouth

*Combine ingredients in a cocktail shaker, with ice. Shake
well, and strain into a chilled cocktail glass.*

CABARET

This recipe drew raves from *Drinkology*'s taste-testers. It's
a truly well-balanced and sophisticated brew.

♂ lemon twist
  2 ounces dry or Plymouth gin
½ ounce sweet vermouth
dash of Pernod or other anise-flavored liqueur
dash of Angostura bitters

*Rim a chilled cocktail glass with the lemon twist. Combine
the other ingredients in a mixing glass, with ice. Stir, and
strain into the cocktail glass. Garnish with the twist.*

CHELSEA SIDECAR

This variation on the classic Sidecar (which uses brandy instead of gin; see page 89) is also known as the Chelsea Hotel or, more straightforwardly, as the Gin Sidecar.

♂ lemon twist
  2 ounces dry or Plymouth gin
½ ounce Cointreau or triple sec
1 teaspoon lemon juice

Rim a chilled cocktail glass with the lemon twist. Combine the other ingredients in a cocktail shaker, with ice. Shake well, and strain into the glass. Garnish with the twist.

CLOVER CLUB

Its brilliant coral color and frothy "head" make this cocktail— named for an early twentieth-century Philadelphia night- club—a fun and tempting drink.

2 ounces dry gin
½ ounce fresh lemon juice
½ ounce grenadine
1 egg white

Combine ingredients in a cocktail shaker, with ice. Shake well, and strain into a cocktail glass.

GIN

CRIMSON

This fruity cocktail is beautifully striped—a layer of deep, velvety red atop a pinkish base.

1½ ounces dry gin
2 teaspoons fresh lemon juice
1 teaspoon grenadine
¾ ounce ruby port

Combine gin, lemon juice, and grenadine in a cocktail shaker, with ice. Shake well, and strain into a cocktail glass. Float port on top.

DEMPSEY

This drink's striking red-orange color won't prepare you for its knockout taste, which, disarmingly, resembles that of a popular cold remedy.

1½ ounces dry or Plymouth gin
1½ ounces applejack
¼ ounce Pernod or other anise-flavored liqueur
¼ ounce grenadine

Combine ingredients in a mixing glass, with ice. Stir, and strain into a chilled cocktail glass.

DIXIE

Is it this cocktail's orangey-peachy color that identifies it with the South? The drink's fruity taste is spiced with a licorice note contributed by the Pernod.

1 ounce dry or Plymouth gin
½ ounce dry vermouth
¼ ounce Pernod or other anise-flavored liqueur
1 ounce orange juice
¼ teaspoon grenadine

Combine ingredients in a cocktail shaker, with ice. Shake well, and strain into a chilled cocktail glass.

DuBARRY COCKTAIL

This elegant cocktail knocked *Drinkology*'s taste-testers' socks off. Luckily, they kept their heads (unlike the cocktail's namesake).

↶ orange peel
1½ ounces dry gin
¾ ounce dry vermouth
½ teaspoon Pernod or other anise-flavored liqueur
dash Angostura bitters

Rim a chilled cocktail glass with the orange peel. Combine the other ingredients in a mixing glass, with ice. Stir, and strain into the cocktail glass. Garnish with the peel.

GIN

ENGLISH ROSE

The English Rose is pale pink, ladylike, and sugary.

lemon wedge
superfine sugar
1½ ounces dry or Plymouth gin
¾ ounce apricot brandy
¾ ounce dry vermouth
¼ ounce fresh lemon juice
¼ teaspoon grenadine

Rim a chilled cocktail glass with the lemon wedge and sugar. Combine the other ingredients in a cocktail shaker, with ice. Shake well, and strain into the prepared glass.

FARMER'S COCKTAIL

This is no slop to throw to the pigs. Its delicate amber tint and superb balance make it a good once-in-a-while alternative to the Martini. It's a *Drinkology* favorite.

1½ ounces dry gin
¾ ounce dry vermouth
¾ ounce sweet vermouth
2 dashes Angostura bitters

Combine ingredients in a mixing glass, with ice. Stir, and strain into a chilled cocktail glass.

GIN

FINE AND DANDY (GIN VERSION)

There's also a blended whiskey–based cocktail of this name (see page 292). The gin version is light, clean, sweet, and icy pink.

1½ ounces dry or Plymouth gin
½ ounce Cointreau or triple sec
½ ounce fresh lemon juice
dash Angostura bitters
♦ maraschino cherry

Combine liquid ingredients in a cocktail shaker, with ice. Shake well, and strain into a chilled cocktail glass. Garnish with the cherry.

FLAMINGO

Why, it's actually pink-flamingo pink! The lime juice nicely balances this delicious drink, preventing it from being too sweet.

1½ ounces dry or Plymouth gin
½ ounce apricot brandy
½ ounce fresh lime juice
1 teaspoon grenadine

Combine ingredients in a cocktail shaker, with ice. Shake well, and strain into a chilled cocktail glass.

GIN

FLYING DUTCHMAN

Icy, sweet, and (because of the twist) subtly lemony, the Flying Dutchman is a *Drinkology* favorite.

♂ lemon twist
2 ounces dry or Plymouth gin
½ ounce Cointreau or triple sec

Rim a chilled cocktail glass with the lemon twist. Combine liquid ingredients in a mixing glass, with ice. Stir, and strain into the cocktail glass. Garnish with the twist.

FOGHORN

Citrusy and tart, the Foghorn is a great gin lowball.

♂ lime wedge
2 ounces dry gin
½ ounce fresh lime juice
ginger ale

Rim an old-fashioned glass with the lime wedge and fill the glass with ice cubes. Pour in the gin and lime juice. Top with ginger ale, stirring briefly. Garnish with the lime wedge.

GIN

FRENCH 75

Purportedly named after a 75mm howitzer of French make, this mixed drink will drive you ballistic if you don't like sour tastes. To ensure that it's refreshing (not just tart), use good gin and decent (and very cold) champagne.

1½ ounces dry gin
1½ ounces fresh lemon juice
1½ teaspoons simple syrup
about 4 ounces chilled dry champagne
♂ maraschino cherry
♂ orange slice

Combine gin, lemon juice, and simple syrup in a cocktail shaker, with ice. Shake well, and strain into a collins glass with ice cubes (or a wine glass filled with crushed ice). Top with champagne. Garnish with the cherry and orange slice.

GIBSON

The Gibson's just a Martini garnished with a cocktail onion instead of an olive. Here's the classic recipe; you'll want to reduce the amount of vermouth if you prefer a drier drink. If the cocktail onions are tiny, use two or three.

2 ounces dry gin
½ ounce dry vermouth
♂ cocktail onion(s)

Combine liquid ingredients in a mixing glass, with ice. Stir, and strain into a cocktail glass. Garnish with the onion(s).

GIN

GIMLET

The Gimlet is a wonderful drink—and, weirdly, it's actually better when prepared with Rose's lime juice than with fresh-squeezed lime. If you insist on using fresh lime juice, keep the proportions the same but add a teaspoon of powdered sugar or half a teaspoon of simple syrup to the mix.

♂ lime wedge
2½ ounces dry or Plymouth gin
½ ounce Rose's lime juice

Rim a chilled cocktail glass with the lime wedge. Combine the liquid ingredients in a mixing glass, with ice. Stir, and strain into the cocktail glass. Squeeze the lime wedge into the drink, and drop it in.

GIN AND TONIC

This, of course, is the unbeatable summertime refresher.

♂ lime wedge
2 ounces dry or Plymouth gin
tonic water

Rim a highball glass with the lime wedge, and fill the glass with ice cubes. Pour in the gin, top with tonic water, and garnish with the lime wedge, squeezing it and dropping it into the drink.

GIN

GIN FIZZ

What a terrifically refreshing concoction this classic high-ball is. If you wish, you may add an egg white to the shaker to create a Silver Fizz.

2 ounces dry or Plymouth gin
1 ounce fresh lemon juice
1 heaping teaspoon powdered sugar
club soda or seltzer

Combine all ingredients except club soda (or seltzer) in a cocktail shaker, with ice. Shake well, and strain into a highball glass filled with ice cubes. Top with soda or seltzer, and stir briefly.

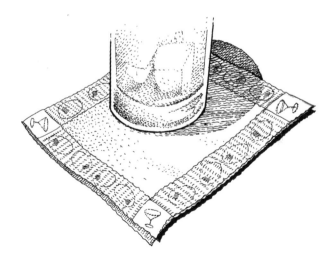

GIN

GIN-GINGER SMASH

Drinkology just loves ginger. If you do, too, you'll idolize this drink. It's dandy when made with dry gin, but better still if you use Plymouth Gin instead.

1 inch-long piece of fresh ginger root, peeled
1 tablespoon simple syrup
2 ounces dry or Plymouth gin
1½ ounces fresh orange juice
ginger ale
🍊 orange slice

Place the piece of ginger root and simple syrup in a double old-fashioned glass and muddle energetically, smashing the ginger root thoroughly. Transfer the muddled ginger and syrup to a cocktail shaker. Add ice, and pour the gin and orange juice into the shaker. Fill the glass with ice cubes. Shake the shaker vigorously, and strain the contents into the ice-filled glass. Top with ginger ale and stir gently. Garnish with the orange slice.

GIN RICKEY

Rickeys are excellent drinks for sweltering summer evenings.

🍸 lime wedge
2 ounces dry gin
½ ounce fresh lime juice
club soda or seltzer

Rim a highball glass with the lime wedge, and fill the glass with ice cubes. Pour in the gin and lime juice, and top with soda (or seltzer). Squeeze the lime wedge into the drink, and drop it in. Stir briefly.

GIN SLING

This is the original sling. (The more famous Singapore Sling, page 148, is a more complex variation.) It's sweeter than a Gin Fizz, but similarly refreshing.

🍸 lemon wedge
2½ ounces dry or Plymouth gin
½ ounce Cointreau or triple sec
½ ounce fresh lemon juice
club soda or seltzer

Rim a highball or collins glass with the lemon wedge, and fill the glass with ice cubes. Combine the gin, Cointreau, and lemon juice in a cocktail shaker; shake well, and strain into the ice-filled glass. Top with club soda (or seltzer). Squeeze the lemon wedge into the drink before dropping it in. Stir briefly.

GIN

GIN SOUR

Less well known than its whiskey-based cousin, the Gin Sour will definitely pucker you up.

2 ounces dry gin
¾ ounce fresh lemon juice
½ ounce simple syrup
♭ maraschino cherry
♭ orange slice

Combine liquid ingredients in a cocktail shaker, with ice. Shake well, and strain into a chilled sour glass. Garnish with the cherry and orange slice.

GOLDEN DAWN

Aromatic and fruity, the Golden Dawn has a lovely, sauterne-like color.

1 ounce dry or Plymouth gin
1 ounce applejack
1 ounce apricot brandy

Combine ingredients in a mixing glass, with ice. Stir, and strain into a chilled cocktail glass.

GIN

GOLDEN DAZE

The orange juice and apricot brandy combine in this vividly yellow drink to produce a surprising, pineapple-like flavor.

1½ ounces dry or Plymouth gin
¾ ounce apricot brandy
1 ounce orange juice

Combine ingredients in a cocktail shaker, with ice. Shake well, and strain into a chilled cocktail glass.

GRAND ROYAL FIZZ

This complexly flavored highball is fruity, fizzy, and creamy—all at once.

2 ounces dry or Plymouth gin
1 teaspoon maraschino liqueur
1 ounce orange juice
¾ ounce fresh lemon juice
2 teaspoons light cream
½ teaspoon powdered sugar
club soda or seltzer

Combine all ingredients except soda (or seltzer) in a cocktail shaker, with ice. Shake well, and strain into a highball glass filled with ice cubes. Top with soda (or seltzer). Stir briefly.

GIN

GREEN DEVIL

The color's a frightening kelly-green shade, but the drink's not bad. The lime juice nicely tempers the mint flavor of the crème de menthe.

1½ ounces dry gin
¾ ounce crème de menthe
½ ounce fresh lime juice

Combine ingredients in a cocktail shaker, with ice. Shake well, and strain into an old-fashioned glass filled with ice cubes.

GYPSY

Equal parts gin and sweet vermouth make for a surprisingly successful combination.

1½ ounces dry gin
1½ ounces sweet vermouth
♦ maraschino cherry

Combine liquid ingredients in a cocktail shaker, with ice. Shake well, and strain into a chilled cocktail glass. Garnish with the cherry.

HONOLULU COCKTAIL

The medley of juices in this recipe produces a cocktail that's surprisingly mild and subtle.

2 ounces dry or Plymouth gin
1 teaspoon fresh lemon juice
1 teaspoon orange juice
1 teaspoon pineapple juice
½ teaspoon powdered sugar
dash Angostura bitters

Combine ingredients in a cocktail shaker, with ice. Shake well, and strain into a chilled cocktail glass.

IMPERIAL COCKTAIL

This subtly flavored drink gets better with every sip. The color is a pale, sauterne-like gold.

1½ ounces dry gin
1½ ounces dry vermouth
½ teaspoon maraschino liqueur
2 dashes Angostura bitters

Combine ingredients in a mixing glass, with ice. Stir, and strain into a chilled cocktail glass.

GIN

INCOME TAX COCKTAIL

If the IRS is on your tail, take refuge in this delicious drink. Its lovely, lively balance of flavors passed *Drinkology*'s taste-testers' audit with flying colors.

1½ ounces dry gin
2 teaspoons dry vermouth
2 teaspoons sweet vermouth
½ ounce orange juice
2 dashes Angostura bitters

Combine ingredients in a cocktail shaker, with ice. Shake well, and strain into a chilled cocktail glass.

JOURNALIST COCKTAIL

Unlike much that goes by the name of journalism, this cocktail is decidedly complex and subtle.

2 ounces dry gin
¼ ounce Cointreau or triple sec
¼ ounce dry vermouth
¼ ounce sweet vermouth
¼ ounce fresh lemon juice
2 dashes Angostura bitters

Combine ingredients in a cocktail shaker, with ice. Shake well, and strain into a chilled cocktail glass.

JUDGE JUNIOR

The grenadine, rum, and lemon juice combine to create an almost herbal flavor in this cheerily pink cocktail.

1 ounce dry gin
1 ounce light rum
1 tablespoon fresh lemon juice
1 teaspoon grenadine

Combine ingredients in a cocktail shaker, with ice. Shake well, and strain into a chilled cocktail glass.

KNICKERBOCKER (GIN VERSION)

This elegant, brass-colored cocktail lives up to its name, evocative of old (and old-money) New York. (A very different rum-based cocktail of the same name appears on page 216.)

⌀ lemon twist
2 ounces dry gin
½ ounce dry vermouth
¼ ounce sweet vermouth

Rim a chilled cocktail glass with the lemon twist. Combine the liquid ingredients in a mixing glass, with ice. Stir, and strain into the cocktail glass. Garnish with the twist.

GIN

Knockout Cocktail

A pale, iridescent green cocktail, the Knockout is dominated by the flavor of Pernod.

1 ounce dry gin
1 ounce dry vermouth
¼ ounce Pernod or other anise-flavored liqueur
dash of white crème de menthe
♺ maraschino cherry (optional)

Combine ingredients in a mixing glass, with ice. Stir, and strain into a chilled cocktail glass. If desired, garnish with the cherry.

Kyoto Cocktail

The Kyoto's brilliant, neon-green color is more reminiscent of some blaring, busy Tokyo districts—Shinjuku, the Ginza—than of the more sedate charms of Japan's ancient capital.

1½ ounces dry gin
½ ounce dry vermouth
½ ounce melon liqueur
¼ teaspoon fresh lemon juice

Combine ingredients in a cocktail shaker, with ice. Shake well, and strain into a chilled cocktail glass.

GIN

LITTLE DEVIL

The Little Devil isn't so devilish. It's milder and subtler than many cocktails flavored with Cointreau.

1 ounce dry gin
1 ounce light rum
½ ounce Cointreau or triple sec
2 teaspoons fresh lemon juice

Combine ingredients in a cocktail shaker, with ice. Shake well, and strain into a chilled cocktail glass.

MAIDEN'S PRAYER

Here's a drink whose name evokes a weird, Victorian mix of piety and prurience. But it's a delicious concoction; its precise balance of tart and sweet is strongly reminiscent of a very good lemon drop.

1 ounce dry or Plymouth gin
1 ounce Cointreau or triple sec
½ ounce fresh lemon juice
½ ounce orange juice

Combine ingredients in a cocktail shaker, with ice. Shake well, and strain into a chilled cocktail glass.

GIN

MARTINEZ COCKTAIL

This cocktail was first concocted in Gold Rush California during the mid-1800s. Some sources say it's the ancestor of the Martini, though that's a highly improbable claim, no doubt based on the similarity of the cocktails' names. The following variation—very tasty, if you like sweet drinks—has a lovely, deep coral color. It needs no garnish.

2 ounces dry or Plymouth gin
½ ounce sweet vermouth
¼ ounce maraschino liqueur
½ ounce simple syrup

Combine ingredients in a mixing glass, with ice. Stir well, and strain into a cocktail glass.

MARTINI (CLASSIC)

"There is something about a Martini": so goes the first line of a 1935 limerick by Ogden Nash. Indeed so, but much has changed since Nash's day, when requesting a Martini meant you'd be given a cocktail very much akin to the "classic" version presented below. Nowadays, there are entire books devoted to Martini preparation and lore, as well as bars that specialize in offering a wide selection of "Martinis," including many combos that contain neither gin nor vermouth. In fact, today's Martini is subject to so many permutations (mostly vodka-based) that the term has lost any fixed meaning.

That's all well and good (many of the newfangled Martinis and Martini-like drinks are excellent), but it's also a bit of a shame, since it leads people to forget just how wonderful a classic Martini—arguably the world's most-quaffed cocktail for more than a hundred years—can be. The classic Martini's reputation, moreover, has been injured by the increasing popularity, over the past fifty years, of the dry (or very dry) Martini. This trend—encouraged by the preferences of famous Martini drinkers (including some fictional characters)—unfairly besmirches the name of the good old-fashioned "4-to-1" Martini. There is nothing whatsoever wrong with—or unglamorous about—preferring your Martini "wetted down" with a relatively hefty dose of vermouth.

Some notes about preparing Martinis: It is, first of all, absolutely necessary that the drink be *very* cold, so use plenty of ice and make sure the Martini glass has been thoroughly chilled. You might even want to keep your gin in the freezer, but, if you do, don't forego the ice when mixing, since the tiny bit of water that escapes the melting ice is essential for harmonizing the cocktail's flavors. It's often convenient to make Martinis in batches, using a glass pitcher (with a pinched or shielded spout that will prevent ice from plopping into the glasses); when mixing a batch of classic Martinis, you might want to reduce the proportion of vermouth slightly. A Martini's taste is a subtle and fragile affair, and can change dramatically depending on the type of gin used and the kind of garnish employed. (A Martini with an olive tastes very unlike a Martini with a twist—and using

GIN

a cocktail onion instead gives the drink such a different flavor that the drink merits a different name: the Gibson; see page 121.) Finding the Martini that best suits your palate may require some experimentation. But that's just fine: after all, people have been experimenting with the Martini since the day the cocktail was born. (Vodka-based Martini recipes are given in the Vodka chapter.)

2 ounces dry or Plymouth gin
½ ounce dry vermouth
🍸 olive(s) or lemon twist

Combine ingredients in a mixing glass, with lots of ice. Stir well, and strain into a chilled cocktail glass. Garnish with the olive(s) or twist. (If using a twist, rim the glass beforehand. If you prefer olives and use more than one, do be careful, since the olives' brininess will affect the drink's flavor.)

MARTINI (DRY)

For those who aren't utterly averse to the taste of vermouth, this 6-to-1 variation on the classic Martini qualifies as "dry."

2 ounces dry gin
⅓ ounce dry vermouth
🍸 olive(s) or lemon twist

Combine ingredients in a mixing glass, with lots of ice. Stir well, and strain into a chilled cocktail glass. Garnish with the olive(s) or twist. (If using a twist, rim the glass beforehand.)

MARTINI (VERY DRY)

Aficionados of the very dry Martini spend (or waste?) life-times devising ways of introducing an infinitesimal amount of vermouth into the drink—enough to vaguely tincture the gin without (in their minds) tainting it. One method recommends that the vermouth be added via an eyedropper; another that a small amount of vermouth be poured into the cocktail glass, swirled around, and then discarded before the ice-chilled gin is added. The following procedure represents a compromise position.

2¼ ounces dry gin
dash dry vermouth
♣ olive(s) or lemon twist

Combine ingredients in a mixing glass, with lots of ice. Stir well, and strain into a chilled cocktail glass. Garnish with the olive(s) or twist. (If using a twist, rim the glass beforehand.)

GIN

MARTINI ("DIRTY")

This variation on the Martini will appeal to olive-lovers (but not to those who don't like little bits of flotsam and jetsam swirling around in their drink).

2 ounces dry or Plymouth gin
½ ounce dry vermouth
¼ ounce olive brine (from the jar)
♂ olive(s)

Combine ingredients in a mixing glass, with lots of ice. Stir well, and strain into a chilled cocktail glass. Garnish with the olive(s).

MONKEY GLAND

This cocktail's gorgeous peachy color and rich, fruity taste are as unusual as its name.

1½ ounces dry or Plymouth gin
¼ teaspoon Bénédictine
1 ounce orange juice
¼ teaspoon grenadine

Combine ingredients in a cocktail shaker, with ice. Shake well, and strain into a chilled cocktail glass.

NEGRONI

This redoubtable drink—its powerful taste is not for every-one—possesses a well-balanced complexity, a distinctive mix of flavors that no other cocktail has. It's astringent (because of the gin), sweet (the vermouth), and bitter (the Campari) all at once. And its brilliant red-orange color is as remarkable as its taste.

The Negroni—purportedly invented around the turn of the twentieth century by a Florentine count, one Camillo Negroni—is sometimes served straight up, but *Drinkology* recommends modulating its brasher qualities by serving it on the rocks. A splash of soda softens the impact and weds the flavors.

1 ounce dry gin
1 ounce Campari
1 ounce sweet vermouth
splash of club soda or seltzer
♂ orange or lemon slice

Fill an old-fashioned glass with ice cubes. Pour in the gin, Campari, and vermouth. Top with the soda (or seltzer), and stir briefly. Garnish with the orange or lemon slice.

OBITUARY COCKTAIL

Among American cities, New Orleans reigns supreme in cocktail creativity. Legend has it that this drink—a dry Martini dosed with absinthe—was invented at the Lafitte's Blacksmith Shop bar, on Bourbon Street. It has an appropriately deathly pallor.

2 ounces dry gin
¼ ounce absinthe or absinthe substitute
¼ ounce dry vermouth

Combine the ingredients in a mixing glass, with ice. Stir, and strain into a chilled cocktail glass.

OPERA COCKTAIL

Dubonnet Rouge makes a very nice mixer with gin, as this cocktail demonstrates.

2 ounces dry gin
½ ounce Dubonnet Rouge
¼ ounce maraschino liqueur

Combine ingredients in a mixing glass, with ice. Stir, and strain into a chilled cocktail glass.

ORANGE BLOSSOM

 The Orange Blossom is basically a short, shaken, gin-based Screwdriver.

1½ ounces dry or Plymouth gin
1½ ounces orange juice
½ teaspoon powdered sugar (optional)
♦ orange slice

Combine gin, orange juice, and (if desired) powdered sugar in a cocktail shaker, with ice. Shake well, and strain into an old-fashioned glass filled with ice cubes. Garnish with the orange slice.

PALL MALL

 The crème de menthe has an unusual effect in this cider-colored brew. You don't taste it while sipping, but afterward it lingers pleasantly on the tongue.

1½ ounces dry gin
½ ounce dry vermouth
½ ounce sweet vermouth
1 teaspoon white crème de menthe
dash Angostura bitters

Combine ingredients in a mixing glass, with ice. Stir, and strain into a chilled cocktail glass.

GIN

PARISIAN COCKTAIL

If you're a fan of cassis, you'll love this dramatically colored cocktail.

1 ounce dry gin
1 ounce crème de cassis
1 ounce dry vermouth

Combine ingredients in a mixing glass, with ice. Stir, and strain into a chilled cocktail glass.

PINK GIN (CLASSIC)

A.k.a. Gin and Bitters, the Pink Gin is an old-time British favorite. Purist Brits don't chill the glass or gin, but *Drinkology's* American sensibilities dictate doing so.

about 1 teaspoon Angostura bitters
3 ounces chilled dry or Plymouth gin

Chill the gin in the freezer for several hours before serving. Pour the bitters into a chilled cocktail glass, then slowly and carefully tilt and twirl the glass until the entire interior is coated. Discard any excess bitters. Pour in the gin.

GIN

PINK GIN ("PINKER" VARIATION)

Peychaud's bitters makes a Pink Gin that's truly pink. This variation's taste is less sharp and a little fruitier than the Angostura bitters version, above.

about 1 teaspoon Peychaud's bitters
3 ounces chilled dry or Plymouth gin

Chill the gin in the freezer for several hours before serving. Pour the bitters into a chilled cocktail glass, then slowly and carefully tilt and twirl the glass until the entire interior is coated. Discard any excess bitters. Pour in the gin.

PINK LADY

The Pink Lady is pinker than pink cotton candy, pinker than a pink Angora sweater. It's as pink as pink can be. For boy-girl get-togethers, try serving Pink Ladies along with Blue Boys (recipe on page 113).

2 ounces dry or Plymouth gin
½ ounce heavy cream
2 teaspoons fresh lemon juice
1 teaspoon grenadine
1 egg white

Combine ingredients in a cocktail shaker, with ice. Shake well, and strain into a chilled cocktail glass.

GIN

RAMOS FIZZ

New Orleans bartender Henry Ramos invented this magnificent (and rich) concoction around the turn of the twentieth century. There are easier variations that use a blender, but *Drinkology* recommends the original, somewhat arduous method given below. Orange flower water—an essential ingredient despite the tiny amount used—can be found in specialty food and cosmetics shops.

2 ounces dry or Plymouth gin
1 ounce heavy cream
½ ounce simple syrup
¼ ounce fresh lemon juice
¼ ounce fresh lime juice
3 or 4 drops of orange flower water
1 egg white
club soda or seltzer

Combine all ingredients except soda (or seltzer) in a standard shaker, with ice. Shake for three full minutes. Strain into a large, chilled red wine glass, and top with the soda (or seltzer). Stir very briefly. (Notes: Use a standard shaker for this drink. If need be, set an oven timer to ensure you don't skimp on the shaking. And hold the shaker—which will become very cold—in a bar towel while shaking.)

RENAISSANCE COCKTAIL

 If the taste of eggnog appeals to you but the overly creamy texture does not, try this cocktail.

1½ ounces dry or Plymouth gin
½ ounce dry sherry
½ ounce heavy cream
freshly grated nutmeg

Combine liquid ingredients in a cocktail shaker, with ice. Shake well, and strain into an old-fashioned glass filled with ice cubes. Sprinkle the nutmeg on top.

SAFFRON SUNSET

 Like infused vodkas, infused gins are gaining in popularity. Among the more intriguing is the gorgeously yellow-or-ange-hued saffron-infused gin made by Gabriel Boudier. This is a subtle, dry, sophisticated, *adult* libation.

2 ounces saffron-infused gin
½ ounce Liqueur Créole Clément *or* Cointreau
↻ orange slice

Rim a chilled cocktail glass with the orange slice and place it in the glass. Combine the ingredients in a mixing glass, with ice. Stir and strain into the cocktail glass. Garnish with the orange slice.

GIN

SAKE-TINI

It's remarkable how the substitution of a tiny amount of sake for the dry vermouth alters a Martini's flavor.

❧ lemon twist
2½ ounces dry gin
¼ ounce *junmai ginjo* sake

Rim a chilled cocktail glass with the twist and drop the twist into the glass. Fill a mixing glass with ice, pour in the gin and sake, and stir. Strain into the cocktail glass.

SALTY DOG (GIN VERSION)

This highball is a gin-based version of the Greyhound (recipe in the Vodka chapter, page 264), but it's made in a glass that's been rimmed with salt.

lemon wedge
salt
2 ounces dry gin
5 or 6 ounces grapefruit juice

Rim a highball glass with the lemon wedge and salt. Discard the lemon wedge. Fill the glass with ice cubes, and pour in the gin and juice. Stir briefly.

GIN

Satan's Whiskers

Such a devilish name for such an innocuous-tasting (though pleasantly fruity) drink!

½ ounce dry or Plymouth gin
½ ounce dry vermouth
½ ounce Grand Marnier
½ ounce sweet vermouth
½ ounce orange juice
dash Angostura or orange bitters

Combine ingredients in a cocktail shaker, with ice. Shake well, and strain into a chilled cocktail glass.

Seventh Heaven

The combination of grapefruit juice and maraschino liqueur gives this icy-looking cocktail a unique, difficult-to-describe taste.

1½ ounces dry gin
½ ounce maraschino liqueur
½ ounce grapefruit juice

Combine ingredients in a cocktail shaker, with ice. Shake well, and strain into a chilled cocktail glass.

GIN

SILVER BULLET

The small dose of scotch in this variation on the dry Martini gives the drink a smoky, dusky flavor.

♂ lemon twist
2½ ounces dry gin
¼ teaspoon blended scotch

Rim a chilled cocktail glass with the lemon twist. Combine the gin and scotch in a mixing glass, with ice. Stir, and strain into the glass. Garnish with the twist.

SINGAPORE SLING

More than any other cocktail moniker, the name *Singapore Sling* evokes an air of mystery, suspense, sultry exoticism. Detective novels, noir-ish films, and even some rather daringly raked women's high-heeled sandals have all been named for the drink. That's pretty odd when you think about it, since this pinkish concoction is so sweet, so fruity—so innocent-seeming, really.

The first Singapore Sling was created in 1915 by a bartender at the famous Long Bar of the Raffles Hotel in (you guessed it) Singapore. There are lots of bartending guides and drink-recipe websites that boast that the Singapore Sling recipe they present is the "original" version—a dubious-seeming claim, since these recipes differ from one another, sometimes quite dramatically. *Drinkology* doesn't give a hoot for this sort of faux-authenticity; we are much more interested in providing you with something that tastes good. The recipe below is the one *Drinkology*'s taste-testers like best. (Note that some Singapore Sling recipes recommend completing the drink with a splash of soda; feel free to do so if you like. Others specify floating the cherry brandy atop the drink; in our experience, the cherry brandy inevitably—and immediately—plunges to the bottom, so why bother trying?)

1½ ounces dry or Plymouth gin
¾ ounce Bénédictine
¾ ounce cherry brandy
¾ ounce Cointreau or triple sec
1½ ounces orange juice
1½ ounces pineapple juice
¾ ounce fresh lime juice
½ teaspoon grenadine
♻ maraschino cherry
♻ pineapple chunk
♻ orange slice

Combine liquid ingredients in a standard cocktail shaker, with ice. Shake well, and strain into a highball glass filled with ice cubes. (This is a large drink, so there may be some overage, depending on the size of the highball glass you're using.) Garnish with the fruit.

GIN

SNOWBALL

Pernod gives this creamy cocktail a subtle licorice flavor—and a vaguely (and vaguely disturbing) greenish tinge, which makes you wonder whether it shouldn't be called the Radioactive Snowball.

1½ ounces dry or Plymouth gin
¼ ounce Pernod
1 ounce heavy cream
1 heaping teaspoon powdered sugar

Combine ingredients in a cocktail shaker, with ice. Shake well, and strain into a chilled cocktail glass.

TAILSPIN

This cocktail's flavor is distinctive—noteworthy, even. Unfortunately, its color borders on the hideous. Best served in a dark room.

♻ lemon twist
1 ounce dry gin
1 ounce green Chartreuse
1 ounce sweet vermouth

Rim a chilled cocktail glass with the lemon twist. Combine the liquid ingredients in a cocktail shaker, with ice. Shake well, and strain into the cocktail glass. Garnish with the twist.

GIN

TOM COLLINS

The name *Tom Collins* has a 1950s ring to it—it's the sort of drink you imagine your parents or your parents' parents serving to friends at a patio party in the midcentury American suburbs. (The sleekly proportioned collins glass, in which it's traditionally served, abets this impression.) But the Tom Collins is actually much older than that—dating back to the mid-nineteenth century, at least. As with so many mixed drinks, there are competing accounts of the Tom Collins's origin, but many sources agree that the name derives from Old Tom gin, with which it seems to have originally been made. (Nobody seems to really know where the drink's surname comes from.)

Given that Old Tom gin is now fairly widely available, you can emulate the original recipe or stick to plain ol' dry gin. If you don't have a set of collins glasses, don't worry overmuch—a highball glass will certainly do, though the visual effect will be a tad less elegant. A collins looks especially handsome garnished with

GIN

a "flag"—a maraschino cherry and orange slice skewered together on a cocktail spear (or toothpick).

2 ounces dry, Plymouth, or Old Tom gin
½ ounce fresh lemon juice
½ ounce simple syrup
club soda or seltzer
♂ maraschino cherry
♂ orange slice

Combine the gin, lemon juice, and simple syrup in a cocktail shaker, with ice. Shake well, and strain into a collins or highball glass filled with ice cubes. Top with soda (or seltzer), and stir briefly. (If you're using a collins glass, stirring the drink can be slightly challenging because of the glass's narrowness; try using the long handle of a bar spoon.) Garnish with the cherry and orange slice, skewered together.

VESPER

This shaken variation on the Martini is named for Vesper Lynd, the "Bond Girl" in Ian Fleming's novel, *Casino Royale.*

♂ lemon twist
2 ounces dry gin
1¼ ounces vodka
½ ounce Lillet Blanc

Rim a chilled cocktail glass with the lemon twist. Combine the other ingredients in a cocktail shaker, with ice. Shake well, and strain into the glass. Garnish with the twist.

WHITE LADY

 The White Lady is very WASPy indeed: icy and sour.

1½ ounces dry gin
¾ ounce Cointreau or triple sec
¾ ounce fresh lemon juice

Combine ingredients in a cocktail shaker, with ice. Shake well, and strain into a chilled cocktail glass.

WHITE LILY

 The White Lily, another icy-looking concoction, is the perfect sweet cocktail for sophisticated drinkers. The sweetness of the Cointreau is modulated by the headiness of the gin-rum mix and the aroma of the Pernod.

¾ ounce dry gin
¾ ounce Cointreau or triple sec
¾ ounce light rum
¼ teaspoon Pernod or other anise-flavored liqueur

Combine ingredients in a cocktail shaker, with ice. Shake well, and strain into a chilled cocktail glass.

GIN

Liqueurs

LIQUEURS ARE PROOF POSITIVE THAT PEOPLE'S INGENUITY IS boundless. Sure, the mapping of the human genome and the compilation of the *Kama Sutra*'s 1,001 sexual positions are impressive achievements, but *Drinkology* is equally agape at the creative fecundity and sheer stick-to-itiveness of those sixteenth-century French Carthusian monks who applied their wits to confabulating the recipe for green Chartreuse—which utilizes no fewer than 130 different herbs and spices. Or so we're told: the actual formula—like that of so many other proprietary liqueurs—remains a closely guarded secret.

Liqueur is, of necessity, a catchall term. It can refer to virtually any spirit—brandy, or whiskey, or rum, or tequila, or what-have-you—that's been flavored with some other stuff and then sweetened to a lesser or greater degree through the addition of sugar or a sweetening syrup. Sorry about that "some other stuff," but it's impossible to be more precise, since liqueurs derive their multiplicity of flavors from everything from apricot pits (amaretto) to coffee (Kahlúa, Tia Maria) to bitter-orange peels (the various curaçaos) to exotic botanicals whose names you've never heard of (Pernod apparently contains an herb called dittany, along with anise and a busload of other ingredients). *Drinkology*'s taste-testers were recently treated to a Transylvanian— Transylvanian!—liqueur that's flavored and tinted with rose petals.

Beyond their myriad flavors and colors, liqueurs also differ markedly by alcohol content and sweetness. The black currant liqueur known as crème de cassis can, depending on the brand, be as low in alcohol as 30 proof (that is, 15 percent, a level only slightly above that of most wines); green Chartreuse, by contrast, is a sobriety-nixing 110 proof (55 percent alcohol). Pernod is, as liqueurs go, relatively dry; Campari is bitter; the scotch-based Drambuie is cloyingly sugary.

Moreover, there's nothing standardized about the methods used to make liqueurs. Some are distilled, some are infused, and others are given their flavors through percolation or maceration (the latter being a process in which mashed-up fruit is marinated in the liquor base, then filtered out). Add to this the fact that there are scores and scores of liqueurs on the market, and you begin to get the picture: to find the time to really get a handle on this subject, why, you'd have to live in a monastery.

Which is exactly where the first liqueurs were made. The dedicated Carthusian brothers who invented Chartreuse were hardly the first holy men to ply this alchemical avocation. That distinction seems to belong to a group of Benedictine monks—also French, wouldn't you know—who developed the formula for (you guessed it) Bénédictine as early as 1510. (Don't ask what's in it, by the way. The secret's been kept for half a millennium, and they're not about to let on.)

Needless to say, those Renaissance-era contemplatives weren't shaking cocktails in the refectory kitchen. Liqueurs were originally designed to be savored slowly, all by their lonesomes—and they're

Lately, the rarefied empire of liqueurs has been invaded by a horde of barbarians known as the do-it-yourselfers. The Internet is crawling with dubious recipes for homemade cordials. Now, *Drinkology* has nothing against the DIY ethic per se, but we'd generally prefer a snifterful of genuine store-bought Chartreuse to a glass of some greenish ick brewed up by your cousin Frank and tasting rather like mowed lawn. We think, that is, that liqueur-making ought in most cases to be left to the professionals.

That said, there is at least one liqueur that can be made by you, at home, with a minimum of fuss and a delicious result. We're thinking of limoncello, the southern Italian liqueur that's a simple amalgam of lemon zest, alcohol, and sugar. There are those who claim that no homemade limoncello—especially one made from ordinary grocery-store lemons—can come close to the exquisite limoncellos produced on Italy's Amalfi coast. We can't argue. (For one thing, your homemade limoncello is likely to look positively anemic when set alongside the best Italian limoncellos, which use ancient lemon varieties, unavailable elsewhere, that impart a vivid yellow color to the infusion.) Still and all, the recipe below, if followed with a modicum of care, will yield an intensely flavorful, nearly candylike drink that makes for mighty pleasant after-dinner sipping.

LIMONCELLO

To make this limoncello, you'll need a 1-liter glass bottle that can be stoppered tightly and a Microplane grater (or some other super-sharp grater) capable of grating lemon zest very finely. You'll also need a kitchen funnel, a long-handled bar spoon (or some similar implement) for forcing the lemon zest through the funnel and into the bottle, a sieve, cheesecloth, and a large (quart-size) spouted measuring cup. Make sure that all your equipment is very clean, with no trace of soap residue. Do be sure to use a good-enough vodka. (We recommend Smirnoff.)

LIQUEURS

12 very fresh lemons
1 750ml bottle vodka
⅓ cup or more simple syrup (see recipe on page 36)

You'll make the limoncello in two steps:

Step 1: Grate the zest of the lemons very finely. As you grate, try your best to avoid grating the white, pithy part of the rind—the albedo. If your grated zest contains too much albedo, the limoncello will be bitter.

Place a funnel in the mouth of a 1-liter bottle. Transfer about a tablespoon of the grated zest to the funnel and pour just enough vodka into the funnel to wash the grated zest into the bottle. Repeat this—washing a little bit of grated zest into the bottle with as little vodka as possible—until all the zest and all the vodka are in the bottle. This procedure probably won't work perfectly, so you may need to force some of the zest through the funnel using the handle of a bar spoon (or some other implement with a long narrow handle).

Now, stopper the bottle tightly and put it in a cool, dark place, where it will rest for three weeks.

Step 2: After three weeks have passed, take the bottle from its hiding place. Prepare the simple syrup, allowing it to cool before using. Rest a sieve atop a large spouted measuring cup and line it with several layers of cheesecloth. Carefully pour the contents of the bottle through the cheesecloth-lined sieve into the measuring cup. Add ⅓ cup simple syrup to the liquid in the measuring cup and stir. Taste the mixture. If it does not seem sweet enough to you, add more simple syrup—a teaspoonful at a time, tasting after each addition—until the desired sweetness is achieved.

Rinse the bottle thoroughly—no bits of lemon zest should remain. Pour the limoncello into the clean bottle and stopper it tightly.

Limoncello is best served icy cold, so store the bottle in the freezer. (The limoncello will remain good indefinitely.)

LIQUEURS

still often enjoyed that way, sipped from a cordial glass or snifter. (A snifter, warmed by the heat of the drinker's hand, makes a particularly effective vehicle for complexly flavored herbal liqueurs like Chartreuse and Strega.)

The invention of modern cocktails—beginning in the early 1800s—immensely expanded the number of parts that liqueurs could play, however. Today, they take the lead in a fair number of mixed drinks, including those in this chapter, and occupy supporting, but essential, roles in a vast number of alcoholic concoctions. A Margarita (page 239) isn't a Margarita without the triple sec (or that more rarified kind of triple sec known as Cointreau). A Black Russian (page 251) contains more vodka than Kahlúa, but without the Kahlúa (or some other coffee-flavored liqueur) it wouldn't be black—wouldn't, in fact, be a mixed drink at all.

ABSINTHE DRIP

Has absinthe lost its allure?

As recently as 2003, when the first edition of *Drinkology* was released, it was difficult for Americans to obtain true absinthe—whose ingredients include the bitter herb called wormwood (*Artemisia absinthium*). That was because the U.S., just like many European countries, had banned absinthe during the years leading up to World War I. Absinthe remained illegal; to get it, you had to travel to Britain, which had never banned the spirit, or to one of the few other countries where it was legally sold, and carry it home with you. (You still faced the risk of having the bottle confiscated by customs.)

Today, everything's changed—or sort of. It's now possible to buy true absinthe (often of several different brands) at better liquor stores in many places across the country. Meanwhile, absinthe's long-standing reputation as a destroyer of minds and despoiler of lives has undergone a total overhaul. The early-twentieth-century bans were enacted because it was believed that absinthe was hallucinogenic, addictive, and ultimately poisonous. According to those pushing for the ban (who included temperance activists as well as winemakers worried about the competition!), drinking absinthe *made you insane.*

Well, that turns out not to be the case. Or not exactly. The notorious deleterious effect of habitual absinthe drinking—a dire mental and physical syndrome once classified as the "disease" of absinthism—most probably resulted from heavy metals introduced during the distillation of the cheap absinthe that was mass produced to meet Belle Époque demand. Wormwood, the ostensible culprit, had nothing to do with it, or so say absinthe's present-day advocates, who contend that high-quality absinthe presents no dangers beyond those posed by any alcoholic beverage.

Most European countries that had prohibited absinthe have lifted their bans. Despite its current easy availability, however, true absinthe is still technically illegal in the United States. How can this be? This quite sensible question has a complicated answer, having to do with the purported absence of a (banned) chemical called thujone (which is a constituent of wormwood) from the absinthes

LIQUEURS

sold here, and with the authorities' reluctance or inability to enforce the law consistently. A commercial absinthe-themed website, www.greendevil.org, does its best to explain the complex legal issues involved—as well as the stratagems employed by absinthe makers and distributors to market their products.

So *has* absinthe lost its allure? A formerly widely banned, hard-to-obtain, and glamorously dangerous beverage has metamorphosed, in these few short years, into a quasi-legal, readily available spirit that, despite your most ardent wishes, will not give you visions or turn you into a schizophrenic-genius poet or painter. Absinthe has become almost tame.

But not quite. Certainly, a gossamer shadow of the Green Fairy's devilish charm perdures. It was, after all, the favored libation of the likes of Baudelaire, Van Gogh, and Rimbaud. And then there's the appealingly solemn ceremony that surrounds an Absinthe Drip's preparation—the slow pouring of the liquor, followed by water, over a sugar cube balanced upon a dagger-shaped slotted spoon.

The Absinthe Drip procedure described here omits the step—favored by some touristy bars—of soaking the sugar cube in liquor and then setting it afire before beginning the pouring. *Drinkology* has nothing against flaming (drinks or anything else), mind you. But that step isn't part of the traditional French ritual. (It's a later Czech innovation.)

Actually, the sugar cube itself may be dispensed with when making an Absinthe Drip nowadays. Absinthe contains no sugar (technically, it's therefore a distilled spirit rather than a liqueur per se), and the mass-produced absinthes of a century and more ago required sweetening because they were often profoundly harsh and bitter. Not so with the many superbly crafted absinthes sold today. (Try the Drip with and without the sugar cube to find out which you prefer.)

What *is* absolutely necessary, however, is the water. Absinthe's alcohol content is very, very high—as high as 75 percent in some cases—and it must be watered down to be drinkable (by most people). Also, adding water to absinthe has a magic effect, visually and taste-wise: The clear green liquid turns whitish and cloudy when mixed with water—a phenomenon called *la louche* (literally, "squint-eyed") in French. (The English word *louche*—meaning "disreputable"—derives from olden-day absinthe addicts' dubious social standing.) And the water—which should be *icy* cold—also serves to release the essential oils in absinthe, making it much tastier than it is when drunk neat.

2 ounces absinthe
1 sugar cube
ice-cold water

Set an absinthe spoon or a small strainer across the mouth of a white wine glass or absinthe glass. Place the sugar cube on the spoon (or in the strainer) and pour the absinthe slowly—very slowly—over the cube. Add water—again, by slowly pouring it over the cube—until the sugar has dissolved and the liquid in the glass has turned cloudy.

Note on equipment: *Ornate stemmed absinthe glasses (some with reservoirs in their stems), absinthe spoons (old silver ones and new ones made of stainless steel), absinthe fountains (modeled on nineteenth-century vessels), and all manner of absinthe paraphernalia are available from online purveyors. But you don't need any of this stuff to enjoy—or elegantly prepare—an Absinthe Drip. For our Absinthe Drips,* Drinkology *uses old French bistro glasses (pictured here) from a set found at a New Orleans antiques shop.*

Note on substitutes: *During the years when absinthe was banned, a number of absinthe substitutes were created. Some of these faux absinthes—which include Pernod, Absente, and the New Orleans spirit called Herbsaint—are quite good. Differing from true absinthe in that they do not contain wormwood (and thus remained legal), they share absinthe's anise/fennel-dominated flavor. Such substitutes can be used instead of true absinthe in the Absinthe Drip, the Sazerac (see page 306), and, if you must, the Absinthe Zap, on the next page.*

ABSINTHE ZAP

Absinthe's widening availability has spurred the creation of numerous new absinthe-based cocktails. Likewise, the incomprehensible popularity of the energy soft drink Red Bull has spawned hundreds of god-awful cocktails whose recipes incorporate that supercaffeinated beverage. So why not a drink that mixes both? We looked for one on the Web, and of course we immediately found one—with a nasty name to match its taste. Here's our (renamed and slightly reformulated) version, which isn't quite as bad as it ought to be. Its turquoise color can only be described as lurid.

1½ ounces absinthe
½ ounce blue curaçao
½ ounce fresh lime juice
Red Bull

Fill a double old-fashioned glass with ice. Combine the absinthe, curaçao, and lime juice in a cocktail shaker, with ice. Shake well, and strain into the glass. Top with Red Bull and stir gently.

ALFONSO SPECIAL

This cocktail—one of the few that uses Grand Marnier as its basis—is light and sweet, but also complex.

1½ ounces Grand Marnier
¾ ounce gin
¾ ounce dry vermouth
¼ teaspoon sweet vermouth
2 dashes Angostura bitters

Combine ingredients in a cocktail shaker, with ice. Shake well, and strain into a chilled cocktail glass.

AMARETTO ALEXANDER

Among drinkers, amaretto lovers constitute a rather exclusive tribe (as exclusive as that of marzipan lovers among those who eat candy). Only they will prefer this drink to a Brandy Alexander—but they'll *really* prefer it.

2 ounces amaretto
1½ ounces white crème de cacao
1 ounce heavy cream
⚘ a few almond slivers

Combine liquid ingredients in a shaker, with ice. Shake well, and strain into a chilled cocktail glass. Garnish with the slivered almonds.

AMARETTO SOUR

This sour doesn't require any sugar because amaretto is so sweet. Its dark, somewhat muddy color belies its refreshingly tart taste.

2 ounces amaretto
1 ounce fresh lemon juice
♦ maraschino cherry

Combine liquid ingredients in a cocktail shaker, with ice. Shake well, and strain into a chilled sour glass. Garnish with the cherry.

AMERICANO

The Americano is the ancestor of the more famous—and, frankly, more interesting—Negroni (page 139). But if you like Campari and prefer a milder, less potent drink, have one of these.

1½ ounces Campari
1½ ounces sweet vermouth
club soda or seltzer
♦ orange slice

Pour the Campari and vermouth into an old-fashioned glass filled with ice cubes. Top with soda (or seltzer), and stir briefly. Garnish with the orange slice. (Note: This combination also works well as a highball; simply use a highball or collins glass and increase the amount of soda.)

LIQUEURS

ANGEL'S TIT

Drinkology wishes this simple—and simply delicious—confection had a less objectionable name. It's one of those wonderful crosses between a dessert and an after-dinner drink. Make sure the crème de cacao is chilled ahead of time.

2 ounces chilled white crème de cacao
whipped cream
♺ maraschino cherry

Pour the crème de cacao into a chilled parfait glass, sour glass, or other small, narrow-bowled stemmed glass. Spoon (or squirt) the whipped cream on top. Garnish with the cherry. Serve with a straw or small, long-handled spoon.

BANSHEE

A banshee, of course, is a fairy who emits a baleful Irish scream (get it?), but there's nothing Gaelic about this combination. It's subtle and nicely foamy.

1 ounce crème de banane
1 ounce white crème de cacao
1 ounce heavy cream

Combine ingredients in a cocktail shaker, with ice. Shake well, and strain into a chilled cocktail glass.

LIQUEURS

BOCCE BALL

This is a very nice, fruity, sweet highball. Without the club soda, it's a little cloying for *Drinkology*'s taste, but omit the soda if you wish.

2 ounces amaretto
about 4 ounces orange juice
club soda or seltzer
⌀ orange slice

Pour the amaretto into a highball glass filled with ice cubes. Add the orange juice, stopping at least one-half inch short of the lip. Top with soda (or seltzer), and stir briefly. Garnish with the orange slice.

BRAIN HEMORRHAGE

Drinkology, for reasons better left uninvestigated, feels the need to present a few concoctions that are truly awful. Here's one that's horrifying looking and sickeningly sweet. We suggest that you prepare it as carefully as Anthony Hopkins prepped Ray Liotta's skull in *Hannibal.*

1½ ounces peach schnapps
1½ ounces Bailey's Irish Cream
a few drops of grenadine

Pour the schnapps into a sherry glass (or other small glass). Slowly and carefully pour in the Irish Cream, allowing it to coagulate into gray-matter-ish clumps. Carefully drip a little grenadine—the "hemorrhage"—on top.

LIQUEURS

BUTTERED TOFFEE

Usually, *Drinkology* recommends heavy cream for cream-based drinks. This one, though, is so incredibly rich that we suggest using light cream or half-and-half instead.

1 ounce amaretto
1 ounce Bailey's Irish Cream
1 ounce coffee liqueur
2 ounces light cream or half-and-half

Fill a red wine glass with ice. Pour in the liqueurs, followed by the cream (or half-and-half). Stir briefly.

BUTTERFINGER

This is about as candylike as an alcoholic beverage gets. Shake it in a standard shaker so that it doesn't slip from your grasp.

2 ounces butterscotch schnapps
1½ ounces Bailey's Irish Cream
6 ounces milk
chocolate syrup

Combine the schnapps, Bailey's, and milk in a standard shaker, with ice. Shake very well, and strain into a highball glass filled with ice cubes. Squirt a few globs of chocolate syrup on top.

LIQUEURS

CAFÉ ROMANO

This subtle, creamy cocktail is a very happy marriage–Italian-style of flavors.

1 ounce coffee liqueur
1 ounce Sambuca
1 ounce heavy cream

Combine ingredients in a cocktail shaker, with ice. Shake well, and strain into a chilled cocktail glass.

CAMPARI AND SODA

Book your trip to Italy while sipping on this classic Mediterranean refresher. *Drinkology* really likes Campari, so we prefer the lowball version of this drink. Feel free to make it as a tall drink, however: just use a highball or collins glass, and up the amount of soda accordingly.

2 ounces Campari
club soda or seltzer
☽ orange slice

Fill a double old-fashioned glass with ice. Pour in the Campari, and top with soda. Stir briefly, and wedge the orange slice into the glass.

CHOCOLATE ALMOND

This rich, mocha-colored lowball is a fine sipping drink.

¾ ounce amaretto
¾ ounce Bailey's Irish Cream
¾ ounce dark crème de cacao

Combine ingredients in a cocktail shaker, with ice. Shake well, and strain into an old-fashioned glass filled with ice cubes.

CLIMAX

This creamy drink is unusual in that the flavors of all the liqueurs remain individually, subtly discernible.

½ ounce amaretto
½ ounce Cointreau or triple sec
½ ounce crème de banane
½ ounce vodka
½ ounce white crème de cacao
1 ounce heavy cream

Combine ingredients in a cocktail shaker, with ice. Shake well, and strain into a chilled cocktail glass.

LIQUEURS

DREAMSICLE

This drink tastes just like you hope it will. It's smashing, and will put you in a very good humor.

1 ounce amaretto
½ ounce orange curaçao
½ ounce vanilla-flavored vodka
2 ounces heavy cream
2 ounces orange juice

Combine ingredients in a cocktail shaker, with ice. Shake well, and strain into an old-fashioned glass filled with ice cubes.

GOLDEN CADILLAC

This classic creamy cocktail isn't as innocent as it looks. The Galliano carries a real—but pleasant—bite, which you'll experience as you swallow each sip.

2 ounces white crème de cacao
¾ ounce Galliano
1 ounce heavy cream

Combine ingredients in a cocktail shaker, with ice. Shake well, and strain into a chilled cocktail glass.

LIQUEURS

GRASSHOPPER

The Grasshopper tastes just like a chocolate-covered after-dinner mint. Extremely popular three decades ago, it's due for a revival.

1 ounce green crème de menthe
1 ounce white crème de cacao
1 ounce heavy cream

Combine ingredients in a cocktail shaker, with ice. Shake well, and strain into a chilled cocktail glass.

GREEN RUSSIAN

Melon liqueur tends to make *Drinkology*'s taste-testers a little green around the gills, but its powerful flavor is nicely modulated when it's combined with vodka and cream.

1½ ounces melon liqueur
1½ ounces vodka
1 ounce heavy cream

Fill an old-fashioned glass with ice cubes. Pour in the melon liqueur and vodka, followed by the cream. Stir.

LIQUEURS

LONDON FOG

The licorice flavor of this cocktail is strongly reminiscent of Good 'n' Plenty candies.

1½ ounces anisette
1½ ounces white crème de menthe
2 dashes Angostura bitters
⌁ thinly cut lemon slice

Combine liquid ingredients in a cocktail shaker, with ice. Shake well, and strain into a chilled cocktail glass. Garnish with the lemon slice, letting it float on top of the drink.

MELON ALEXANDER

Melon liqueur is best when combined with ingredients that soften and attenuate its flavor, as in this honeydew-colored take on the classic Brandy Alexander.

1½ ounces melon liqueur
1 ounce brandy
1 ounce cream

Combine ingredients in a cocktail shaker, with ice. Shake well, and strain into a chilled cocktail glass.

LIQUEURS

NUTTY IRISHMAN

This utterly simple combination produces a drink that's anything but simple-minded. The delicious mix of Irish cream and hazelnut—exploited in many a cream-based drink—is at its undiluted best here.

1½ ounces Bailey's Irish Cream
1½ ounces Frangelico

Combine ingredients in a cocktail shaker, with ice. Shake well, and strain into an old-fashioned glass filled with ice.

ORGASM

Try not to scream in ecstasy.

1 ounce amaretto
1 ounce Bailey's Irish Cream
1 ounce coffee liqueur

Combine ingredients in a cocktail shaker, with ice. Shake well, and strain into an old-fashioned glass filled with ice.

LIQUEURS

PEPPERMINT STICK

This is a sensational concoction. At holiday time, serve it garnished with a small candy cane hooked over the lip of the flute.

1½ ounces white crème de cacao
1 ounce peppermint schnapps
1 ounce heavy cream

Combine ingredients in a cocktail shaker, with ice. Shake well, and strain into a chilled champagne flute.

PERNOD COCKTAIL

Drinkology guesses that you either love Pernod or you *hate* it. Most of our taste-testers fall into the former camp, though dissenting murmurs have been heard.

½ ounce water
½ teaspoon powdered sugar
2 dashes Angostura bitters
crushed ice
2 ounces Pernod or other anise-flavored liqueur

Combine the water, sugar, and bitters in an old-fashioned glass. Stir, then pack the glass with crushed ice. Pour in the Pernod, and stir again.

PIMM'S CUP

The whole thing's weird. First, there's the Pimm's Cup No. 1 itself—an impossible-to-classify mix of gin, fruit liqueurs, and herbs. Then there's the cucumber-spear garnish—a truly oddball touch. Then there's the lemon-lime soda: *Drinkology* hates lemon-lime soda, but we *love* it in this drink. Bizarre. But very tasty.

3 ounces Pimm's Cup No. 1
lemon-lime soda
♦ cucumber spear (peeled)

Pour the Pimm's Cup into a highball glass filled with ice cubes. Top with lemon-lime soda, and stir. Garnish with the cucumber spear.

PINK SQUIRREL

Many recipes for this classic cream-based cocktail call for crème de noyaux. If you can't find it, substitute amaretto, which makes for a Squirrel that's more beige than pink.

1 ounce crème de noyaux or amaretto
1 ounce white crème de cacao
1 ounce heavy cream

Combine ingredients in a cocktail shaker, with ice. Shake well, and strain into a chilled cocktail glass.

LIQUEURS

When it comes to Pousse-Cafés, *Drinkology*—alone among bartending guides—is decidedly *un*enthusiastic. Sure, a perfectly executed P.C. is a wonder to behold. But, tell us, are you *really* going to spend the time needed to learn to pour a Pousse-Café properly? And, even if you do, are you actually going to *drink* it—or worse, foist it in on your friends? Face it, combinations of half a dozen or so liqueurs (and sometimes other ingredients) that are chosen *not* according to the complementarity of their flavors but according to how pretty they look when poured one atop the other are not likely to *taste* good. In a word, blechh.

We should, we guess, get over ourselves, and just give you the facts. Pousse-Cafés appeared in France during the early nineteenth century; they landed in this country in that bastion of francophilia, New Orleans, sometime in the 1840s. The Pousse-Café—the name refers not to a specific recipe but to a wide range of possible drinks, all made by *layering* liqueurs—was invented as an after-dinner delectation (*pousse-café* literally means "pushes the coffee").

Drinkology's disdain aside, Pousse-Cafés are indeed dramatic-looking libations. Their existence relies on the same law of physics that causes the oil and vinegar in salad dressing to separate: to wit, that liquids of different *specific gravities* resist mixing unless shaken or stirred. Since every liqueur has its own specific specific gravity, different liqueurs will stratify—just like the layers in a geological formation—if they're poured into a glass very carefully, beginning with the heaviest (i.e., the one with the highest specific gravity) and working one's way up to the lightest.

Easier said than done. To pour a Pousse-Café successfully, you must begin with a pousse-café glass or other reasonably straight-sided glass. The heaviest liquid gets poured directly into the glass, but each subsequent layer is added very deliberately; infinite care must be taken not to shake the drink or otherwise disturb the layers during the pouring.

Various guides propose various methods for accomplishing this. To their surprise, *Drinkology*'s taste-testers found that the simplest method provides a fair chance of success. (No warranties are proffered, however.) After pouring in the bottom layer, position the bowl of a bar spoon (or other long-handled spoon) inside the glass, with the back (convex) side of the bowl turned up and the edge of the bowl held fast against the glass's interior, *just above* the level of the liquid. Very slowly, pour the next layer onto the back of the spoon. If you're lucky and steady-handed, it will flow across the surface of the layer below without mixing. After each layer, wipe the spoon off so that no residue remains. As you work your way up, adding layer upon layer, remember *never* to let the edge of the spoon penetrate the layer below the one you're pouring.

Got it? (You *are* allowed to give up right now.) In any case, book-learning will only take you so far. Pousse-Cafés demand rigorous practice, and even the slightest temblor

LIQUEURS

on the countertop may destroy all your beautiful liquidness. What's more, no Pousse-Café recipe that uses any generic liqueurs—liqueurs that, like crème de cacao, are made by multiple distillers—can guarantee its own success, since the specific gravity of such a liqueur may well differ from brand to brand.

That's probably enough said about a cocktail we were somewhat reluctant even to include. Here's one classic Pousse-Café recipe; you may want to increase the amount of each liquid, depending on the size of your glass, but make sure the amounts are equal.

¼ ounce grenadine
¼ ounce yellow Chartreuse
¼ ounce crème de cassis
¼ ounce white crème de menthe
¼ ounce green Chartreuse
¼ ounce brandy

Pour the grenadine into a pousse-café glass or other straight-sided glass. Carefully layer the other ingredients, one atop the other, in the order given.

San Francisco Cocktail

This gaily colored concoction is *only* for those who like sloe gin and vermouth in equal measure.

1 ounce sloe gin
1 ounce dry vermouth
1 ounce sweet vermouth
1 dash Peychaud's bitters
🍒 maraschino cherry

Combine liquid ingredients in a cocktail shaker, with ice. Shake well, and strain into a chilled cocktail glass. Garnish with the cherry.

Slippery Nipple

O.K., the name embarrasses *Drinkology*, too. But you'll find it hard to wean yourself from this passionate combination of Irish and Italian liqueurs.

1½ ounces Bailey's Irish Cream
1½ ounces Sambuca

Combine ingredients in a cocktail shaker, with ice. Shake well, and strain into an old-fashioned glass filled with ice.

LIQUEURS

SLOE GIN COCKTAIL

Drinkology's taste-testers surprised themselves by not minding this bright-red concoction. It is what it is, and it's not too bad. (It's better when made with Peychaud's rather than Angostura bitters.)

2 ounces sloe gin
½ ounce dry vermouth
dash Peychaud's or Angostura bitters

Combine ingredients in a cocktail shaker, with ice. Shake well, and strain into a chilled cocktail glass.

SLOE GIN FIZZ

Many a prom dress has been sent to the dry cleaner bearing telltale traces of this concoction. Actually, the version presented here is somewhat less jejune. It's fun—*if* you like sloe gin.

2 ounces sloe gin
1 ounce fresh lemon juice
½ ounce simple syrup
club soda or seltzer
⚲ maraschino cherry

Combine sloe gin, lemon juice, and simple syrup in a cocktail shaker, with ice. Shake well, and strain into a highball glass filled with ice cubes. Top with soda or seltzer. Stir briefly, and garnish with the cherry.

LIQUEURS

SLOE SCREW

The Screwdriver (page 275) begat the Sloe Screw, which in turn begat the Sloe Comfortable Screw (page 277). This lowball's for those whose tastes remain as adolescent as their sense of humor.

1½ ounces sloe gin
orange juice

Fill a double old-fashioned glass with ice cubes. Pour in the sloe gin, and top with orange juice. Stir briefly.

SOMBRERO

This creamy lowball is a perennial favorite for the very good reason that it is delicious.

2 ounces coffee liqueur
1½ ounces heavy cream

Combine ingredients in a cocktail shaker, with ice. Shake well, and strain into an ice-filled old-fashioned glass.

LIQUEURS

TATTOO

This *Drinkology* original was a bona fide hit with taste-testers. It proves the worth of experimenting with combinations that you believe just might work.

2 ounces white crème de cacao
1½ ounces heavy cream
½ teaspoon crème de cassis

Combine the crème de cacao and cream in a cocktail shaker, with ice. Shake well, and strain into a chilled cocktail glass. Drizzle the cassis over the surface of the drink.

TOASTED ALMOND

Amaretto-loving coffee drinkers will find it hard to imagine a better combination than this.

1 ounce amaretto
1 ounce coffee liqueur
1 ounce heavy cream

Combine ingredients in a cocktail shaker, with ice. Shake well, and strain into an old-fashioned glass filled with ice.

LIQUEURS

VELVET HAMMER
(LIQUEURS-AND-BRANDY VERSION)

 The vodka-based version of this drink (page 278) is better known, but *Drinkology* prefers this variation. Most cream-based drinks, no matter how delicious, are fairly straight-forward in taste; this one, however, is subtly and complexly flavored. Do *not* substitute triple sec for Cointreau in this drink.

1 ounce Cointreau
1 ounce white crème de cacao
½ ounce brandy
1 ounce heavy cream

Combine ingredients in a cocktail shaker, with ice. Shake well, and strain into a chilled cocktail glass.

LIQUEURS

Rum
and Cachaça

"SMASH, SMASH, SMASH! SMASH THE DEMON RUM!" HER BATTLE cry echoed off saloon walls from Kansas City to New York. While the good sisters of the Women's Christian Temperance Union stood by singing hymns, the axe-wielding prohibitionist Carry Nation took aim at bottles of Caribbean rum and left their contents drizzled over many a barroom floor. She had her reasons. This most American of spirits had been wreaking havoc ever since 1493, when Columbus swiped sugarcane from the Canary Islands and planted it in the West Indies. It didn't take long for the locals there to figure out that this tall, reedy grass tasted even better fermented. Debauchery ensued.

American colonists knocked back 12 million gallons of the stuff each year—nearly four gallons each—giving "sugar high" an altogether different meaning long before M&Ms came on the market. Although Lord Byron claimed it brought him closer to the divine ("There's nought, no doubt, so much the spirit calms/As rum and true religion"), rum was singularly responsible for much of the drunkenness across the pond from where he waxed poetic. Rum's nefarious effects were, unfortunately, not limited to those who imbibed. New

Englanders turned West Indian molasses into the first commercially distilled spirit in the Colonies. They sold a lot and drank even more. But they always saved some rum to ship to Africa, where it was exchanged for slaves. Demonic, indeed.

Rum was also at the root of early calls for a kind of campaign finance reform. None other than George Washington distributed untold gallons of rum among the voters of Virginia, who subsequently elected him to the House of Burgesses in 1758. Rum even played a part in inspiring revolution: a 1765 tax on non-British molasses helped fuel the outrage that ultimately found its voice in the Boston Tea Party. The following decade, one Paul Revere would use it to fortify his galloping *cri de guerre*. Rum's long association with smuggling ("rum runners"), piracy, and drunken sailors has not helped its reputation. People thought it so low that its very name, lengthened to "rummy," became a stand-in for wanton inebriates of all stripes. What a complicated, unsettling history for a liquor that's so simple and so good.

RUMS, YOUNG AND OLD

Although rum can, in fact, be made from sugarcane (see the sidebar on cachaça, page 222), it's usually distilled from molasses, a byproduct of refining sugarcane into the white crystals we put in coffee and tea. Rum is characterized as light, medium, or heavy: the longer molasses, water, and yeast are allowed to stew, the darker and more flavorful, or heavy, the rum. The heaviest rums are fermented for about three weeks, the lightest for only a few days.

The yeast cultures themselves are peculiar to each distillery, and because they contribute to the rum's ultimate taste, they are guarded like gold. In fact, the finest distilleries no longer add fresh yeast, but instead use *dunder,* the yeast-rich residue left in the stills after decades and decades of cooking this goo. The distillate is aged in oak for anywhere from six months for the clear, light rums to six years for the heavier varieties. Rum that has been aged for six years or more is labeled *añejo,* which is simply a Spanish word for "old." (Highly aromatic, añejo rums are delicious sipped neat from a snifter.)

Jamaica is known for its dark rum, Haiti and Barbados for their medium-bodied varieties. Cuba produces some of the world's best light rum—if you can get it. Puerto Rico's light rum is mighty fine, too, and far easier to find in the States. "Overproof" rum (generally referred to as 151-proof rum, or, if it's distilled in Guyana, as Demerara rum) is a wickedly strong distillation; in cocktails, it's generally used to add potency and bite to the drink. Because it ignites easily, 151 rum is also useful for flaming drinks.

Befitting a liquor with a checkered past, no one is quite sure where rum's name comes from. One theory links it to *saccharum,* the Latin word for sugarcane, but there's a whole mess of Latin nouns that end in *−rum,* and a more likely abbreviation would be "sac," anyway. A more colorful explanation has groggy British sailors naming it after Old Rummy, a kindly old admiral who plied them with the demon water to treat their scurvy. (It turned out the real remedy was the lemon juice the sailors mixed it with, but they downed it in quantities that left them stupefied anyway.) But it seems more likely that his nickname derived from Old Rummy's drinking habits, and not the other way around. The most credible derivation is from *rumbustiousness,* meaning uncontrollable exuberance, or the British slang *rumbullion,* a rambunctious uproar or melee; Carry Nation would undoubtedly agree with these etymologies.

ACAPULCO

Reminiscent of a Margarita, this is an extraordinarily refreshing cocktail. *Drinkology* tested the recipe using both fresh lime juice and the bottled variety; we surprised ourselves by preferring the latter.

2 ounces light rum
½ ounce Cointreau or triple sec
½ ounce Rose's lime juice
½ ounce simple syrup

Combine ingredients in a cocktail shaker, with ice. Shake well, and strain into a chilled cocktail glass.

BACARDI COCKTAIL

This classic drink—whose garnet color could be called Jazz Age Red—is perhaps the only cocktail that comes with a legal brief attached. A 1936 New York State court ruling declared that it *must* be made with Bacardi rum. Well, O.K. *Drinkology* has tried it with both the light and gold varieties, and definitely prefers the latter.

2 ounces Bacardi Gold rum
1 ounce fresh lime juice
½ ounce grenadine

Combine ingredients in a cocktail shaker, with ice. Shake well, and strain into a chilled cocktail glass.

BEACHCOMBER

The Beachcomber, like so many rum-based drinks, conjures images of surf, swaying palms, and taking it oh-so-easy.

lime wedge
superfine sugar
2 ounces gold rum
¼ ounce cherry brandy
¼ ounce maraschino liqueur
⚬ maraschino cherry

Rim a chilled cocktail glass with the lime wedge and sugar. (Discard the wedge.) Combine the rum, cherry brandy, and maraschino liqueur in a cocktail shaker, with ice. Shake well, and strain into the prepared glass. Garnish with the cherry.

BEE'S KNEES

If you like orangey, robustly flavored drinks, you'll think the Bee's Knees is the cat's pajamas.

⚬ orange peel
1½ ounces gold rum
½ ounce Cointreau or triple sec
½ ounce fresh lime juice
½ ounce orange juice
1 teaspoon powdered sugar

Rim a chilled cocktail glass with the orange peel. Combine liquid ingredients and sugar in a cocktail shaker, with ice. Shake well, and strain into the glass. Garnish with the orange peel.

BOLERO (APPLEJACK VERSION)

Bolero recipes differ rather dramatically: some are dry, others sweet and fruity. This applejack-and-vermouth version of the cocktail is outstanding—dry and highly aromatic, with just a hint of apple flavor.

1½ ounces light rum
¾ ounce applejack
½ teaspoon sweet vermouth

Combine ingredients in a mixing glass, with ice. Stir, and strain into a chilled cocktail glass.

BOLERO
(DARK RUM AND BRANDY VERSION)

This pineapple-yellow version of the Bolero is utterly unlike the previous one—*except* in its subtlety. It's one of the few fruity rum-based drinks whose flavor is genuinely complex.

2 ounces dark rum
½ ounce brandy
½ ounce fresh lime juice
½ ounce orange juice
½ ounce simple syrup

Combine ingredients in a cocktail shaker, with ice. Shake well, and strain into a chilled cocktail glass.

BOSTON COOLER

The pale, translucent-yellow Boston Cooler is a truly excellent summertime highball: light, tart, and clean-tasting.

☙ lemon twist
2 ounces light rum
½ ounce fresh lemon juice
1 teaspoon powdered sugar
club soda or seltzer

Rim a highball glass with the lemon twist, and fill the glass with ice cubes. Combine the rum, lemon juice, and sugar in a cocktail shaker, with ice. Shake well, and strain into the highball glass. Top with club soda (or seltzer). Stir briefly, and garnish with the twist.

B.V.D.

You can enjoy this cocktail even if you're not a jockey or a boxer. By the way, the drink sometimes goes by the name Brown Cocktail, but *Drinkology*'s delicate sensibilities won't let us call it the Brown B.V.D.

1 ounce light rum
1 ounce dry vermouth
1 ounce gin
☙ lemon twist or olive

Combine liquid ingredients in a mixing glass, with ice. Stir, and strain into a chilled cocktail glass. Garnish with the lemon twist or olive. (If using a twist, rim the glass beforehand.)

RUM

CARIBBEAN MILLIONAIRE

Frankly, this drink *sounds* awful—garishly overproduced in a *nouveau riche* sort of way. But it's really very good.

1 ounce gold or dark rum
1 ounce crème de banane
½ ounce apricot brandy
½ ounce fresh lemon juice
¼ teaspoon sloe gin
❧ banana slice

Combine liquid ingredients in a cocktail shaker, with ice. Shake well, and strain into an ice-filled collins or highball glass. Garnish with the banana slice.

CASABLANCA

Rick's American Bar was, in Bogie's famous phrase, a gin joint, but the Casablanca is made with rum. The cocktail's taste is as crisp as its icy-white appearance. Like Bogart and Bergman, it's an enchanting balance of the sour and the sweet.

2½ ounces light rum
½ ounce Cointreau or triple sec
½ ounce maraschino liqueur
½ ounce fresh lime juice

Combine ingredients in a cocktail shaker, with ice. Shake well, and strain into a chilled cocktail glass.

CHOCOLATE RUM

The light café-au-lait color of this cocktail is as appealing as its chocolaty taste.

1½ ounces gold rum
¾ ounce dark crème de cacao
½ teaspoon white crème de menthe
½ ounce heavy cream

Combine ingredients in a cocktail shaker, with ice. Shake well, and strain into a chilled cocktail glass.

CONTINENTAL

This elegantly named, elegant-looking cocktail deftly combines the flavors of lime and mint. It's perfect for those who like Mojitos but don't like the muddling mess.

2 ounces light rum
¼ ounce green crème de menthe
½ ounce fresh lime juice
¼ teaspoon simple syrup
⚮ lemon twist

Rim a chilled cocktail glass with the lemon twist. Combine the other ingredients in a cocktail shaker, with ice. Shake well, and strain into the glass. Garnish with the twist.

RUM

CREOLE

Don't serve this drink to your vegan friends. Even among carnivores, opinion is divided, though *Drinkology* tends to like the Creole's no-holds-barred taste.

2 ounces light rum
2 ounces beef broth or bouillon
½ ounce fresh lemon juice
2 dashes Tabasco sauce
freshly ground salt and pepper

Combine the rum, broth, lemon juice, and Tabasco in a cocktail shaker, with ice. Shake well, and strain into an old-fashioned glass filled with ice cubes. Sprinkle with salt and pepper, to taste. (If you're using canned beef broth, go lightly on the salt.)

CUBA LIBRE

How dare we feature a drink as insipid as the Cuba Libre (which, by the way, should be pronounced KOO-bah LEE-bray)? After all, it's just a rum and Coke, right?—a combination that, while it may bliss out youthful revelers, is an affront to adult sensibilities. *Drinkology* begs to differ. Made well—which means going heavy on the lime and using Mexican Coca-Cola (which is still made with cane sugar)—the Cuba Libre can certainly hold a *candela* to other highball coolers.

Named not, as you might imagine, by some anti-Castro zealot but by an American soldier taking a break from "liberating" Cuba during the Spanish-American War, the Cuba Libre has retained its popularity for more than a century for one simple reason: it tastes good. The rum and lime undercut the cloying characteristics of the cola and bring out its subtler, more herbal attributes. (We're serious, so stop laughing.)

The Cuba Libre's two main ingredients inspired the lyric of what, during the 1940s, became the most popular calypso record of all time, the Andrews Sisters' "Rum and Coca-Cola"—a relentlessly upbeat number about U.S. GIs consorting with cheerful local prostitutes while stationed in Trinidad.

½ large lime
2 ounces rum
Coca-Cola (preferably bottled in Mexico)

Fill a highball glass with ice cubes. Squeeze the half-lime into the drink, dropping in the hull. Pour in the rum, and top with the Coke. Stir briefly.

CUBAN SPECIAL

This pale, pale yellow cocktail has a clean and highly refreshing taste.

1½ ounces light rum
¼ ounce Cointreau or triple sec
½ ounce fresh lime juice
½ ounce pineapple juice
↻ a few pineapple chunks

Combine liquid ingredients in a cocktail shaker, with ice. Shake well, and strain into a chilled cocktail glass. Garnish with the pineapple chunks, skewered together.

CURAÇAO COOLER

Did you know that Cointreau is a type of curaçao—that is, a liqueur made (at least in part) from the dried peel of bitter oranges? You can use any curaçao (except blue) in this cooler, though *Drinkology,* as always, prefers Cointreau.

1 ounce gold or dark rum
1 ounce Cointreau
1 ounce fresh lime juice
club soda or seltzer
↻ orange slice

Combine the rum, Cointreau, and lime juice in a cocktail shaker, with ice. Shake well, and strain into an ice-filled highball glass. Top with the club soda (or seltzer), and garnish with the orange slice.

DAIQUIRI (CLASSIC)

 Today's bar-goers mostly know the Daiquiri in its innumerable frozen incarnations. Many of those icy, fruity, blender-blended concoctions are quite tasty (*Drinkology* includes a few such recipes in the Frozen Drinks chapter). But the near-oblivion into which the classic Daiquiri has sunk is a nonetheless a crying shame. The classic Daiquiri is simplicity itself—just rum, lime, and sugar syrup—and in this case less is definitely more.

Like the Cuba Libre (page 195), the Daiquiri appears to have been invented by an American in Cuba, though it's likely that he (one Jennings S. Cox, a mining engineer working in the eastern part of the island in the wake of the Spanish-American War) simply adapted a rum-, lime-, and sugar-based recipe that had been enjoyed by the locals for centuries.

⚘ lime wedge
2 ounces light rum
1 ounce fresh lime juice
½ ounce simple syrup

Rim a chilled cocktail glass with the lime wedge. Combine the other ingredients in a cocktail shaker, with ice. Shake well, and strain into the glass. Squeeze the lime wedge into the drink, and drop it in.

DARK AND STORMY

The Dark and Stormy originated in sunny Bermuda, where it is always made with Bermudian ingredients: Gosling's Black Seal rum and Barritt's ginger beer. If you can't find those, any good dark rum (e.g., Mount Gay) and ginger beer (*not* ginger ale) will do.

2 ounces dark rum
ginger beer
♘ lime wedge

Rim a highball glass with the lime wedge and fill the glass with ice cubes. (Reserve the wedge.) Pour in the rum, and gently top with the ginger beer. Squeeze the lime wedge and drop it into the drink.

EL SALVADOR

The rum is overshadowed by the hazelnut flavor of Frangelico in this pretty pink drink.

1½ ounces light rum
¾ ounce Frangelico
½ ounce fresh lime juice
1 teaspoon grenadine

Combine ingredients in a cocktail shaker, with ice. Shake well, and strain into a chilled cocktail glass.

EYE-OPENER

Pernod dominates the unusual flavor of this canary-yellow cocktail. If you don't hate it, you'll love it.

1½ ounces light rum
1 teaspoon Cointreau or triple sec
1 teaspoon white crème de cacao
½ teaspoon Pernod or other anise-flavored liqueur
1 egg yolk
1 teaspoon powdered sugar

Combine ingredients in a cocktail shaker, with ice. Shake very well, and strain into a chilled cocktail glass.

FRAP FRAPPÉ

Starbucks' mocha-flavored Frappucino soft drink makes a great base for this delicious beverage. The aged rum we use is Anniversario Venezuelan *ron añejo*, but feel free to substitute any dark and flavorful rum.

1½ ounces aged rum (*ron añejo*)
½ ounce Godiva chocolate liqueur
2 ounces mocha-flavored coffee soft drink
↋ chocolate-flavored maraschino cherry

Fill a double old-fashioned glass with ice cubes. Combine ingredients in a cocktail shaker, with ice. Shake well, and strain into the glass. Garnish with the chocolate-flavored cherry.

GORILLA TIT

 Though it will definitely grow hair on your breast, this cola-colored drink isn't the atrocious, frat-house concoction the name suggests. Unaccountably, the combination of three strong, dark flavors works very well.

¾ ounce dark rum
¾ ounce bourbon
¾ ounce coffee liqueur

Fill an old-fashioned glass with ice cubes. Pour in the rum, bourbon, and coffee liqueur. Stir briefly.

HAVANA COCKTAIL

 This frothy, pale yellow concoction's pineapple and lemon flavors are deliciously balanced. It rates as a *Drinkology* favorite.

2 ounces light rum
2 ounces pineapple juice
½ ounce fresh lemon juice

Combine ingredients in a cocktail shaker, with ice. Shake well, and strain into a chilled cocktail glass.

HEATWAVE

This fruity highball's a terrific thirst-quencher when the temperature's risin'.

1 ounce dark rum
½ ounce peach schnapps
pineapple juice
¼ ounce grenadine

Fill a highball glass with ice cubes. Pour in the rum and schnapps, and fill the glass almost to the top with the pineapple juice. Add the grenadine, and stir briefly.

HONEYBEE

Rum and honey are as natural a combination as rum and sugar. You'll be surprised by how gently the taste of honey infuses this icy-white drink. A mild-flavored honey (like clover) works best in this recipe.

2 ounces light rum
1 tablespoon honey
2 teaspoons fresh lemon juice

Combine ingredients in a cocktail shaker, with ice. Shake very well (to thoroughly dissolve the honey), and strain into a chilled cocktail glass.

HOP TOAD

Some Hop Toad recipes call for light rum and skip the bitters. *Drinkology* prefers this darker, more robust version of the drink.

1½ ounces dark rum
1 ounce apricot brandy
½ ounce fresh lime juice
dash Angostura bitters

Combine ingredients in a cocktail shaker, with ice. Shake well, and strain into a chilled cocktail glass.

HURRICANE

Hardly tempestuous, the Hurricane is fruity and mild. Double this recipe if you intend to serve the drink in the traditional manner—that is, in a hurricane glass.

1 ounce dark rum
1 ounce light rum
½ ounce fresh lime juice
½ ounce passion-fruit juice
¼ ounce simple syrup

Combine ingredients in a cocktail shaker, with ice. Shake well, and strain into a chilled cocktail glass.

JADE

It's astonishing how closely the color of this cocktail resembles that of the semiprecious stone after which it's named. The taste is sweet and pleasant—not overwhelmed by the crème de menthe. The cocktail will look all the more jewel-like if you cut the lime slice very thin and allow it to float on top of the drink.

1½ ounces gold rum
½ teaspoon Cointreau or triple sec
½ teaspoon green crème de menthe
½ ounce fresh lime juice
1 heaping teaspoon powdered sugar
♂ thinly cut lime slice

Combine liquid ingredients and sugar in a cocktail shaker, with ice. Shake well, and strain into a chilled cocktail glass. Garnish with the lime slice.

KINGSTON COCKTAIL

The deep-amber-colored Kingston Cocktail has a very distinctive taste. It's a *Drinkology* favorite.

2 ounces Jamaican rum
1 ounce coffee liqueur
1 teaspoon fresh lime juice

Combine ingredients in a cocktail shaker, with ice. Shake well, and strain into a chilled cocktail glass.

MAI TAI

The Mai Tai is an artifact of the craze for all things "Polynesian" that swept America during the 1940s and 1950s. Actually, it's about as Polynesian as a plastic lei, an inflatable palm tree, or Hawaiian Punch (whose taste it inadvertently mimics). It's the kind of drink—decorated with paper parasols and other kitschy paraphernalia—that loud, loudly dressed, loutish tourist-types used to guzzle too many of at the Trader Vic's chain of Polynesian-themed restaurants. (Purportedly, it was invented in 1944 by "Trader Vic"—Victor Bergeron—himself, who christened it with a Tahitian phrase meaning "out of this world." Regarding the veracity of this claim, *Drinkology*'s guess is as good as yours.)

The Mai Tai is, in a word, *awful*. But it's so flamboyantly, so grandiosely awful that it wins a place in *Drinkology*'s otherwise unforgiving heart.

Note that most Mai Tai recipes call for orgeat syrup—an almond-based goop that can be as difficult to find as it is hard to pronounce (or-ZHAH, in case you're interested). Almond syrup, which is carried by many specialty food shops, is a more-than-acceptable substitute. Be careful when you're shaking a Mai Tai: with ice, the drink's so huge that it virtually fills the cup of a standard shaker, and some spillage is almost inevitable.

1 ounce dark rum
1 ounce light rum
1 ounce Cointreau or triple sec
½ ounce orgeat syrup or almond syrup
½ ounce fresh lime juice
½ ounce grenadine
☙ maraschino cherry and fresh fruit (orange slice, pineapple chunk, or whatnot)

Combine liquid ingredients in a standard shaker, with ice. Shake well, and strain into a large, chilled red wine glass filled with ice cubes or crushed ice. Garnish liberally with the fruit.

MIAMI

This cocktail looks icy and cool, and its frosty, refreshing taste delivers on the promise. Cut the lime slice very thin, and allow it to float on top of the drink.

2 ounces light rum
½ ounce white crème de menthe
½ teaspoon fresh lemon juice
☙ thinly cut lime slice

Combine liquid ingredients in a cocktail shaker, with ice. Shake well, and strain into a chilled cocktail glass. Garnish with the lime slice.

MOJITO

A Cuban version of the Mint Julep, the Mojito has ridden the wave of enthusiasm for Cuban culture to become an immensely popular summertime cooler. As with the Mint Julep, *Drinkology* prefers a drink that's sweet and mighty minty.

8 or more large fresh mint leaves
¾ ounce simple syrup
½ lime
crushed ice
2 ounces light rum
club soda or seltzer
♂ sprig of fresh mint

In the bottom of a highball glass, muddle the mint leaves and simple syrup, thoroughly crushing the leaves. (Because of the height of the glass, this will be difficult if you don't have a muddler. If you're using a spoon or the handle of a wooden citrus reamer, perform the muddling in a small, sturdy ceramic bowl, then carefully scrape the muddled leaves and syrup into the highball glass.) Squeeze the lime-half into the glass, drop in the hull, and stir briefly. Fill the glass with crushed ice, pour in the rum, and fill the glass with the soda or seltzer. Garnish with the mint sprig.

NAVY GROG

The grog that was rationed out to eighteenth-century British sailors consisted of rum and water. This highball is somewhat more elaborate. It's terrific—a classic rum-and-fruit punch. Use a standard (not a Boston) shaker for this large drink.

1 ounce dark rum
1 ounce gold rum
1 ounce light rum
½ ounce fresh lime juice
½ ounce orange juice
½ ounce passion-fruit juice
½ ounce pineapple juice
½ ounce orgeat syrup or almond syrup
♂ sprig of fresh mint

Combine liquid ingredients in a standard cocktail shaker, with ice. Shake well, and strain into a highball glass filled with ice cubes. Garnish with the mint sprig.

OLD SAN JUAN

This light pink cocktail looks like a Cosmopolitan, but it's uncompromisingly tart.

⌀ lime wedge
1½ ounces gold rum
½ ounce cranberry juice
1 ounce fresh lime juice

Rim a chilled cocktail glass with the lime wedge. Combine the other ingredients in a cocktail shaker, with ice. Shake well, and strain into the glass. Squeeze the lime wedge into the drink, and drop it in.

PAGO PAGO

This potent lowball's oddball name gets all the odder when you find out it's pronounced "pango pango." (BTW, Pago Pago is the capital city of the Pacific island protectorate of American Samoa.)

3 ounces Jamaican rum
1 teaspoon green Chartreuse
1 teaspoon white crème de cacao
1 ounce fresh lime juice
1 ounce pineapple juice

Combine ingredients in a cocktail shaker, with ice. Shake well, and strain into an old-fashioned glass filled with ice cubes.

PARISIAN BLONDE

This concoction is surprisingly mild in flavor and light in texture, with subtle notes of orange.

1 ounce light rum
1 ounce orange curaçao
1 ounce heavy cream

Combine ingredients in a cocktail shaker, with ice. Shake well, and strain into a chilled cocktail glass.

PIÑA COLADA (SHAKEN)

To quote the Coco Lopez website: "Once upon a time there was no Piña Colada. . . . THE HORROR!" Many a lover of tropical drinks would doubtless agree.

This most renowned of Caribbean drinks was actually made possible by the invention of Coco Lopez by a Puerto Rican culinary genius named Ramón Lopez Irizarry, who in the mid-twentieth century devised a way of extracting coconut "cream" from the pulp of that hard-shelled fruit, mixing it with sugar to create the sweet, viscous, pearly white goo that serves as the basis for the Piña Colada and a range of other tropical concoctions.

The drink itself appears to have been invented in the early 1950s—probably by another Ramón (Ramón "Monchito" Marrero, bartender at the Caribe Hilton in San Juan), who had the brilliant idea of mixing Coco Lopez with rum and a goodly dose of pineapple juice. (The drink's name, so exotic-sounding to Anglophone ears, actually has a humdrum, workaday meaning: "strained pineapple.")

The Piña Colada's popularity crested in the 1970s—but it's well worth a retro revival. Today's Piña Colada drinkers mostly know it in its frozen, blended variation (see page 344), but it was originally a shaken drink. *Drinkology* recommends using a standard shaker (rather than a Boston shaker) for the Piña Colada; it reduces the chance of mishap.

2 ounces light or gold rum
6 ounces pineapple juice
2 ounces cream of coconut
♂ pineapple and maraschino cherry "flag"

Combine liquid ingredients in a standard cocktail shaker, with ice. Shake very well, and strain into a large red wine glass filled with ice cubes. Garnish with the flag (pineapple chunks and maraschino cherries skewered on a cocktail spear or toothpick).

PLANTER'S COCKTAIL

Not to be confused with the Planter's Punch (see opposite), this golden cocktail is very simple (and quite good).

2 ounces dark rum
¾ ounce fresh lemon juice
1 heaping teaspoon powdered sugar

Combine ingredients in a cocktail shaker, with ice. Shake well, and strain into a chilled cocktail glass.

PLANTER'S PUNCH

The Planter's Punch is one of that multitude of famous drinks whose origin is contested. Some say it was created by the Myers's Rum Company in the 1890s; others place its invention some 50 years earlier, giving credit to an antebellum bartender at St. Louis's Planter's Hotel. There are numerous "original" recipes; here's one *Drinkology*—without laying any claim to its "authenticity"—happens to like. The size of this drink necessitates using a standard shaker (rather than a Boston shaker) to reduce the chance of spillage.

2 ounces dark rum
¼ teaspoon Cointreau or triple sec
3 ounces orange juice
½ ounce fresh lemon juice
2 heaping teaspoons powdered sugar
¼ teaspoon grenadine
✧ maraschino cherry
✧ orange slice

Combine all ingredients except the garnishes in a standard cocktail shaker, with ice. Shake well, and strain into a high-ball glass filled with ice cubes. Garnish with the cherry and orange slice.

RUM AND TONIC

Beware: this drink is insipid if made with light rum. Use a good dark rum—one whose flavor is powerful enough to compete with the tonic water—and it's delicious.

↧ quarter lime
2 ounces dark rum
tonic water

Rim a highball glass with the quarter lime, and fill the glass with ice cubes. Pour in the rum, and fill the glass with tonic water. Squeeze the lime into the drink, and drop it in. Stir briefly.

RUM RICKEY

Dark rum makes an exceptional rickey. You could hardly ask for a more flavorful refresher.

2 ounces dark rum
½ ounce fresh lime juice
club soda or seltzer
↧ lime wedge

Rim a highball glass with the lime wedge, and fill the glass with ice cubes. Pour in the rum and lime juice, and top with soda (or seltzer). Squeeze the lime wedge into the drink, and drop it in. Stir briefly.

Rum Runner

Think a drink this complicated can't be any good? Wrong. The shaken version of the Rum Runner is definitely a *Drinkology* favorite. If you can get 'em, use Peychaud's bitters rather than Angostura in this recipe. And, to prevent spills, shake this drink in a standard (not a Boston) shaker.

¼ lime
1 ounce gold rum
1 ounce light rum
2 ounces pineapple juice
1 ounce simple syrup
½ ounce fresh lime juice
1 egg white
2 dashes Peychaud's or Angostura bitters
♺ 2 or 3 pineapple chunks

Squeeze the quarter-lime into an empty highball glass, and drop it in. Fill the glass with ice cubes. Combine the other ingredients (except for the pineapple chunks) in a standard shaker, with ice. Shake well, and strain into the highball glass. Garnish with the pineapple chunks.

RUM SANGAREE

Sangarees—cold drinks that incorporate wine (or fortified wine) and spices—have been around since the early eighteenth century, at least. This Rum Sangaree's rich taste is sharpened by the freshly grated nutmeg.

2 ounces dark rum
½ ounce Cointreau or triple sec
½ ounce ruby port
freshly grated nutmeg

Combine liquid ingredients in a mixing glass, with ice. Stir, and strain into a red wine glass filled with ice cubes. Sprinkle nutmeg on top.

SAN SALVADOR

The San Salvador is a lowball, lighter take on the Planter's Punch.

1½ ounces dark rum
1 ounce orange curaçao
1½ ounces orange juice
½ ounce fresh lime juice
⚘ lime slice

Combine liquid ingredients in a cocktail shaker, with ice. Shake well, and strain into a double old-fashioned glass filled with ice cubes. Garnish with the lime slice.

SCORPION

Like the Mai Tai and the Zombie, the Scorpion is one of those Tiki Bar–type concoctions that go down easy but will sting you if you're not careful.

pineapple chunk
maraschino cherry, stem removed
1 ounce gold rum
1 ounce brandy
1 ounce orange juice
¾ ounce fresh lemon juice
½ ounce orgeat syrup or almond syrup
½ ounce simple syrup
♂ pineapple and maraschino cherry "flag"

In the bottom of a cocktail shaker, muddle the pineapple chunk and de-stemmed cherry. (Really pulverize them.) Add ice to the shaker, and pour in the liquid ingredients. Shake very well, and strain into a large, ice-filled red wine glass. Garnish with the flag (pineapple chunks and cherries skewered on a cocktail spear or toothpick).

SHERRY-RUM KNICKERBOCKER

 This Knickerbocker couldn't be more different from the gin-based drink that shares the name (see page 131). Pedro Ximénez sherry (the sweetest of all sherries) lends unexpectedly depth to the lushly tropical concoction.

2 ounces Mount Gay rum
½ ounce Liqueur Créole Clément or Cointreau
½ ounce Pedro Ximénez sherry
2 ounces pineapple juice
2 dashes orange bitters
⚬ pineapple and maraschino cherry "flag"

Pack a double old-fashioned glass with crushed ice. Combine all ingredients in a mixing glass (without ice), stir, and pour into the prepared glass. Garnish with the flag (pineapple chunks and maraschino cherries skewered on a cocktail spear or toothpick).

SWIZZLE

The secret to this traditional Caribbean highball is all in the swizzling.

crushed ice
2 ounces dark rum
¾ ounce fresh lime juice
1 teaspoon simple syrup
3 dashes Angostura bitters
club soda or seltzer
☙ lime wedge

Pack a highball glass with crushed ice. Pour in the rum, lime juice, and simple syrup, and shake in the bitters. Sink a long-handled spoon to the bottom of the glass, and stir the drink by swizzling (holding the handle of the spoon between your palms and turning it rapidly by rubbing your palms together). Top with club soda or seltzer, and garnish with the lime wedge, squeezing it into the drink before dropping it in.

THIRD RAIL

This recipe really belongs to that class of drinks known as Corpse Revivers (see page 80), all of which utilize equal parts of three different liquors. The Third Rail's better than most such concoctions, though—surprisingly light for a drink that's basically straight booze.

1 ounce dark rum
1 ounce applejack
1 ounce brandy
dash of Pernod or other anise-flavored liqueur

Combine ingredients in a mixing glass, with ice. Stir, and strain into a chilled cocktail glass.

TIGER'S MILK

This lightly flavored, milkshake-like drink isn't so forbidding. It purrs rather than roars.

1 ounce dark rum
1 ounce brandy
4 ounces half-and-half
2 heaping teaspoons powdered sugar
freshly grated nutmeg

Combine rum, brandy, half-and-half, and sugar in a standard cocktail shaker, with ice. Shake well, and strain into a large, chilled red wine glass. Sprinkle the nutmeg on top.

WHITE LION

The White Lion is actually pink. It's lemony and sweet—
like pink lemonade.

1½ ounces light rum
¾ ounce fresh lemon juice
1 teaspoon simple syrup
½ teaspoon grenadine
2 dashes Angostura bitters

*Combine ingredients in a cocktail shaker, with ice. Shake
well, and strain into a chilled cocktail glass.*

XYZ COCKTAIL

The XYZ is a lemony take on the Daiquiri. Cut the lemon
slice very thin, and allow it to float on top of the drink.

2 ounces light rum
1 ounce Cointreau or triple sec
1 ounce fresh lemon juice
🍋 thinly cut lemon slice

*Combine liquid ingredients in a cocktail shaker, with ice.
Shake well, and strain into a chilled cocktail glass. Garnish
with the lemon slice.*

Yellow Bird

Drinkology wonders whether the Yellow Bird was named for the mid-1950s calypso hit. No matter. If you're a Galliano fan, you're sure to like this beautifully colored drink.

2 ounces gold rum
½ ounce Cointreau or triple sec
½ ounce Galliano
½ ounce fresh lime juice

Combine ingredients in a cocktail shaker, with ice. Shake well, and strain into a chilled cocktail glass.

Zombie

Ah, the Zombie. What a fitting finale to the rum recipes: a drink that, if you have more than a couple, will certainly transport you to the land of the living dead.

It's often reported that this witch-doctor's brew was first created in the late 1930s by Don Beach, proprietor of Hollywood's Don the Beachcomber restaurant. But not everyone agrees, and New York–centric *Drinkology* prefers an alternate tale: that the death-dealing drink was first served up at the Hurricane Bar at the 1939 New York World's Fair.

As with so many cocktails, there are numerous claimants to the Zombie's "original" recipe. What's certain is that a Zombie *must* include at least two types of rum, and usually a hefty dose of some other liquor, as well. (This drink really wants to snatch your body away from you.) Many Zombie recipes insist that the drink be completed by floating half an ounce or so of 151-proof rum on top. This strikes *Drinkology* as, shall we say, *de trop*, but you may do so if you just can't control yourself.

The Zombie demands to be accessorized with garnishes—the more extravagant the better. Our recommendation—pineapple chunk, mint sprig, and cherry—is meant as the bare minimum. Note that this is a *large* drink; shake it in a standard shaker, and make sure your wine goblet is big enough to handle it.

1 ounce dark rum
1 ounce light rum
1 ounce orange curaçao or Cointreau
1½ ounces orange juice
1½ ounces papaya nectar
½ ounce fresh lemon juice
½ ounce fresh lime juice
¼ ounce grenadine
2 dashes Angostura or orange bitters
↧ maraschino cherry
↧ pineapple chunk
↧ sprig of fresh mint

Combine all ingredients except garnishes in a standard shaker, with ice. Shake well, and strain into a large red wine glass filled with ice cubes. Garnish with the fruit and mint sprig.

CACHAÇA

Like rum's history, that of the Brazilian sugarcane spirit called cachaça (kah-SHAH-suh) is intertwined with slavery. Cachaça was first created in the early sixteenth century on Brazilian sugarcane plantations: The African slaves working the plantations were "rewarded" (and, undoubtedly, kept docile) with fermented sugarcane juice—the juice being a byproduct of the sugar-milling process. At some point, someone realized that this brew could be rendered more potent by being distilled, and cachaça was born. (Cachaça's potency is attested by the common Brazilian slang word for the drink—*pinga*, which means "drop" in Portugese. Cachaça, in other words, is so strong that it's best consumed drop by drop.)

For a long, long time, cachaça remained a humble liquor—the kind of hooch poor people would imbibe to forget their troubles and put a little luster on their gritty lives. Something of cachaça's "everyman" reputation survives, especially in its native country. Brazilians today consume an average, annually, of two gallons of cachaça per person—but it's mostly of the cheap, unaged variety, bottled directly after distillation. In fact, many Brazilian farmers continue to make their own cachaça, selling it themselves at little roadside stands or through cooperatives that impose a modicum of quality control.

But there are cachaças and then are cachaças. Sugarcane liquor benefits greatly from ageing in wood, and a variety of better-grade cachaças—aged for at least a year, sometimes much longer, in barrels made of tropical hardwoods—have long been produced in Brazil. All kinds of cachaça—downmarket and up—were virtually unknown outside Brazil, however, until the Brazilian diaspora of the 1980s. Driven by economic need to relocate themselves, hundreds of thousands of Brazilians immigrated to North America and Europe, and (like all immigrants, always) brought their culture, including their drinking culture, along with them.

The wider world was introduced to cachaça at the Brazilian bars and restaurants these immigrants established. Brazil's "national drink," the Caipirinha (kyc-pccr-EEN-yuh)—a muddled lime, sugar, and cachaça cocktail—gained an international following, and the outflow of cachaça from Brazil rose from trickle to flood: Cachaça is, by some accounts, now the second-most-popular alcoholic beverage in Germany (following beer, of course); in the United States, cachaça imports have increased at least sixfold over the past decade.

Despite cachaça's burgeoning popularity, it's still difficult to find better-quality, aged cachaças in many areas of the U.S. The brand called Pitú (whose name means "lobster," and whose label sports a bright red crustacean) is ubiquitous; unfortunately, it's not very good. (This is polite understatement.) A much better choice, and nearly as widely available, is the upstart brand Leblon (named for a beach in Rio), whose highly distinctive, pungently fruity flavor is conferred by ageing in casks previously used for ageing cognac. Luckily, *Drinkology* lives hard by one of the country's largest "Little Brazils," in Newark, New Jersey. A scouting expedition to the Brazilian-owned liquor stores of Ferry Street—the main corridor of Newark's Ironbound neighborhood—found fifteen different cachaça brands on sale.

For our Caipirinha recipe, we use Leblon cachaça. But for the traditional Brazilian blended drinks, called batidas, that we offer on the following pages, we opted for an aged cachaça of a more traditional Brazilian style—Velho Barreiro. If you can't find it, substitute Leblon or experiment with whatever brand or brands your local grog shop purveys.

CACHAÇA

CAIPIRINHA

There's no better combo for quenching a tropical thirst.

1 lime, quartered
1 tablespoon simple syrup
2 ounces Leblon cachaça
club soda or seltzer (optional)

Place the lime quarters in the bottom cup of a Boston shaker, add the simple syrup, and muddle, thoroughly crushing the lime pieces. Add the cachaça to the shaker cup. Fill a double old-fashioned glass with ice cubes, then add these to the shaker, as well. Shake vigorously, and transfer contents to the glass. If you wish, top with soda (or seltzer).

CORN BATIDA

This traditional Brazilian batida, one of the more unusual drinks in *Drinkology's* repertoire, is definitely for the mixo-logically adventurous. (The recipe produces two drinks, so bring a friend along on this adventure.)

¾ cup Velho Barreiro or other cachaça
1 cup sweet corn kernels, drained (about half of an
    11-ounce can)
1 tablespoon evaporated milk
2 teaspoons simple syrup

Pack two old-fashioned glasses with crushed ice. Combine ingredients in a blender and blend until smooth. Strain into the prepared glasses.

PEANUT BUTTER BATIDA

 Brazilians use all manner of unusual (to us) ingredients in the blended drinks they call batidas (*batida* means "blended" in Portuguese). Here's *Drinkology's* milkshake-like take on a peanut-flavored batida.

ice cubes
½ cup evaporated milk
¼ cup freshly ground peanut butter
¼ cup vanilla ice cream
2 ounces Velho Barreiro or other cachaça
2 teaspoons simple syrup
♦ chocolate-flavored maraschino cherry

Fill a highball glass with ice cubes, then transfer the cubes to the carafe of a blender. (Make sure the blender you use is capable of crushing ice.) Add the other ingredients to the carafe, and blend until smooth. Pour the blended drink into the glass and garnish with the cherry. Serve with a straw.

CACHAÇA

STRAWBERRY BATIDA

With its light, almost fluffy, texture, this batida is like a strawberry smoothie—with a pleasantly peppery bite.

ice cubes

2 ounces Velho Barreiro or other cachaça

4 fresh strawberries, hulled

2 ounces evaporated milk

1 teaspoon simple syrup

♦ 1 additional strawberry, not hulled

Fill a highball glass with ice cubes, then transfer the cubes to the carafe of a blender. (Make sure the blender you use is capable of crushing ice.) Add the other ingredients to the carafe, and blend until smooth. Pour the blended drink into the glass and garnish with the unhulled strawberry. Serve with a straw.

Sake

YOU'VE NO DOUBT HEARD SAKE DESCRIBED AS "RICE WINE," OR possibly as "rice beer." Well, it's a little of both and a lot of neither. Good sake shares something of good wine's subtlety—and sake's devotees resemble committed oenophiles in their passion and discrimination. But sake is *not* wine for the obvious reason that it isn't made from grapes (or from any fruit). Like beer, it's a beverage made from fermented grain, but the method of its brewing differs from that of beer, it's not carbonated, it's colorless—and, needless to say, its taste is *entirely* dissimilar. So why bother trying to fit it into one category or the other? Sake is . . . sake.

Sake was first made in China in prehistoric times, but sake-making was introduced into Japan sometime around the third century AD, and the beverage would forever after be identified with its adoptive home-land. That identification runs so deep that the word *sake,* in Japanese, means "alcoholic beverage." Sure, Japan makes (great) beer and (very good) whiskey, but neither of these beverages, introduced after Japan's "opening" to the West in the nineteenth century, has anything like sake's resonance in Japanese history and culture.

The rice used in sake-making isn't ordinary table rice; it's rice that's been specially bred so that the starches are concentrated in the center of the grain. The first step in making sake involves milling, or "polishing," the rice—removing the grains' outer layers so that only this starchy center (the *fermentable* part) remains. We can't cover all the intricacies of sake-making here, but one interesting step bears mention: after the polished rice for a batch of sake has been steamed, but before fermentation, a portion of the rice is treated with a mold called *koji-kin* (scientific name: *Aspergillus oryzae*). That sounds yucky, but the rationale is the same as that for malting barley before brewing beer. Just as in malting—in which the barley is allowed to begin sprouting—the *koji* process produces enzymes that break down starch molecules into simple sugars, which the yeast used in fermentation find much more easily digestible. (Lesson: Everything about alcohol finally comes down to yeast and what those little demons prefer to eat.)

The complexities of sake—the several different classifications, the variations in style among different makers—rival those of wine. If anything, they're more intimidating—at least to non-Japanese-speakers—since gaining even the most basic knowledge about sake requires you to memorize a number of Japanese terms, and selecting a bottle of imported sake requires that you be able to read the Japanese labels. Yikes.

Fortunately for those interested in using sake in cocktails, these complexities are somewhat irrelevant. Sake is such a good basis for certain cocktails in part because its flavor is so unobtrusive, which also means that mixing sake with other ingredients tends to obscure subtle differences between types and brands. What you *do* need to know—and this is extremely important—is that sake, like almost all beer, is best drunk soon after bottling. When buying sake, you'll be wise to patronize a store that carries and sells a lot of sake, because it's likelier that the sake will be reasonably fresh and that the staff will be knowledgeable enough to assist you in making your selection. (Note, too, that better liquor stores refrigerate their sake.)

For American cocktail drinkers, it's also fortunate that there is an American sake brewery (or "sakery") whose products are exceptional: the SakéOne company of Forest Grove, Oregon. Its sake bottles' labels are (of course) in English, and each label provides the sake's bottling date (letting you instantly determine freshness). What's more, the company has built a good distribution network, so its sakes are fairly widely available. Each of the recipes here was created using a SakéOne product: either its Momokawa Silver *junmai ginjo* sake (a dry, clear sake) or its Momokawa Pearl, a *nigori*-style sake (a cloudy, "roughly" filtered sake whose appearance and flavor are creamier than those of fully filtered sakes). (Note: For the sake-tinctured Martini known as the Sake-tini, see page 146.)

SAKE

ASIAN PEAR

This combination produces a cocktail that tastes astonishingly like a tree-ripened fresh pear. Round, brown Asian pears are available in most supermarkets nowadays.

2 ounces *junmai ginjo* sake
1 ounce Pear William pear brandy
1 ounce pear nectar
♣ 2 or 3 thin, crescent-shaped slices of Asian pear

Combine ingredients in a cocktail shaker, with ice. Shake well, and strain into a chilled cocktail glass. Float the pear slices on the drink.

CODE ORANGE

Use the cloudy, partly unfiltered sake known as *nigori* for this orangiest of drinks.

3 ounces *nigori* sake
1 ounce Grand Marnier
2 ounces freshly squeezed orange juice
2 dashes orange bitters
♣ orange slice

Fill a double old-fashioned glass with ice cubes. Combine ingredients in cocktail shaker, with ice. Shake well, and strain into the glass. Garnish with the orange slice.

PLUM BLOSSOM

The nectarlike sweetness of Japanese *ume* plum wine is a wonderful foil to the sake's astringency and the orange juice's acidity in this perfectly balanced brunch drink.

2 ounces *junmai ginjo* sake
2 ounces *ume* plum wine
3 ounces fresh-squeezed orange juice
🍊 orange slice

Fill a highball glass with ice cubes. Combine ingredients in a standard shaker (not a Boston shaker), with ice. Shake well and strain into the glass. Garnish with the orange slice.

TOMI COLLINS

The drink's name—too obviously a play on "Tom Collins"—comes from the Japanese male moniker *Tomi*, which literally means "red." That makes the name doubly appropriate for this pink-hued summer cooler.

3 ounces *junmai ginjo* sake
3 teaspoons frozen pink lemonade concentrate (*not* diluted)
splash of Rose's Lime Cocktail
🍋 ¼ lime

Fill a collins glass with ice cubes. Combine ingredients in a standard shaker (not a Boston shaker), with ice. Shake well, and strain into the glass. Squeeze the quarter-lime into the drink and drop it in.

Tequila

L ET'S GET THE WHOLE WORM THING STRAIGHT RIGHT NOW, *muchachos.* If there's a worm at the bottom of your tequila bottle, you've either purchased gag-inducing hooch aimed at gullible gringos, or your top-shelf booze is infested by some kind of alcohol-breathing, alien bug.

There *is* sometimes a worm—or, more correctly, a pickled caterpillar—inside bottles of mezcal, a liquor made from a plant related to the blue agave, from which tequila is distilled. There is no mescaline in mezcal (the words are unrelated), and although eating this worm, or *gusano,* may freak out your friends and provide you with a portion of your minimum daily protein requirement, it won't, despite irrepressible legends to the contrary, bring you any closer to seeing God or make you sexually irresistible. If you have visions after swallowing this larva, it's because it's been soaking in very strong alcohol for years. If suddenly everyone at the party wants to bed you—well, remember they're probably drinking heavily, too.

There *is* mescaline in peyote, which comes from a cactus that often grows alongside blue agave, but agave is not a cactus, and Mexicans do not make alcohol from cacti of any kind. Agave is related to the lily and amaryllis and looks like a basketball-player-size aloe plant with a 200-pound pineapple at its core. There are more than 130 species of agave, which is also known as maguey, but just one may be used to make tequila, and it grows only in the Mexican state of Jalisco.

The Aztecs and their descendants have been making alcoholic drinks from different agave plants for thousands of years, but it was the Spanish who introduced them to distilling. Still, concocting tequila is so difficult and complicated it's a wonder that anyone ever bothered to figure out how to do it. The heart of the plant, or *piña* (named after the pineapple, which it resembles), must first be harvested. This in itself is no small feat. The *piña* usually weighs more than the *jimador* (he's the poor guy picking it), and it is surrounded by hundreds of seven-foot-long, thorn-covered spikes—so it's kind of like trying to wrangle a giant, sugary porcupine. Once corralled, the *piña* is steamed, baked, roasted, shredded, juiced, cooked, ground, crushed, and otherwise clobbered. These giant nuggets are so tough and fibrous that distilleries often sell their discarded pulp to construction companies, which use it to make bricks.

Each distillery has its own method for humbling its *piñas* into submission, and the variation in technique and timing accounts, in part, for the difference in taste among tequilas. The juice strained from the resulting mash is known, poetically, as *aguamiel,* or honeywater; after it's extracted, it's mixed with pure H_2O, fermented, and twice distilled.

Blanco (white) tequila (also called *plata*, or silver) is filtered and then bottled immediately or after very brief ageing in a neutral container. Bottles marked *joven* (young) or *oro* (gold) are white tequila mixed with a little bit of aged tequila or colored with caramel or other additives. *Reposado* (rested) tequila is ripened in oak barrels for between two months and a year; *añejo* (aged) tequila must be oak-mellowed for at least one year. And as of 2006, there's a new classification: *extra añejo* (extra aged), which is kept in oak for a minimum of three years.

The Mexican town of Tequila, founded in the sixteenth century by a Spanish conquistador, is where it all began, and almost all its residents are still involved in the tequila industry—from agave cultivation to tequila sales and marketing. The origin of the word *tequila*, however, is open to debate. In the language of the indigenous Nahuatl, the word means (depending on who you ask) "the place of harvesting plants," "the place of wild herbs," "the place of tricks," or even "the rock that cuts," supposedly for the jagged obsidian in the hills surrounding the town. But trust *Drinkology*. Once you've begun drinking tequila, you won't care about the etymology of its name.

BLUE AGAVE

Both tequila and agave syrup (an increasingly popular lower-carb sweetener) are made from blue agave. *Drinkology* thought it might be interesting to combine them—and to make the cocktail itself blue by adding blue curaçao.

3 ounces white tequila
1 ounce blue curaçao
1 ounce agave syrup
1 ounce fresh lime juice
♭ lemon slice

Combine ingredients in a cocktail shaker, with ice. Shake well, and strain into a chilled margarita or cocktail glass. Garnish with the lemon slice.

Blue Margarita (Shaken)

This azure-colored variation on the classic Margarita (page 239) has become immensely popular for the simple though unaccountable reason that people—or *some* people—really like drinking bright-blue libations.

lime wedge
kosher salt
3 ounces white tequila
1 ounce blue curaçao
1 ounce Cointreau or triple sec
1 ounce fresh lime juice

Rim a chilled margarita glass with the lime wedge and salt. (Discard the wedge.) Combine the tequila, curaçao, Cointreau, and lime juice in a standard cocktail shaker, with ice. Shake well, and strain into the prepared glass.

Brave Bull

Drinkology loves Black Russians, but actually prefers this tequila variation. It's incredible how very well tequila and coffee liqueur complement one another.

1½ ounces white tequila
1 ounce coffee liqueur

Pour the tequila and coffee liqueur into an ice-filled old-fashioned glass. Stir briefly.

CHAPALA

Named for a large lake in Jalisco State—where the agave used in tequila is grown—this coral-colored cocktail is fruity but has a pleasant tequila bite.

1½ ounces white tequila
½ teaspoon Cointreau or triple sec
½ ounce fresh lemon juice
½ ounce orange juice
2 teaspoons grenadine
♂ orange slice

Combine liquid ingredients in a cocktail shaker, with ice. Shake, and strain into a double old-fashioned glass filled with ice cubes. Garnish with the orange slice.

EL DIABLO

The devil hath the power to assume a pleasing appearance and taste, as this unusually colored lowball demonstrates.

½ lime
1½ ounces tequila
¼ ounce crème de cassis
ginger ale

Squeeze the half-lime into an empty old-fashioned glass, drop in the hull, and fill the glass with ice cubes. Pour in the tequila and crème de cassis. Top with ginger ale, and stir briefly.

FREDDY FUDPUCKER

This is the tequila version of the Harvey Wallbanger (page 265); Fred's flavor—dominated by the orange juice and, of course, the Galliano—is virtually indistinguishable from Harv's.

2 ounces white tequila
about 5 ounces orange juice
½ ounce Galliano

Pour the tequila and orange juice into a highball glass filled with ice. Stir, then float the Galliano on top.

FRIDA COOL-O

This foamy and refreshing cooler is a *Drinkology* original. We named it in honor of that most celebrated of Mexican painters, Frida Kahlo.

1½ ounces white tequila
1 ounce Cointreau or triple sec
1 ounce fresh lime juice
1 ounce pineapple juice
1 egg white

Combine ingredients in a cocktail shaker, with ice. Shake very well, and strain into a highball glass filled with ice cubes.

HOT PANTS

The salt and peppermint make for an interesting combination of flavors in this powerful lowball.

lemon wedge
kosher salt
1½ ounces tequila
½ ounce peppermint schnapps
½ ounce grapefruit juice
1 teaspoon powdered sugar

Rim an old-fashioned glass with the lemon wedge and salt. (Discard the wedge.) Fill the glass with ice cubes. Combine the tequila, schnapps, grapefruit juice, and sugar in a cocktail shaker, with ice. Shake well, and strain into the prepared glass.

MARGARITA (CLASSIC)

There's definitely a woman to blame for the name of this cocktail. Trouble is, it's hard to say just who she was. Differing claims about the Margarita's namesake abound. She was either (a) a Mexican bartender's girlfriend, name of Margarita; (b) an American showgirl named Marjorie King (Marjorie ≈ *Span.* Margarita); (c) 1940s actress/pinup Rita Hayworth (real name = Margarita Cansino); (d) a Texas socialite called Margarita Sames; or (e) somebody else.

What's more certain is that the cocktail first appeared—in hotspots in Mexico and then in southern California nightclubs—in the 1930s and 1940s. It's been going strong ever since (Margarita tabs fortify the cash flow of many a Mexican restaurant), though, for the past couple of decades, the Frozen Margarita (page 339) has far outdistanced the original version in popularity.

Ever nostalgic, *Drinkology* prefers a good old shaken Margarita. We also insist that the glass be rimmed with salt beforehand: it's essential to a Margarita's identity. (You may, of course, ignore our demand.) *Drinkology*'s chum Betsy Keller—the wonderworker behind several of this book's recipes—isn't nearly so purist; she dispenses with the salt, uses gold tequila rather than white, and adds a bit of orange juice to the mix. Her recipe follows the classic version given below.

lime wedge
kosher salt
3 ounces white tequila
2 ounces Cointreau or triple sec
1 ounce fresh lime juice
⚘ thinly cut lime slice

Rim a chilled margarita glass with the lime wedge and salt. (Discard the wedge.) Combine the tequila, Cointreau, and lime juice in a standard cocktail shaker, with ice. Shake well, and strain into the prepared glass. Garnish with the lime slice, allowing it to float on top of the drink.

MARGARITA (GOLD VARIATION)

Mixological *maîtresse* Betsy Keller contributed this recipe to *Drinkology*'s repertoire.

2½ ounces gold tequila
1½ ounces Cointreau or triple sec
1 ounce fresh lime juice
1 ounce orange juice
⚘ thinly cut lime slice

Combine the tequila, Cointreau, and juices in a standard cocktail shaker, with ice. Shake well, and strain into a chilled margarita glass. Garnish with the lime slice, allowing it to float on top of the drink.

MATADOR

Among traditional tequila-based drinks, the Matador is one of the tartest.

1½ ounces gold tequila
3 ounces pineapple juice
½ ounce fresh lime juice

Combine ingredients in a cocktail shaker, with ice. Shake well, and strain into an ice-filled old-fashioned glass.

MEXICANA

This peachy-colored lowball is exquisitely tangy.

1½ ounces white tequila
1½ ounces pineapple juice
1 ounce fresh lemon juice
1 teaspoon grenadine

Combine ingredients in a cocktail shaker, with ice. Shake well, and strain into a double old-fashioned glass filled with ice cubes.

PIPE CLEANER

Aloe vera juice has a system-cleansing reputation. Hence the name of this refreshing cooler, which, curiously, tastes something like grape Kool-Aid. (The idea for the drink comes from *Drinkology* friend Alyson Nehren.)

1½ ounces tequila
6 ounces aloe vera juice drink
¾ ounce fresh lime juice
¾ ounce simple syrup
½ egg white (optional)
♪ lime slice

Fill a highball glass with ice cubes. Combine ingredients in a standard shaker (not a Boston shaker), shake well, and strain into the glass. Garnish with the lime slice.

SALTY CHIHUAHUA

Needless to say, this is the "Mexican" version of the Salty Dog (pages 146 and 275); the taste is a bit sharper than that of the gin- and vodka-based breeds.

lemon wedge
salt
2 ounces white tequila
5 or 6 ounces grapefruit juice

Rim a highball glass with the lemon wedge and salt. (Discard the wedge.) Fill the glass with ice cubes, and pour in the tequila and juice. Stir briefly.

TEQUILA FIZZ

Tequila's subtle bite gives the classic fizz a very pleasant edge. *Drinkology*'s taste-testers were shocked— shocked!—to discover they prefer it to their beloved Gin Fizz (page 123).

2 ounces white tequila
1 ounce fresh lime juice
1 heaping teaspoon powdered sugar
club soda or seltzer

Combine the first three ingredients in a cocktail shaker, with ice. Shake well, and strain into a highball glass filled with ice cubes. Top with soda (or seltzer), and stir briefly.

TEQUILA GHOST

This lowball's milky green color is ethereal, but the taste is definite and sharp. If you hate Pernod, give up this ghost; if you like it, get into the spirit.

2 ounces white tequila
1 ounce Pernod or other absinthe substitute
½ ounce fresh lemon juice

Combine ingredients in a cocktail shaker, with ice. Shake well, and strain into an ice-filled old-fashioned glass.

TEQUILA MOCKINGBIRD

Drinkology would love to make the acquaintance of the master punster who gave this unusual drink its name.

2 ounces white tequila
1 ounce white crème de menthe
½ ounce fresh lime juice
✂ thinly cut lime slice

Combine liquid ingredients in a cocktail shaker, with ice. Shake well, and strain into a chilled cocktail glass. Garnish with the lime slice, allowing it to float on top of the drink.

TEQUILA SHOOTER

In the younger day, *Drinkology* squandered many an evening "doing" tequila shooters. Ah, the memories! (Or, wait, where *are* those memories?)

salt
shot glass of tequila (white or gold)
lime wedge

Prepare for this shooter by pouring the shot of tequila and making sure the salt and lime wedge are within easy reach. Lick the back of your hand in the area just below the index finger. Sprinkle salt on the saliva-moistened area. Then lick off the salt, quickly down the shot, and bite into the lime wedge. It is traditional to grimace throughout this process and to emit a yelp of victory immediately after.

TEQUILA SUNRISE

Drinkology thinks this is just another drink. It's pretty, sure, but there are better things to do with your tequila (and your life).

1½ ounces white tequila
orange juice
½ ounce grenadine

Fill a highball glass with ice cubes, and pour in the tequila. Then fill the glass almost to the top with orange juice, then drop in the grenadine (it will spread through the drink like dawn's rosy fingers). Do not stir.

TOREADOR

This curious drink is really quite delicious. The Indians of pre-Conquest Mexico invented both tequila and chocolate, so maybe it shouldn't be surprising that these tastes go together so well.

1½ ounces white tequila
½ ounce white crème de cacao
1 tablespoon heavy cream
whipped cream
unsweetened cocoa powder

Combine tequila, crème de cacao, and cream in a cocktail shaker, with ice. Shake well, and strain into a chilled cocktail glass. Float a dollop of whipped cream on top, and lightly dust the entire surface of the drink with cocoa powder.

Vodka

AMERICANS DITHER ABOUT STICKS AND STONES. IN RUSSIA, they say, "Call me what you like, only give me some vodka." While Poles, Ukrainians, Russians, Byelorussians, Balts, and Scandinavians will all argue that *their* ancestors invented vodka, it was probably introduced to all of them by Genoese merchants, who learned about distilling from early Italian explorers visiting the East. Vodka was, however, perfected by northern and eastern Europeans, who made the drink their own.

Vodka was first introduced stateside by the Smirnoff family, who had been the exclusive vodka supplier to the czars but fled Russia after the Bolshevik revolution. We Americans resisted its charms, however, until World War II was well under way. A Los Angeles bartender who'd ordered too much ginger beer tried to get rid of it by mixing it with gin and with whiskey, but never received requests for another round. When this alchemist added it to vodka and squeezed in a little lime, however, he struck gold: the Moscow Mule was born, and with it Americans' enduring love affair with this most durable liquor. Even as the Cold War iced relations with vodka's mother country, the great thaw in America's relationship with its enemy's number-one pastime was on. It is now the most popular liquor in the States, accounting for over 20 percent of all distilled spirits consumed.

That impressive figure pales, however, in comparison to the gusto with which Russians guzzle the stuff. If you've heard the old saw that they drink vodka like water, . . . well, believe it. The word itself is a diminutive form of *voda,* Russian for "water," and by the mid-1990s, annual Russian vodka consumption was equivalent to more than 30 liters for every man, woman, and child.

The Russians' relationship with vodka has not been entirely one-sided, however, as evidenced by another age-old Russian proverb: "Vodka spoils everything but the glasses." Although Ivan the Terrible invented the officer's club in the sixteenth century, building *kabaks,* or taverns, exclusively for his palace guard, subsequent czars were ambivalent, and ordered them closed and reopened according to their own morals and whims. But the genie was already out of the bottle, so to speak, and one economically minded czar nationalized vodka production, monopolized its sale, and levied heavy taxes on it, using the proceeds to finance conquest and repression. This proved to be as habit-forming as the alcoholism that decimates characters in the novels and plays of Dostoyevsky and Chekhov.

A need for sober troops during World War I saw the introduction of prohibition, which was supported wholeheartedly by Lenin, a notorious teetotaler. But despite the father of Soviet communism's belief that "the proletariat has no need of intoxication, because it derives its strongest stimulant from the communist ideal," the production and sale of "rotgut" was soon a revenue stream for Russia's socialist leaders, too. (In the mid-twentieth century, it was the sales tax on vodka that put

Cosmonauts in orbit.) Then, in the 1980s, political reformer Mikhail Gorbachev—much more popular in the West than in his homeland—curtailed vodka production and gamely tried to control his people's propensity to abuse the stuff. Gorby's *perestroika* worked, but—guess what?—his prohibitionist efforts failed miserably.

COLORLESS, ODORLESS, TASTELESS (WELL, ALMOST)

If liquor were religion, vodka would be Zen Buddhism. It is valued for its lack of exactly those things prized in other spirits: aroma, color, and palate. Vodka is allowed to distill until its alcohol content is quite high, then filtered through charcoal to remove any remaining impurities. Because it is distilled and redistilled until nearly every trace of its source has dissipated, vodka's base materials are more or less irrelevant to its flavor, and vodka is generally classified only by its country of origin. While Poles sometimes make it from potatoes, it is more often distilled from rye, wheat, barley malt, sugar beets, or (especially) corn. Though some Polish and Russian vodka is aged in oak, most vodka-drinkers' preference is for double- or triple-distilled vodka straight from the tap.

Vodka's most pronounced characteristic is not taste, but its ineffably smooth, buttery mouth-feel—a sensation that's enhanced when the liquor is chilled. Drunk neat, vodka should be ice cold: keep it in your freezer and leave it there until you are ready to serve it. And if you *are* drinking it straight, never pour it over ice—the cubes may impart unwanted flavor to this most minimalist of spirits.

Its spiritual agnosticism makes vodka the perfect mixer. The drink of the czars combines equally well with vegetable juice, fruit juice, tonic water, soda water, and, of course, other liquors. Flavored vodka, too, is quite popular. Russians are fond of peach and cherry; the Scandinavians of *akvavit*, a vodka that's been flavored and redistilled with caraway and dill. Americans are becoming partial to lemon-, vanilla-, pepper-, and orange-flavored vodkas. (For *Drinkology's* tips on making your own tea-infused vodka, see page 262.)

For the twentysomething set, vodka—flavored or not—has replaced gin as the base of most Martinis, which are now being mixed in combinations and colors that would make James Bond cringe.

But 007 be damned. Drink it any way you please. And to insure any toast made with vodka, do what the Russians do: smash your tumblers in the fireplace afterward. Just don't use the good crystal. It seems that vodka spoils the glasses after all.

AGENT ORANGE

When choosing your poison, you might try this strongly orange-flavored concoction.

  ♂ orange peel
    1½ ounces vodka
  ¾ ounce Grand Marnier
  ¼ ounce Cointreau or triple sec
  ½ ounce orange juice

Rim a chilled cocktail glass with the orange peel. Combine other ingredients in a cocktail shaker, with ice. Shake well, and strain into the glass. Garnish with the orange peel.

APPLE MARTINI

My, how the Martini has changed. *Drinkology* is slightly disapproving, but bows to fashion.

1½ ounces vodka
¾ ounce green apple schnapps
¾ ounce apple juice
♺ several thin slices of Granny Smith apple

Combine liquid ingredients in a cocktail shaker, with ice. Shake well, and strain into a chilled cocktail glass. Garnish with the apple slices.

BLACK RUSSIAN

Most bartenders use Kahlúa in their Black Russians, though another coffee liqueur, Tia Maria, also performs admirably.

2 ounces vodka
1 ounce coffee liqueur

Pour the vodka and liqueur into an old-fashioned glass filled with ice. Stir.

VODKA

BLOODY BULL

This variation on the Bloody Mary is just the thing for a pre-run brunch in Pamplona.

2 ounces vodka
2 ounces beef broth or bouillon
2 ounces tomato juice
¼ ounce fresh lemon juice
¼ teaspoon fresh, grated horseradish
2 or 3 dashes Worcestershire sauce
1 or 2 dashes Tabasco sauce
salt, if needed
⚘ lemon wedge

Rim a highball glass with the lemon wedge, and fill the glass with ice cubes. Combine the other ingredients (except salt) in a cocktail shaker, with ice. Shake well, and strain into the glass. Squeeze the lemon wedge into the drink, and drop it in. Taste before salting (the beef broth may be salty enough).

Ever spent a Sunday afternoon in a fog because you've imbibed a few too many of these at brunch? *Drinkology* has, too. But let's not give ourselves too much grief. The personage after whom this classic concoction was purportedly named did things that were much worse. The fanatical Mary Tudor—the daughter of Henry VIII and his first wife, Catherine of Aragon—captured the English throne in 1553; for the next five years, Queen Mary I proceeded mercilessly to persecute those who'd adopted her father's Protestant faith. By the time she died in 1558, her spate of Oedipally-themed vengeance had earned her the moniker Bloody Mary. Such horror stories could drive one to drink.

The historical origin of the beloved mixed drink is an altogether gentler tale. It was apparently first concocted in the late 1920s or early '30s by one Fernand (a.k.a. "Pete") Petoit, a bartender at Harry's New York Bar, in Paris. (An alternate account of the drink's naming credits it to a regular at Harry's, who reportedly told Pete that the tomato-red brew reminded him of a gal called Mary whom he'd met at a Chicago watering hole called the Bucket of Blood Club. *Drinkology* is dubious. Plus, that story's sort of boring.)

Anyhow, in 1934 Pete crossed the Atlantic and started a gig at the King Cole Bar in Manhattan's St. Regis Hotel, where he introduced American drinkers to his creation. Legend has it that the New Yorkers Pete served found his original recipe—just vodka and tomato juice—too bland,

and urged him to fire it up a bit. Knowing New Yorkers as we do, *Drinkology* finds this plausible.

2 ounces vodka
4 ounces tomato juice
½ ounce fresh lemon juice
¼ teaspoon fresh, grated horseradish
¼ teaspoon Tabasco sauce
2 or 3 dashes Worcestershire sauce
salt
♌ lemon wedge
♌ celery stalk

Rim a highball glass with the lemon wedge, and fill the glass with ice cubes. Combine the vodka, tomato juice, lemon juice, horseradish, Tabasco, and Worcestershire in a standard cocktail shaker, with ice. Shake well, and strain into the glass. Squeeze the lemon wedge into the drink, and drop it in. Salt to taste, stir briefly, and garnish with the celery stalk.

BRASS MONKEY

This excellent highball is a glorified—nay, a beatific—Screwdriver. The Galliano gives it a rich, almost buttery taste.

1 ounce vodka
¾ ounce light rum
about 4 ounces orange juice
¼ ounce Galliano

Pour the vodka, rum, and orange juice into an ice-filled collins or highball glass. Stir briefly. Float the Galliano on top.

BULLFROG

One of the lightest of summertime coolers, the Bullfrog tastes like lemon-flavored seltzer.

⚘ lemon wedge
2 ounces vodka
1 ounce Cointreau or triple sec
½ ounce fresh lemon juice
club soda or seltzer

Rim a highball glass with the lemon wedge, and fill it with ice cubes. Pour in the vodka and Cointreau, and top with soda. Squeeze the lemon wedge into the drink, and drop it in. Stir briefly.

Bullshot

 Widely regarded as a hangover cure, the Bullshot is an uncompromisingly meaty eye-opener.

♦ lemon wedge
2 ounces vodka
4 ounces beef broth or bouillon
¼ ounce fresh lemon juice
2 or 3 dashes Worcestershire sauce
1 or 2 dashes Tabasco sauce
salt, if needed

Rim a highball glass with the lemon wedge, and fill it with ice cubes. Combine the vodka, beef broth, lemon juice, Worcestershire, and Tabasco in a standard cocktail shaker, with ice. Shake well, and strain into the glass. Squeeze the lemon wedge into the drink, and drop it in. Taste before salting (the beef broth may be salty enough).

Cape Codder

 If you like a sea breeze and salty air (and cranberry juice), you're gonna fall in love with the ol' Cape Codder.

♦ lime wedge
2 ounces vodka
about 5 ounces cranberry juice

Rim a highball glass with the lime wedge, and fill it with ice cubes. Pour in the vodka and cranberry juice, and stir briefly. Squeeze the lime wedge into the drink, and drop it in.

CHOCOLATE MARTINI ("CHOCOTINI")

Drinkology turns up its snooty nose at most newfangled "Martinis." But our taste-testers *love* this drink. The unusual rimming technique makes for a very pretty effect.

white crème de cacao and unsweetened cocoa powder, for
    rimming the glass
2 ounces vodka
1 ounce white crème de cacao
♦ Hershey's Kiss or chocolate chips

Rim a chilled cocktail glass with the crème de cacao and cocoa powder. (To do this, pour a small amount of crème de cacao onto a saucer or small plate, swishing it around until it covers the plate's surface. Spoon some cocoa powder onto a separate plate, and spread it around as evenly as you can. Now, upend the cocktail glass onto the crème de cacao–covered plate, immediately transferring it to the cocoa-covered plate. Twist the glass until the entire rim is coated.) Combine the vodka and crème de cacao in a mixing glass, with ice. Stir, and strain into the prepared cocktail glass. Garnish with the Hershey's Kiss or a few chocolate chips.

VODKA

CLAMDIGGER

Sometimes called a Bloody Caesar (who knows why?), this is a chowderheaded variation on the Bloody Mary.

◊ lemon wedge
2 ounces vodka
4 ounces Clamato juice (or 2 ounces tomato juice and 2 ounces clam juice)
¼ ounce fresh lemon juice
2 or 3 dashes Worcestershire sauce
1 or 2 dashes Tabasco sauce
salt

Rim a highball glass with the lemon wedge, and fill the glass with ice cubes. Combine the other ingredients (except salt) in a standard cocktail shaker, with ice. Shake well, and strain into the glass. Squeeze the lemon wedge into the drink, and drop it in. Salt to taste.

VODKA

CONFIDENTIAL COCKTAIL

There are so many delicious tea-based soft drinks on the market these days that *Drinkology* just *had* to find a way to use one in a mixed drink. This delicately pink libation employs one of the pomegranate-flavored teas made by Pom Wonderful.

1½ ounces vodka
½ ounce crème de mûre (blackberry liqueur)
2 ounces Pom Wonderful pomegranate-blackberry tea
½ teaspoon grenadine
½ teaspoon fresh lime juice
2 or 3 fresh raspberries, for garnish

Combine liquid ingredients in a cocktail shaker, with ice. Shake and strain into a chilled cocktail glass. Garnish with the raspberries. Options: *In the fall, try garnishing with a few pomegranate seeds instead of raspberries. If neither raspberries nor pomegranates are in season, garnish with a thin slice of lime.*

COSMOPOLITAN

The Cosmopolitan is the youngest of the "classic" drinks. Invented in the late 1980s, this pretty-in-pink cocktail *really* took off in the 1990s. There was a moment (well, more like a couple of years) when it seemed that "Cosmos" were all that anyone—movie star, dot-com mogul, administrative assistant—was drinking. It's easy to pooh-pooh such trends, but in this case, the immense popularity was merited. If made well, the Cosmopolitan is a superbly refreshing drink. (If made less than well, it can be disappointing: too much vodka renders it oily and unpleasant; too little Cointreau or too much lime juice will give the drink a sour edge it shouldn't have.) The original recipe apparently called for lemon-flavored rather than plain vodka, and that's *Drinkology's* recommendation, as well. Note that Rose's lime juice can be substituted for fresh lime juice, but the resulting drink will be sweeter.

♦ lemon twist
2 ounces lemon-flavored vodka
¾ ounce Cointreau or triple sec
1½ ounce cranberry juice
2 teaspoons fresh lime juice

Rim a chilled cocktail glass with the lemon twist. Combine the other ingredients in a cocktail shaker, with ice. Shake well, and strain into the glass. Garnish with the lemon twist.

INFUSING VODKA

Drinkology has no real argument with the do-it-yourself ethic, but there's a problem. *Drinkology* is *lazy*. Theoretically, we'd like to make all kinds of infused vodkas—hot pepper vodkas, coffee-flavored vodkas, you name it—but when it comes right down to it, we just cannot muster the effort. Our exacting publisher, however, suggested we include a vodka-infusing recipe in the book's new edition, so we were, of course, eager to comply.

But which sort of infused vodka should we do? Internet research revealed scores of possibilities. Each recipe, though, seemed more complicated than the last, and the writers of such recipes seemed always to be cautioning that, no matter how diligently you try, your vanilla bean– or herb-infused vodka might not turn out perfectly satisfactorily. For *Drinkology*, this is the kiss of death.

Then, one afternoon, we happened to have lunch at a Manhattan restaurant that pretends that it's a truck stop somewhere in, say, Alabama. It was early summer, and we were intrigued by the summery name of the restaurant's cocktail of the day: the Firefly. We inquired and were told that the drink combined sweet tea–infused vodka and lemonade. We ordered one; it was good, if a tad sugary. Later, at home, we discovered on our trusty friend the Internet that *Firefly* is the brand-name of one of the sweet tea–infused vodkas that have become very popular in the South—and that it takes its name from a traditional Southern summertime drink that mixes together (nonalcoholic) sweet tea and lemonade.

We had our idea. We would make an infused vodka using tea, which, after all, the Good Lord created for the *express purpose* of infusing. Then we'd combine it with homemade lemonade. (I guess we're not all that lazy.) We'd sweeten the lemonade, of course, but

INFUSING VODKA

not the tea-flavored vodka, so as to concoct a refreshing cooler some-what less cloying than the eponymous Firefly. And, not wanting to step on any trademarked toes, we'd call our beverage the Lightning Bug. And so we did. And it was as easy as we needed it to be.

INFUSING VODKA WITH TEA

When infusing vodka with tea or anything else, don't use a pricey premium vodka. The flavoring will overwhelm and erase whatever subtle distinctiveness the premium vodka lays claim to. (This same principle applies to any and all mixed drinks made with vodka except, perhaps, plain dry vodka Martinis.) Instead, use the tried-and-true, excellent but decidedly non-snooty Smirnoff.

The tea we chose was Earl Grey. We figured (rightly, as it turned out) that the small bits of bergamot peel in the Earl Grey blend would give us our infusion a slight citrus edge that would go well with the lemonade. And we used teabags rather than loose tea, wanting to avoid having to strain and filter the vodka once we'd infused it. Here are the recipes for the infused vodka, the lemonade, and the Lightning Bug:

EARL GREY–INFUSED VODKA

If you use teabags with strings and printed paper tags, cut off the tags before placing the teabags in the vodka. You don't want any ink leaching into the infusion.

> 1 750ml bottle Smirnoff
> 4 teabags of Earl Grey tea

Pour the vodka into a pitcher and add the teabags. Cover the mouth of the pitcher with plastic wrap. Wait for about an hour and a half—or just until the infusion develops the rich amber color of undiluted tea. Remove the teabags. To store, transfer the infused vodka to a stoppered bottle; it should remain fine and drinkable for a good long while. (As of this writing, the tea-infused vodka is still delicious many weeks after making.) Store the bottle in the freezer, if you're so inclined.

LEMONADE

It's much easier to use simple syrup (see the recipe on page 36) than granulated sugar when making lemonade, since you don't have to stir and stir to get the sugar to dissolve.

1 cup fresh lemon juice, strained
1½ cups simple syrup
1 quart water

Combine ingredients in a pitcher and stir. Covered and refrigerated, the lemonade should stay fresh for two to three days, but it's best if used immediately.

LIGHTNING BUG

This is a fantastic summer party drink, so you may want to make it by the pitcherful, using the same proportions (two parts lemonade to one part infused vodka) as in the individual-drink recipe below.

⅔ cup lemonade
⅓ cup Earl Grey–infused vodka
♌ lemon slice

Fill a highball glass with ice cubes. Add the lemonade and vodka, stir, and garnish with the lemon slice.

FUZZY NAVEL

Some Fuzzy Navel recipes dispense with the vodka (and call for two or three times as much schnapps), but that's a mistake. This version is much less cloying, yet—since peach schnapps tastes so strongly of peaches—it's still wonderfully fruity.

1 ounce vodka
1 ounce peach schnapps
4 or 5 ounces orange juice

Pour the vodka and schnapps into a highball glass filled with ice. Top with orange juice, and stir.

GREYHOUND

The Greyhound is a tarter, more astringent alternative to the Screwdriver.

2 ounces vodka
5 or 6 ounces grapefruit juice

Pour the vodka and grapefruit juice into a highball glass filled with ice cubes. Stir briefly.

HARVEY WALLBANGER

This variation on the Screwdriver dates from the 1970s. A Google search reveals various implausible theories about how the drink got its name; *Drinkology* has the feeling it was just made up by a copywriter at whatever ad agency was handling the Galliano account at the time.

2 ounces vodka
about 5 ounces orange juice
½ ounce Galliano

Pour the vodka and orange juice into a highball glass filled with ice. Stir, then float the Galliano on top.

ICEBERG

This lowball certainly looks the part. Make sure the vodka is as chilly as the North Atlantic in winter.

Pernod or other anise-flavored liqueur
2 ounces lemon-flavored vodka

Pour a small amount of Pernod into an empty old-fashioned glass. Tilt and slowly twirl the glass until the interior is entirely coated. Discard any excess. Fill the glass with ice cubes, and pour in the vodka.

KAMIKAZE

This is a classic shooter, meant to be drunk in one gulp. Decide for yourself whether to yell "Banzai!" just before downing it.

2 ounces vodka
1 teaspoon fresh lime juice

Combine ingredients in a mixing glass half-filled with ice. Stir well, and strain into an old-fashioned glass. Drink in one quick motion.

KAMIKAZE COCKTAIL

This more refined version of the Kamikaze is meant for sipping. Its pearly, icy color is very appealing; the clean taste has just the right mix of tart and sweet.

2 ounces vodka
½ ounce Cointreau or triple sec
¼ ounce fresh lime juice

Combine ingredients in a cocktail shaker, with ice. Shake well, and strain into a chilled cocktail glass.

KRETCHMA COCKTAIL

The Kretchma is a gorgeous, pale-pink cocktail whose taste—combining lemon and chocolate flavors—reminds *Drinkology* of a birthday cake.

♂ lemon twist
1 ounce vodka
1 ounce white crème de cacao
½ ounce fresh lemon juice
¼ teaspoon grenadine

Rim a chilled cocktail glass with the lemon twist. Combine the liquid ingredients in a cocktail shaker, with ice. Shake well, and strain into the glass. Garnish with the twist.

LEMON DROP

The Lemon Drop, whose flavor perfectly balances the tart and the sweet, is a *Drinkology* favorite.

lemon wedge
superfine sugar
1½ ounces lemon-flavored vodka
½ ounce Cointreau or triple sec
1 ounce fresh lemon juice
½ ounce simple syrup

Rim a chilled cocktail glass with the lemon wedge and sugar. (Discard the lemon wedge.) Combine the other ingredients in a cocktail shaker, with ice. Shake well, and strain into the prepared glass.

LONG ISLAND ICED TEA

The Long Island Iced Tea has a nasty reputation that's both deserved and undeserved. Because it really does look and taste like iced tea—which means it goes down awfully easy—it's become a byword for overindulgence. Many a frat-house hangover owes its origin to one (or two, or three) too many Long Island Iced Teas. But in this case one should blame the sinner, not the sin: the drink's a delicious work of mixological genius, and it certainly can be enjoyed in moderation. By the way, the Long Island Iced Tea really does hail from Long Island: its invention is credited to a Hampton Bays bartender named Robert Butt. *Drinkology*'s version is less potent than Butt's original, which reportedly called for one ounce each of the component liquors.

🍸 lemon wedge
½ ounce vodka
½ ounce gin
½ ounce light rum
½ ounce tequila
½ ounce Cointreau or triple sec
½ ounce fresh lemon juice
cola

Rim a collins glass with the lemon wedge, and fill it with ice cubes. Combine the vodka, gin, rum, tequila, Cointreau, and lemon juice in a cocktail shaker, with ice. Shake well, and strain into the glass. Top with the cola, and garnish with the lemon wedge.

LOVE POTION

Drinkology suffered a sudden infatuation with this berry-flavored, berry-colored cocktail.

1½ ounces lemon-flavored vodka
¾ ounce Chambord
¾ ounce cranberry juice

Combine ingredients in a cocktail shaker, with ice. Shake well, and strain into a chilled cocktail glass.

MADRAS

Drinkology is of the opinion that this drink should "bleed"—just like the brightly colored Indian fabric after which it's named. (But do stir it if you wish.)

2 ounces vodka
3 ounces orange juice
2 ounces cranberry juice

Pour the vodka and orange juice into a highball glass filled with ice cubes. Top with the cranberry juice, allowing the drink to mix gradually as it is sipped.

MARTINI (VODKA)

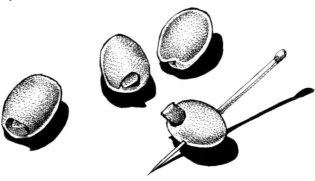

This is the upstart that's supplanted the traditional, gin-based Martini. The recipe given here is the classic four-to-one blend, though you're certainly welcome to make your vodka Martinis dry, extra dry, "dirty," or whatever. (For those proportions and ingredients, consult the Martini recipes in the Gin chapter, pages 134–138.) But, really, if you're in the habit of ordering bone-dry vodka Martinis, why not do yourself a favor and have an ice-cold vodka, neat, instead?

2 ounces vodka
½ ounce dry vermouth
☙ olive(s) or lemon twist

Combine liquid ingredients in a mixing glass, with lots of ice. Stir well, and strain into a chilled cocktail glass. Garnish with the olive(s) or twist. (If using a twist, rim the glass beforehand.)

MOSCOW MULE

As is mentioned in this chapter's introduction, the Moscow Mule was the first vodka-based drink to really make a splash in America. The recipe calls for ginger beer, but if that's too sharp and spicy for your taste, feel free to substitute ginger ale. (You sissy.)

2 ounces vodka
1 ounce fresh lime juice
about 4 ounces ginger beer (or ginger ale)
ᶁ lime wedge

Pour the vodka and lime juice into a highball glass filled with ice cubes. Top with ginger beer (or ginger ale), and stir briefly. Squeeze the lime wedge into the drink, and drop it in.

MUDSLIDE

This creamy lowball is mild-flavored but potent.

1 ounce vodka
1 ounce Bailey's Irish Cream
1 ounce coffee liqueur
1 ounce heavy cream

Combine ingredients in a cocktail shaker, with ice. Shake well, and strain into an ice-filled double old-fashioned glass.

ORANGE MARTINI

If a hard-drinking brunch guest sneers at your Screwdrivers or Mimosas, impress the boozehound with one of these. The orange zest–flecked rimming intensifies the cocktail's super-citrusy flavor.

orange wedge
grated orange zest
superfine sugar
3 ounces lemon- or orange-flavored vodka
¼ ounce Lillet Blanc
drop of orange flower water (optional)
⚶ orange peel

Pour some superfine sugar onto a saucer or small plate, spreading it around until it evenly covers the plate's surface. Grate some orange zest onto the sugar, distributing it as evenly as possible. Rim a chilled glass with the orange wedge and this sugar-and-zest mix. (Discard the wedge.) Combine the vodka and Lillet in a mixing glass, with ice. (If you're using lemon-flavored vodka, you may want to dribble in a drop of orange flower water.) Stir, and strain into the prepared glass. Garnish with a long, looping spiral of orange peel.

POMEGRANATE MARTINI

 The Pomegranate Martini was, for a time, the must-serve cocktail at weddings. During that time, we met "Pom-Martinis" at every nuptials we attended, and we mostly didn't like them. So we decided to create one we *do* like: as fresh 'n' pretty as a blushing bride. (Ahem.)

2 ounces lemon–flavored vodka
1 ounce Pom Wonderful pomegranate juice
½ ounce fresh lemon juice
¼ teaspoon grenadine
♗ lemon twist

Rim a chilled cocktail glass with the twist, and drop it in. Combine ingredients in a cocktail shaker, with ice. Shake well, and strain into the glass.

VODKA

PURPLE PENIS

This no-longer-novel novelty drink is more interesting than *Drinkology* would like to admit. The dark, opaque purple concoction—which tastes something like raspberry sorbet—fills a collins glass to the brim. Prepare it in a standard shaker, lest the contents prematurely ejaculate.

2 ounces vodka
1½ ounces blue curaçao
1½ ounces Chambord
2 ounces cranberry juice
1 ounce fresh lemon juice
1 ounce simple syrup

Combine ingredients in a standard cocktail shaker, with ice. Shake well, and strain into a chilled collins glass (no ice).

SALTY DOG (VODKA VERSION)

The "dog" is, of course, a Greyhound (page 264). This highball differs from that drink only in that the glass is rimmed with salt beforehand.

lemon wedge
salt
2 ounces vodka
5 or 6 ounces grapefruit juice

Rim a highball glass with the lemon wedge and salt. Discard the lemon wedge. Fill the glass with ice cubes, and pour in the vodka and juice. Stir briefly.

SCREWDRIVER

This classic Sunday brunch highball is simplicity itself—just vodka and orange juice. Use fresh-squeezed juice if at all possible.

2 ounces vodka
5 or 6 ounces orange juice
♦ orange slice

Pour the vodka and orange juice into a highball glass filled with ice cubes. Stir briefly, and garnish with the orange slice.

VODKA

SEA BREEZE

Vodka truly lends itself to mild, fruity highballs—the Greyhound, the Madras, the Screwdriver. Here's another classic concoction.

♻ lime wedge
2 ounces vodka
about 3 ounces grapefruit juice
about 2 ounces cranberry juice

Rim a highball glass with the lime wedge, and fill the glass with ice cubes. Pour in the vodka and juices, and stir briefly. Squeeze the lime wedge into the drink, and drop it in.

SEX ON THE BEACH

Opinion differs on whether this by-now classic highball is as good as the activity after which it's named. *Drinkology* finds the scrape of gritty, cold, wet sand on hot flesh decidedly unsexy, and prefers the drink.

1 ounce vodka
1 ounce peach schnapps
about 3 ounces grapefruit juice
about 2 ounces cranberry juice
♻ maraschino cherry

Pour the liquid ingredients into a highball glass filled with ice cubes. Stir briefly. Garnish with the cherry.

SHIRLEY TEMPLE OF DOOM

Fashion dictates that we include a couple of Red Bull cocktails in *Drinkology*'s new edition. This one tastes like a Shirley Temple. But the Good Ship Lollipop is flying the Jolly Roger.

2 maraschino cherries
1 orange slice
2 teaspoons simple syrup
2 ounces vodka
ginger ale
Red Bull

Place the cherries and orange slice in a double old-fashioned glass, add the simple syrup, and muddle well. Fill the glass with ice cubes (do not remove the fruit), and pour in the vodka. Top with equal parts ginger ale and Red Bull. Stir briefly.

SLOE COMFORTABLE SCREW

The cleverness of its name wears thin, and the drink itself is overpoweringly sweet, but *Drinkology* includes it because . . . well, because *somebody's* gonna look it up in the index.

1½ ounces vodka
½ ounce sloe gin
½ ounce Southern Comfort
orange juice

Fill a highball glass with ice cubes. Pour in the vodka, sloe gin, and Southern Comfort, and top with orange juice. Stir.

VODKA

Southern Cosmopolitan

Southerners like *Drinkology*'s friend Susan Sully are very cosmopolitan indeed. This peachy twist on the Cosmo was concocted by Susan and longtime *Drinkology* cohorts Eric Mueller and Ramona Ponce.

3 mint leaves
1½ ounces peach-flavored vodka
½ ounce Cointreau
1 ounce peach nectar
¼ ounce fresh lime juice
♺ sprig of mint

Rim a chilled cocktail glass with one of the mint leaves. (Discard the leaf.) Place the remaining two mint leaves in a cocktail shaker, fill with ice, and add the vodka, Cointreau, peach nectar, and lime juice. Shake vigorously and strain into the glass. Garnish with the mint sprig.

Velvet Hammer (Vodka Version)

Sometimes called the Russian Bear, the vodka-based version of the Velvet Hammer is very different from—and much milder-flavored than—the liqueurs-and-brandy version (page 184).

1½ ounces vodka
1 ounce crème de cacao
1 ounce heavy cream

Combine ingredients in a cocktail shaker, with ice. Shake well, and strain into a chilled cocktail glass.

VODKA RICKEY

Of all the rickey variations, this is the mildest-flavored.

♦ lime wedge
2 ounces vodka
½ ounce fresh lime juice
club soda or seltzer

Rim a highball glass with the lime wedge, and fill the glass with ice cubes. Pour in the vodka and lime juice, and top with soda (or seltzer). Stir briefly. Squeeze the lime wedge into the drink, and drop it in.

VODKA TONIC

A linguist might be able to tell us how the "and" got dropped from this drink's name. It's beyond *Drinkology* why so many people prefer this innocuous concoction to its more robustly flavored predecessor, the Gin *and* Tonic. But they do.

2 ounces vodka
tonic water
♦ lime wedge

Rim a highball glass with the lime wedge, and fill it with ice cubes. Pour in the vodka, and top with tonic water. Squeeze the lime wedge into the drink, and drop it in.

WHITE RUSSIAN (ON THE ROCKS)

There are two ways of fashioning this wonderful, classic drink. *Drinkology* can't decide which it likes better, so we present both.

2 ounces vodka
1 ounce coffee liqueur
½ ounce heavy cream

Pour the vodka and coffee liqueur into a highball glass filled with ice cubes. Stir briefly. Float the cream on top. (Do not mix in the cream; let it gradually infiltrate the drink as it's sipped.)

WHITE RUSSIAN (UP)

It's no wonder that this cocktail has remained so popular for decades. It's an absolutely scrumptious combination.

2 ounces vodka
1 ounce coffee liqueur
1 ounce heavy cream

Combine ingredients in a cocktail shaker, with ice. Shake well, and strain into a chilled cocktail glass.

Whiskey

"SHOW US THE WAY TO THE NEXT WHISKEY BAR." THAT LYRIC—penned in 1929 by German playwright Bertolt Brecht, set to music by his collaborator Kurt Weill, and decadently covered by Jim Morrison and The Doors in their 1967 debut LP—is one that *Drinkology* has been repeating, mantra-like, for more years than we care to remember.

Drinkology has whiskey on the brain (and, undoubtedly, in the liver). It gives us a warm, glowing feeling that, we imagine, must be akin to what those who indulge in sports fandom experience. Just thinking about whiskey gives us a lump in the throat, a swelling in the breast, a tear at the corner of the eye. Devotion. Loyalty. Words can't really express the emotion.

MAD FEDS AND IRISHMEN

Over its history, whiskey has inspired a range of emotions, some of them downright treasonous. The first serious trouble that George Washington, as the newly elected president of the republic, ran into was an armed revolt against the fledgling U.S. government by a group of western Pennsylvania distillers. Congress, you see, had decided that levying a 25-percent excise tax on whiskey would be a fine and dandy way of lining up the revenues needed to pay down the country's Revolutionary War debt. The Pennsylvania hooch-makers violently disagreed, and in 1794 Washington had to send in 13,000 federal troops to put down what came to be dubbed the Whiskey Rebellion.

Like the alcohol in a bottle that's been left uncapped, resistance evaporated. Many of the rebels simply headed south, to the hills and hollers of Kentucky and Tennessee. There, some of their descendants invented fine bourbons and sour mash whiskeys; others—a scrappier lot—created that raw, fiery, untaxed rotgut known as moonshine, and have continued to be chased by federal agents ever since.

But enough about U.S. sin taxes and their discontents. Whiskey, of course, isn't originally American, and its genealogy goes back way past the late eighteenth century. *Way* past. The Celtic peoples of Great Britain and Ireland were the first whiskey-makers, though it's unclear whether the Scottish Gaelic–speaking Scots or the Irish Gaelic–speaking Irish hold the more aboriginal responsibility. Both ancient languages have a word that translates, literally, as "water of life," and either the Scottish *uisgebeatha* or the Irish *uisegebaugh* might be the root of the English *whiskey*. What's certain from the historical record is that the joy-juice was being produced on the Emerald Isle at least as early as the twelfth century; its prior lineage is lost in the Irish mists of time.

GRIST FOR YOUR SWILL

As every snooty single-malt sipper knows—along with anyone who's ever had the sudden, overpowering urge to take up clog-dancing in an Irish pub on St. Paddy's Day—Scotland and Ireland continued to produce the world's most celebrated whiskeys. The Scots and the Irish have been joined, more recently, by the Americans (bourbon, Tennessee whiskey, rye) and the Canadians (Canadian blended whiskey). In modern times, even Japan has gotten into the act; that country's Suntory distillery makes some truly excellent red-eye.

If you've ever sampled more than one kind of whiskey (scotch and bourbon, for example), you don't need *Drinkology* to tell you that the various styles of this spirit don't taste at all alike—so much so that those who worship at the altar of scotch may consider bourbon the devil's own brew, and vice versa. Despite the marked differences among various whiskeys' flavors, however, all are made in basically the same way. Both God and the devil are in the details.

In very broad strokes, the whiskey-making process goes like this: Some sort of grain (barley, corn, wheat, rye) is ground into grist. Some of the grain is *malted* first, which means that it's allowed to sprout, then roasted.) Water is added to the ground grain, and this soup is cooked, releasing starches from the grist. The grist is strained away, leaving behind a liquid known as *wort,* to which yeast is added. The soon-fermented brew—at this stage it's called *beer,* though you wouldn't want to drink it—is then distilled to produce *raw whiskey* (which is about 80 percent alcohol). The raw whiskey is watered down, and the resulting solution is aged in wooden barrels.

Though many factors influence a whiskey's flavor—the grain or combination of grains it's made from, the fuel that fires the flame in the still, the water used in the brewing, and even the atmosphere surrounding the distillery—it's the barrel and the amount of time a whiskey spends aging that have the greatest impact on its taste. Bourbon is aged in new casks made of charred oak; Canadian whiskey in white-oak barrels; and many scotch and Irish whiskeys in seasoned (i.e., "pre-owned") barrels that were previously used to age sherry or bourbon. As with brandy, it's true as a general rule that the older the whiskey (of whatever type), the better; this is why, despite efforts by some enterprising Appalachian white-lightning makers to market their products legally and develop a following for them, straight-from-the-still moonshine has no connoisseurs. (We might mention, in passing, that *Drinkology* carries no recipe for that moonshine-and-grape-juice "punch" known as Purple Jesus; if you want to find out how to make it, go Google yourself.)

MANHATTAN IS NOT IN SCOTLAND

Some whiskeys are blends; others aren't. The specific terms applied to unblended whiskeys vary: an unblended scotch is called a *single-malt* scotch; unblended bourbons and ryes are referred to by the term *single barrel*. (Technically, *single barrel* means that all the whiskey in the bottle was aged in the same cask; since there are relatively few actual single-barrel bourbons and ryes on the market, however, it's usually more accurate to refer to premium "unblended" bourbons and ryes as *small batch*.)

The term *straight whiskey* has a different sort of meaning. U.S. law dictates that all whiskey be labeled either "straight" or "blended"; all that "straight" means, in this sense, is that at least 51 percent of the whiskey in the bottle was distilled from a single kind of grain. A blended whiskey, by contrast, can contain up to 80 percent other stuff (including whiskeys distilled from other grains, neutral grain spirits, and even fruit juices). Generally speaking, blended whiskeys are lighter-bodied and smoother than unblended whiskeys.

And then there's the matter of the spelling of the word *whiskey*. Or, rather, *whisky*. Which is it? Well, it usually depends on where the hooch hails from. In general, the spelling *whisky* is used by Scottish, Canadian, and Japanese makers, while American and Irish makers plug an "e" between the "k" and the "y." The reason for the divergence is historical—but not terribly interesting. Besides which, some American producers (with Scottish roots) continue to call their products *whisky*. To simplify matters—and to keep our copyeditor (or should it be *copy editor*?) from going crazy, *Drinkology* decided to adhere, throughout, to the more common American spelling *whiskey*. The purists will never forgive us, but you, we hope, will.

There's *scads* more to know about this subject—especially about single-malt and blended scotches. Mercifully, the knowledge that you, as a budding mixologist, need in order to make successful whiskey-based cocktails can be summarized in relatively few sentences.

First, *never* use single-malt scotch in a mixed drink. Stick with the blended stuff, but make sure the blended scotch you use is a good one. *Drinkology* prefers the darker-amber "call" brands like Dewar's, Johnny Walker Red Label, Famous Grouse, and White Horse, to name just a few possibilities. (Similarly, you should use blended Canadian and Irish whiskeys in mixed drinks calling for these liquors, but, since all Canadian whiskeys and most of the Irish whiskeys readily available in this country are blends, this is unlikely to present a problem.)

This rule does not apply to bourbon and rye, which by definition are straight whiskeys. In general, the more powerful a bourbon's (or rye's) flavor, the better. In fact, some bourbon- and rye-based drinks simply cry out for the bare-knuckled taste only a premium small-batch bourbon or rye can provide.

Second, when making a mixed drink you must never, ever substitute another sort of whiskey for the one the recipe calls for. (Granted, a few recipes permit you a choice of whiskeys.) If you make a Manhattan with scotch, you haven't made a Manhattan at all—you've made a Rob Roy, which is an utterly different drink. And if you make a Mint Julep with Irish, . . . well, who cares what you've made, but the state of Kentucky should issue an all-points bulletin for your arrest.

Enough. We're tired of lecturing you. Just show us the way to the next whiskey bar, please. We're feeling a devotional urge coming on.

ALABAMA SLAMMER

Drinkology's taste-testers are among those who generally dislike Southern Comfort (which isn't really whiskey per se, but rather a bourbon-based liqueur). So our initial reaction to this recipe was, "Gee, that sounds *dreadful.*" It turns out to be quite good—fruity and complex.

1 ounce Southern Comfort
1 ounce amaretto
1 ounce sloe gin
1 ounce orange juice

Combine ingredients in a cocktail shaker, with ice. Shake, and strain into a double old-fashioned glass filled with ice cubes.

BLARNEY STONE

The Pernod's flavor dominates this pale golden cocktail, despite the small amount used.

♂ lemon twist
2 ounces Irish whiskey
¼ ounce Cointreau
¼ ounce Pernod or other absinthe substitute
dash of maraschino liqueur

Rim a chilled cocktail glass with the lemon twist. Combine the other ingredients in a mixing glass, with ice. Stir, and strain into the glass. Garnish with the twist.

BOBBY BURNS

Unsurprisingly, the names of scotch-based drinks often hearken back to Scottish history and culture. The Bobby Burns—a *Drinkology* favorite—is named for the poet who penned "Auld Lang Syne."

2 ounces blended scotch
1 ounce sweet vermouth
¼ ounce Bénédictine

Combine ingredients in a mixing glass, with ice. Stir, and strain into a chilled cocktail glass.

BOURBON COBBLER

Drinkology is wild about cobblers. If blackberries, blueberries, or raspberries are in season, you might consider using a few to garnish the drink—rather than the more mundane cherry and orange slice.

2½ ounces bourbon
½ ounce simple syrup
crushed ice
♦ maraschino cherry
♦ orange slice

Pack a large red wine glass with crushed ice. Pour in the bourbon and simple syrup, and stir very briefly. Garnish with the cherry and orange slice.

BOURBON CRUSTA

Crustas are all about *presentation*. Without the sugar rimming and the long spiral of lemon peel, it ain't a crusta.

lemon wedge
superfine sugar
♌ lemon peel cut into a long spiral
2 ounces bourbon
½ ounce Cointreau or triple sec
½ ounce fresh lemon juice

Prepare a chilled sour glass by rimming it with the lemon wedge and sugar. (Discard the wedge.) Loop a long spiral of lemon peel around the glass's interior. Combine the liquid ingredients in a cocktail shaker, with ice. Shake well, and strain into the prepared glass.

BOURBON DAISY

This gorgeously red cooler tastes strongly of bourbon.

♌ lemon twist
2½ ounces bourbon
1 ounce fresh lemon juice
½ ounce grenadine
crushed ice

Rim a highball glass with the lemon twist, and pack it with crushed ice. Combine the bourbon, lemon juice, and grenadine in a cocktail shaker, with ice. Shake well, and strain into the glass. Garnish with the twist.

WHISKEY

BROOKLYN COCKTAIL

The classic Brooklyn Cocktail recipe calls for Amer Picon, a French bitters that is nigh unto impossible to come by, so we substitute the Italian bitters Torani Amer. If you can't find it either, use a dash or two of Angostura instead. (But don't tell anyone we advised you to do so.)

♂ lemon twist
1½ ounces rye
¾ ounce dry vermouth
dash maraschino liqueur
dash Torani Amer

Rim a chilled cocktail glass with the lemon twist. Combine the other ingredients in a mixing glass, with ice. Stir, and strain into the cocktail glass. Garnish with the twist.

CANADIAN COCKTAIL

This pale golden cocktail is aptly named, as it makes very good use of Canadian blended whiskey.

2 ounces Canadian blended whiskey
½ ounce Cointreau or triple sec
½ teaspoon simple syrup
dash Angostura bitters

Combine ingredients in a cocktail shaker, with ice. Shake well, and strain into a chilled cocktail glass.

CLAREMONT

The Claremont is like an Old Fashioned (page 300), but with the fruitiness ratcheted up a couple of notches.

2 maraschino cherries
2 orange slices
¾ ounce orange curaçao
2 or 3 dashes Angostura bitters
1½ ounces bourbon or rye
club soda or seltzer

De-stem one of the cherries. In an old-fashioned glass, carefully muddle one of the orange slices and the de-stemmed cherry with the curaçao and bitters. Discard the orange rind. Add three or four ice cubes to the glass, and pour in the bourbon. Top with soda or seltzer, stir briefly, and garnish with the remaining cherry and orange slice.

WHISKEY

EVERYBODY'S IRISH

Not only is every*body* Irish, but this cocktail seems to make every*thing* Irish, as well. Chartreuse? Crème de menthe? Olives? It's as multiethnic as the politicians in a St. Patrick's Day parade. And, for the moment, harmony prevails.

2 ounces Irish whiskey

1 teaspoon green Chartreuse

1 teaspoon green crème de menthe

♦ olive (green, of course)

Combine liquid ingredients in a mixing glass, with ice. Stir, and strain into a chilled cocktail glass. Garnish with the olive.

FINE AND DANDY (WHISKEY VERSION)

This recipe produces a rosy-amber drink that's an elegant variation on the Manhattan.

♦ lemon twist

2 ounces Canadian blended whiskey

½ ounce Cointreau or triple sec

½ ounce Dubonnet Rouge

Rim a chilled cocktail glass with the lemon twist. Combine the liquid ingredients in a mixing glass, with ice. Stir, and strain into the cocktail glass. Garnish with the twist.

JOHN COLLINS

The John Collins is the offspring of the Tom Collins (page 151). Like its dad, it's a terrific summertime refresher. Don't be afraid to make it in a highball glass if you don't have collins glasses.

2 ounces bourbon or Canadian blended whiskey
½ ounce fresh lemon juice
½ ounce simple syrup
club soda or seltzer
⚬ maraschino cherry
⚬ orange slice

Combine the whiskey, lemon juice, and simple syrup in a cocktail shaker, with ice. Shake well, and strain into a collins or highball glass filled with ice cubes. Top with soda (or seltzer), and stir briefly. (If you're using a collins glass, stirring the drink can be slightly challenging because of the glass's narrowness; try using the long handle of a bar spoon.) Garnish with the cherry and orange slice, skewered together.

KENTUCKY COLONEL

The Colonel is one of *Drinkology*'s favorite bourbon-based cocktails.

♂ lemon twist
2½ ounces bourbon
½ ounce Bénédictine

Rim a chilled cocktail glass with the lemon twist. Combine the bourbon and Bénédictine in a mixing glass, with ice. Stir, and strain into the cocktail glass. Garnish with the twist.

MANHATTAN (CLASSIC)

Let's fess up. The classic Manhattan is *Drinkology*'s absolutely favorite cocktail. A well-made Manhattan is beautiful to the eye, delectable to the tongue, and comforting to the soul and body. Several of our taste-testers are in agreement that the Manhattan's intoxicating effect is qualitatively different from that of any other cocktail: it's deeply calming, profoundly cheering. The only trouble is that the feeling of well-being a Manhattan produces can be a little *too* attractive. After two Manhattans you may be on cloud nine; indulge in a third, however, and you're likely to feel a tad tattered and torn.

As with so many classic cocktails, there's controversy over what a Manhattan should contain and about the proper proportions of the ingredients. The recipe below, which employs Canadian blended whiskey, is the one

Drinkology likes best, though many Manhattan aficionados insist that the drink be made with bourbon or rye. Historically, rye makes better sense, since it's likely that the original Manhattan recipe—concocted by a bartender at New York City's Manhattan Club for an 1874 party hosted by Lady Randolph Churchill—employed rye whiskey. (Lady Churchill, by the way, was Winston Churchill's mother.) Rye—or bourbon, for that matter—is a little too strong-flavored for the drink, however; it tends to tilt the cocktail's balance too far in the whiskey direction.

Drinkology's Manhattan recipe is distinctive in that it suggests including just a tiny bit of syrup from the maraschino cherry jar. If that makes the drink too sweet for your taste, feel free to drop that ingredient. *Drinkology* definitely recommends that the Manhattan be served "up"—that is, in a chilled cocktail glass. (You may certainly use this recipe for an on-the-rocks Manhattan, but it's our strong opinion that pouring the drink over ice makes it too watery.)

2 ounces Canadian blended whiskey (or bourbon or rye)
¾ ounce sweet vermouth
¼ teaspoon maraschino cherry syrup (from the jar)
2 dashes Angostura bitters
♻ maraschino cherry

Combine liquid ingredients in a mixing glass, with ice. Stir, and strain into a chilled cocktail glass. Garnish with the cherry.

MANHATTAN
(FERNET BRANCA VARIATION)

Drinkology was introduced to this excellent variation on the classic Manhattan recipe by Saed Ibrhim, bartender at Bistro Les Amis, in New York City's SoHo district. The Fernet Branca—an Italian *digestivo*—invests the drink with a sultry, darkly herbal favor.

2 ounces Canadian blended whiskey
¾ ounce sweet vermouth
¼ teaspoon Fernet Branca
⚘ maraschino cherry

Combine liquid ingredients in a mixing glass, with ice. Stir, and strain into a chilled cocktail glass. Garnish with the cherry.

MANHATTAN (DRY)

Only those who are constitutionally opposed to sweet-flavored drinks will prefer a dry Manhattan to the classic variety. It's for them that we include this recipe.

⚘ lemon twist
2 ounces Canadian blended whiskey
¾ ounce dry vermouth
dash Angostura bitters

Rim a chilled cocktail glass with the lemon twist. Combine the other ingredients in a mixing glass, with ice. Stir, and strain into the cocktail glass. Garnish with the twist.

MANHATTAN (PERFECT)

"Perfect" cocktails employ equal parts dry and sweet vermouth. Though *Drinkology* recommends garnishing a Perfect Manhattan with a twist, it's allowable to substitute a maraschino cherry.

♂ lemon twist
2½ ounces Canadian blended whiskey
½ ounce dry vermouth
½ ounce sweet vermouth
dash Angostura bitters

Rim a chilled cocktail glass with the lemon twist. Combine the other ingredients in a mixing glass, with ice. Stir, and strain into the cocktail glass. Garnish with the twist.

MINT JULEP

Oh, the controversies that rage over the proper fabrication of a Mint Julep—only slightly less savage than the War Between the States. Every Southern family, it seems, has its own recipe, and factionalism and disagreement over basic principles are as rife as they are among adherents of the Baptist Church. (*Drinkology* knows one lady Methodist minister who's a mean Mint Julep maker, but that's a different story.) The sweet, extra-minty recipe offered below is guaranteed to earn *Drinkology* some enemies; we can only pray that it wins us a few friends as well.

The Mint Julep hails from Kentucky—or so Kentuckians like to claim. They're certainly the best-known quaffers of the drink, which is the featured beverage at Churchill Downs racetrack on the first Saturday of every May, when the Kentucky Derby is run. Actually, the julep has a long, complex, and somewhat obscure history, which extends at least as far back the fifteenth century. Originally, juleps seem to have been concoctions of water, sugar, and various floral or herbal extracts, used for medicinal purposes. In America, brandy-based juleps predate those using bourbon. (There are also juleps based on rum and even scotch.)

Drinkology's taste-testers enjoyed their Mint Juleps in high style. One of us, you see, grew up in Cincinnati—just upriver from Louisville, Kentucky—and throughout his boyhood and young manhood was presented with a monogrammed, pewter julep cup on birthdays, graduations, and whenever he served as an usher at a debutante ball. He amassed quite a set. Although it's perfectly "acceptable" to sip your julep from an old-fashioned glass, *Drinkology* highly recommends that you invest in a set of pewter—or, even better, silver—julep cups if you intend to enjoy the drink frequently. The metal conducts the cold from the ice—it's *essential* that you use crushed ice in this drink—and the frosty condensation that gathers on the outside of the cup is very attractive indeed. (By the way, it's also advisable to use a good bourbon in your juleps. The drink is well worth it.)

a dozen or more fresh mint leaves (medium to large)
1 heaping teaspoon superfine sugar
1 teaspoon water
crushed ice
2½ ounces bourbon
♧ 2 or 3 sprigs of mint

In the bottom of a julep cup or old-fashioned glass, muddle the mint leaves, sugar, and water. Pack the cup or glass with crushed ice. Pour in the bourbon and stir. Top with more ice, and garnish with the mint sprigs. Serve with a straw.

NEW YORK COCKTAIL

If you find whiskey-based cocktails too heavy for summer drinking, try this light, lemony mixture.

♧ lemon twist
2 ounces Canadian blended whiskey
½ ounce fresh lemon juice
½ ounce simple syrup
dash grenadine

Rim a chilled cocktail glass with the lemon twist. Combine the other ingredients in a cocktail shaker, with ice. Shake well, and strain into a chilled cocktail glass. Garnish with the twist.

OLD FASHIONED

 You wouldn't think there'd be much argument over the method of preparing an Old Fashioned. After all, the name itself bespeaks tradition and a time-honored way of doing things. The drink's origins are relatively uncontroversial: numerous sources credit its invention to a bartender at the Pendennis Club of Louisville, Kentucky, who created it for a local distiller named Colonel Pepper sometime around the turn of the twentieth century. But that's where the agreement ends.

There appear to be as many different Old Fashioned recipes as there are aficionados of the drink. Some employ bourbon, others rye, still others Canadian blended whiskey. (There are even a few recipes that call for scotch.) Some recipes require that the fruit—or some of it—be muddled; others dispense with the muddling. (And a few recipes actually dispense with the fruit altogether!) Many—but by no means a majority of—Old Fashioned recipes advise that the drink be topped off with a splash of water or soda. Others denounce this as a travesty. Dear God.

Drinkology, of course, has its own opinions on the subject. Acknowledging the drink's Kentucky home, our taste-testers vote for bourbon (or, if you prefer, rye). We definitely belong to the muddling (if not the muddled) camp. And we hold with those upstarts who recommend using soda in the drink. (Adding a splash of soda to the muddled fruit helps blend the flavors; topping with soda sharpens the taste.) Our old-fashioned manners, however, permit gentlemanly disagreement.

One cautionary note: Muddling is an energetic process; don't use your fine crystal when preparing an Old Fashioned.

2 orange slices (one for muddling, one for garnish)
2 maraschino cherries (one for muddling, one for garnish)
1 teaspoon superfine sugar
2 dashes Angostura bitters
2½ ounces bourbon or rye
club soda or seltzer

De-stem one of the cherries. In an old-fashioned glass, carefully muddle the sugar, the bitters, one of the orange slices, and the de-stemmed cherry. Discard the orange rind. Add a splash of soda to the muddled mixture and stir briefly. Add three or four ice cubes and the bourbon. Top with soda (or seltzer), stir briefly, and garnish with the remaining orange slice and cherry.

PADDY WAGON

Also known (a tad more politely) as the Paddy Cocktail, this is *Drinkology*'s favorite Irish whiskey–based concoction.

2½ ounces Irish whiskey
¾ ounce sweet vermouth
2 dashes Angostura bitters
♣ maraschino cherry

Combine liquid ingredients in a mixing glass, with ice. Stir, and strain into a chilled cocktail glass. Garnish with the cherry.

POMATTAN (POMEGRANATE MANHATTAN)

Snobbish *Drinkology* disdained pomegranate liqueur—until, that is, we tasted the splendid Pama. It smoothes out bourbon's rougher edges even better than sweet vermouth. The Pomattan is hereby declared a *Drinkology* favorite.

3 ounces bourbon
1 ounce Pama pomegranate liqueur
¼ teaspoon grenadine (optional)
2 dashes orange bitters
♂ maraschino cherry *or* pomegranate seeds (in season)

Combine ingredients in a mixing glass, with ice. (Note that the grenadine, if added, will redden and sweeten the drink.) Stir well, and strain into a chilled cocktail glass. Add the maraschino cherry; if pomegranates are in season, garnish with four or five pomegranate seeds instead.

PRESBYTERIAN (LOW-CHURCH VERSION)

Presbyterians pride themselves on doing things "decently and in order." The order of this surprisingly decent lowball (ice, then scotch, then ginger ale) couldn't be simpler.

2½ ounces blended scotch
ginger ale

Fill a double old-fashioned glass with ice cubes. Pour in the scotch, top with ginger ale, and stir.

PRESBYTERIAN (HIGH-CHURCH VERSION)

The trouble with the ordinary Presbyterian (previous page) is, let's face facts, that it is somewhat dull. Wanting more pomp, *Drinkology* created this "high-church," highball version. (Bottled ginger juice, by the way, is sold at most health-food stores.)

2 ounces blended scotch
1 ounce ginger juice
1 ounce simple syrup
¾ ounce fresh lemon juice
½ egg white
club soda or seltzer
↻ thin strip of fresh ginger

Fill a tumbler with ice cubes. Combine all ingredients except the soda (or seltzer) in a shaker, with ice. Shake vigorously and strain into the tumbler. Pouring very slowly and carefully so that the foaming drink does not overflow the glass, top with soda (or seltzer). Garnish with the strip of ginger.

WHISKEY

ROB ROY (CLASSIC)

Named for the Robin Hood–like hero of a Sir Walter Scott novel, the Rob Roy is nothing other than a scotch-based Manhattan. (And, like a Manhattan, a Rob Roy can be served either "up," as in this recipe, or on the rocks in an old-fashioned glass.) A Rob Roy's taste is sharper, more biting, than a Manhattan's.

2½ ounces blended scotch
½ ounce sweet vermouth
dash Angostura bitters
♂ maraschino cherry

Combine liquid ingredients in a mixing glass, with ice. Stir, and strain into a chilled cocktail glass. Garnish with the cherry.

ROB ROY (DRY)

Like its transatlantic cousin, the Manhattan, the Rob Roy also has dry and "perfect" variants. Here they are.

♂ lemon twist
2½ ounces blended scotch
½ ounce dry vermouth
dash Angostura bitters

Rim a chilled cocktail glass with the twist. Combine the other ingredients in a mixing glass, with ice. Stir, and strain into the cocktail glass. Garnish with the twist.

ROB ROY (PERFECT)

♻ lemon twist
2½ ounces blended scotch
¼ ounce dry vermouth
¼ ounce sweet vermouth
dash Angostura bitters

Rim a chilled cocktail glass with the twist. Combine the other ingredients in a mixing glass, with ice. Stir, and strain into the cocktail glass. Garnish with the twist.

RUSTY NAIL

Back in the '60s, when it was invented, the Rusty Nail had a reputation as a swinger's drink. It's sweet and aromatic. (Don't overdo the Drambuie, or it will become cloying.)

♻ lemon twist
2 ounces blended scotch
½ ounce Drambuie

Rim an old-fashioned glass with the twist. Fill the glass with ice cubes, and pour in the scotch and Drambuie. Stir briefly, and garnish with the twist.

SAZERAC

 Although less well known (especially outside Louisiana, where it has been designated the official state cocktail), the Sazerac vies with the Manhattan, the Martini, and a few others for the title of Best Mixed Drink Ever. It is a work of genius.

The Sazerac's history is genuinely storied. It first appeared on this blessed planet at the Merchants Exchange Coffeehouse, in New Orleans' French Quarter, in the 1850s. But the original recipe was different from today's: it used a cognac called Sazerac-de-Forge et Fils. The libation proved so popular that the name of the establishment was eventually changed to the Sazerac Coffee House.

The recipe changed sometime after 1870, when the coffeehouse was bought by a gentleman called Thomas Handy. Handy substituted rye whiskey for the cognac, in part to accommodate American drinkers' taste and in part because cognac—distilled from wine—was becoming difficult to get because the *Phylloxera* epidemic was ravaging Europe's grapevines. Somewhere along the line, a tiny bit of absinthe got added to the mix, more or less completely transforming a drink that was originally a combination of cognac, sugar, and bitters.

The Sazerac Coffee House underwent another transformation in 1949, when it was bought by the Roosevelt Hotel, moved there, and became the Sazerac Bar. That barroom—with evocative period murals by New Orleans artist Paul Ninas—is one of the city's treasures; seriously damaged by Hurricane Katrina, it has now been fully restored. It's a swelligant spot to savor a Sazerac cocktail.

As is your own lovely home. The recipe below differs from the Sazerac Bar's "official" version in prep method, and it substitutes simple syrup for the traditional sugar cube. But these are minor variances adopted for convenience. Do take care with the ingredients: The rye should probably be Sazerac-brand rye. Use real absinthe or, if you can't get it, the New Orleans absinthe substitute called Herbsaint. And the bitters *must* be Peychaud's, whose color and flavor are essential to the drink. Some purists claim that the lemon peel ought to be discarded after rimming the glass; *Drinkology* respectfully disagrees.

about ½ teaspoon absinthe or Herbsaint

2 ounces rye

1 teaspoon simple syrup

4 dashes Peychaud's bitters

⚮ large strip of lemon peel (about 2 inches long by ¾ inch wide)

Rim a chilled old-fashioned glass with the lemon peel. (Reserve the peel.) Pour the absinthe into the glass and swirl until the inside of the glass is entirely coated; discard any excess absinthe. Place the glass in the freezer.

Now, place four or five ice cubes in a mixing glass and add the rye, simple syrup, and bitters. Stir well. Retrieve the old-fashioned glass from the freezer and strain the contents of the mixing glass into it. Drop in the lemon peel.

TWIN HILLS

This marvelous drink really deserves to be better known. It belongs to that family of cocktails known as sours, but it's much more complex than the others in the category.

2 ounces rye
½ ounce Bénédictine
¼ ounce fresh lemon juice
¼ ounce fresh lime juice
¼ ounce simple syrup
☙ thinly cut lemon slice
☙ thinly cut lime slice

Combine liquid ingredients in a cocktail shaker, with ice. Shake well, and strain into a chilled cocktail glass. Garnish with the lemon and lime slices, letting them float on top of the drink.

WARD EIGHT

Invented in Boston, this cocktail hearkens back to the heyday of that city's Democratic Party machine. (It's perhaps the only alcoholic concoction named for an election district.)

2 ounces bourbon or rye
1 ounce fresh lemon juice
1 ounce orange juice
dash of grenadine
♂ maraschino cherry
♂ orange slice

Combine liquid ingredients in a cocktail shaker, with ice. Shake well, and strain into a chilled cocktail glass or an ice-filled old-fashioned glass. Garnish with the cherry and orange slice.

WHISKEY FIZZ

Bourbon, rye, and blended whiskeys all make terrific, full-flavored fizzes. The drink's taste differs, of course, according to the kind of whiskey used.

2 ounces whiskey (blended scotch, bourbon, Canadian blended, Irish, or rye)
1 ounce fresh lemon juice
½ ounce simple syrup
club soda or seltzer

Combine the whiskey, simple syrup, and lemon juice in a cocktail shaker, with ice. Shake well, and strain into a highball glass filled with ice cubes. Top with soda (or seltzer), and stir briefly.

WHISKEY RICKEY

As with the fizz, almost any sort of whiskey is suitable for a rickey.

꙳ lime wedge
2 ounces whiskey (blended scotch, bourbon, Canadian blended, Irish, or rye)
½ ounce fresh lime juice
club soda or seltzer

Rim a highball glass with the lime wedge, and fill the glass with ice cubes. Pour in the whiskey and lime juice, and top with soda (or seltzer). Squeeze the lime wedge into the drink, and drop it in. Stir briefly.

WHISKEY SOUR

This is the mother of all sours.

2 ounces bourbon or Canadian blended whiskey
¾ ounce fresh lemon juice
½ ounce simple syrup
꙳ maraschino cherry
꙳ orange slice

Combine bourbon, lemon juice, and simple syrup in a cocktail shaker, with ice. Shake well, and strain into a chilled sour glass. Garnish with the cherry and orange slice.

Wine

D O NOT, UNDER ANY CIRCUMSTANCES, USE THAT BOTTLE OF Rioja that Ernest Hemingway gave your great-grandfather during the Spanish Civil War to make sangria. But if you're a puritanical oenophile who believes that wine must only be drunk unmixed with anything else, you're really missing something. In fact, some of the best wine-based concoctions come pre-bottled.

The ancient Romans liked to flavor their wine with all manner of things, including pepper, poppies, aloe, chalk, tar, boiled seawater, and asafetida—a bitter, foul-smelling resin. Modern Europeans have refined this palette, and sip Dubonnet (the *rouge* version of which is flavored with quinine) and white and red Lillet, which are mixtures of wine, brandy, fruit, and herbs. Vermouth is nothing more than white wine spiked with extra alcohol and *aromatized* with herbs, spices, and a variety of other ingredients. (Sweet vermouth gets its redddish-brown color from the addition of caramel.)

The Portuguese add brandy to wine made from local grapes to create the sweeter, richer, more potent beverage known as Port. Other *fortified* wines—each subjected to a distinctive ageing tech-

WINE

nique—include Sherry, from Andalusia in southern Spain; Marsala, from Sicily; and Madeira, made on the Portuguese-owned islands of that name off the African coast.

Technically, nearly anything can be—and has been—fermented. But it is the grape that takes to fermentation like nothing else, and today the word for *wine* in any language unambiguously refers to fermented grape juice.

Humans have been making wine for as long as they have been keeping recipe cards (we're including the clay-tablet variety). The earliest evidence of winemaking is some 7,000 years old. Oft mentioned in the Bible, wine became an important part of Judeo-Christian religious rites. And (do note how quickly *Drinkology* travels from the sublime to the ridiculous), when Ricky Ricardo took Lucy to Europe, she wound up barefoot in a vat of grapes, trading insults (and grape mash) with an Italian *viticoltore* and absorbing local color in more ways than one. (Italy, by the way, today runs a close second to France in the amount of wine produced, with Spain in third place and the United States a somewhat distant fourth. Dionysus and his vines certainly outdid Johnny Appleseed: grapes are now grown and made into wine on every continent except Antarctica.)

WINEMAKING AND WINE-TALK

To make red wine, grapes are picked, de-stemmed, and crushed to produce what's called *must,* which is then pumped into a fermentation vat, where yeast is added. To make white, the juice is separated from the skins before fermentation begins. In Winespeak, *dry* is the opposite of *sweet,* and means that the yeast consumed most of the available sugar before dying off.

After fermenting, most white wines are stabilized in stainless-steel tanks, and many reds (and some whites) are transferred to wooden barrels for ageing. Specific ageing techniques differ from place to place and from one type of wine to another, but it's not just the winemaking technique (or the variety of grape used) that makes each wine distinctive. The climate and soil of the vineyard—its *terroir*—is just as important to the wine's ultimate flavor.

Most white wines are made from light-skinned grapes, but it ain't necessarily so. As long as the juice—even from dark-skinned grapes—is separated from the skins during crushing, a white wine will result. Quality rosé wines are made by leaving (dark) grape skins in the must for a short time. Grape skins don't just color the brew; they also contain *tannins,* astringent compounds that contribute texture and structure to red wine. Tannins give young red wines that pucker-inducing quality, which diminishes as the wine continues to age in the bottle.

People have been talking about wine for as long as they've been drinking it, developing their own—often alienating—vocabulary. One major source of confusion is that Europeans tend to name their wines for their place of origin, but elsewhere wine is often named for the variety of grape from which it's made. So a California cabernet sauvignon can't be a Bordeaux, but a Bordeaux might be a cabernet. Got it? Don't worry. (Well, maybe you should worry just a *little* bit: *Drinkology* has never been so embarrassed for anyone as for an airport-restaurant waitress who offered us two kinds of wine: "light" and "dark.")

If you want to look like you know what you're doing when you open a bottle, pour a little bit into a glass, swirl it, smell it, and take a sip. You'll not only impress friends and strangers, but you'll also enjoy the experience more.

ARMCHAIR EXPLORATION

Some of the world's greatest thinkers were devoted wine enthusiasts. Thomas Jefferson, himself an amateur vintner, proudly proclaimed, "By making this vine known to the public, I have rendered my country as great a service as if I had enabled it to pay back the national debt." And in *A Moveable Feast,* Papa Hemingway wrote, "In Europe, drinking wine was not a snobbism nor a sign of sophistication nor a cult; it was as natural as eating and to me as necessary."

And so it should be. Don't be put off if you don't know a *terroir* from a terrier: open a bottle of wine and you become an armchair explorer. Sail (in your imagination) around the Cape of Good Hope and sample a sauvignon blanc from Stellenbosch, in South Africa; savor an Australian shiraz without making the day-long flight; refresh yourself with one of Portugal's famous vinho verde whites, and still be home in time for dinner.

And, please, don't turn up your nose at the idea of mixing the grape and the . . . well, any number of other things. Remember that fortified wines (such as port, sherry, Madeira, and Marsala) and aromatized wines (Dubonnet, Lillet, vermouth) are *already* mixtures. Aromatized wines make splendid pre-prandial drinks—so much so that they're often called *aperitif* wines. Fortified wines—as befits their heavier, richer nature—are often served at the end of a meal. And both aromatized and fortified wines are used in a panoply of cocktails—sometimes playing supporting parts, sometimes in the starring roles.

ADONIS

The Adonis is a classic European-style aperitif. If you can find it, use Peychaud's bitters rather than Angostura in this drink.

♢ lemon twist

2 ounces dry sherry

1 ounce sweet vermouth

2 dashes Peychaud's or Angostura bitters

Rim a chilled cocktail glass with the lemon twist. Combine the other ingredients in a mixing glass, with ice. Stir, and strain into the glass. Garnish with the twist.

THE BISHOP

Though it goes against the received wisdom, you should chill the red wine for this punchlike drink.

1 ounce fresh lemon juice

1 ounce orange juice

½ ounce simple syrup

4 ounces light, dry red wine (merlot, for example)

♢ orange slice

Combine the juices and simple syrup in a cocktail shaker, with ice. Shake well, and strain into a red wine glass filled with ice cubes. Pour in the wine, and stir briefly. Garnish with the orange slice.

WINE

BRANDIED MADEIRA

Adding brandy to Madeira is, in one sense, a study in redundancy, since Madeira has already been fortified with brandy. But in this case, more is definitely more; Brandied Madeira is a wonderfully aromatic and subtle brew.

꙼ lemon twist
1½ ounces Madeira
1½ ounces brandy
¾ ounce dry vermouth

Rim a red wine glass with the lemon twist, and fill it with ice cubes. Combine the liquid ingredients in a mixing glass, with ice. Stir, and strain into the red wine glass. Garnish with the twist.

BRANDIED PORT

Brandying tawny port produces a gorgeous, dusty-rose--colored concoction. The lemon juice and maraschino liqueur add sour and sweet notes to this superb mix.

1½ ounces tawny port
1½ ounces brandy
¾ ounce fresh lemon juice
2 teaspoons maraschino liqueur
꙼ orange slice

Combine the liquid ingredients in a mixing glass, with ice. Stir, and strain into a red wine glass filled with ice cubes. Garnish with the orange slice.

DUBONNET COCKTAIL

As this cocktail demonstrates, Dubonnet Rouge mixes admirably with gin.

♂ small wedge of lemon
1½ ounces Dubonnet Rouge
1 ounce gin
dash Angostura bitters

Rim a chilled cocktail glass with the lemon wedge. Combine the liquid ingredients in a mixing glass, with ice. Stir, and strain into the glass. Garnish with the lemon wedge, squeezing it into the drink and dropping it in.

FERRARI

The amaretto makes this light, refreshing lowball unusually sweet for a vermouth-based aperitif.

♂ lemon twist
2 ounces dry vermouth
1 ounce amaretto

Rim an old-fashioned glass with the lemon twist, and fill it with ice cubes. Pour in the vermouth and amaretto, and stir briefly.

WINE

FRENCH KISS

The French Kiss is simply an equal-parts mix of dry and sweet vermouths, over ice. If served up, it's called a Vermouth Cocktail.

2 ounces dry vermouth
2 ounces sweet vermouth
♂ lemon twist

Rim an old-fashioned glass with the lemon twist, and fill it with ice. Pour in the vermouths, and stir briefly. Garnish with the twist.

JAMAICA GLOW

This oddball—though very good—concoction is predominantly gin. But it's the red wine that gives it its distinctive taste (and mauve color), which is why it's included in the Wine chapter.

1½ ounces gin
½ ounce dry red wine
½ ounce dark rum
½ ounce orange juice

Combine ingredients in a cocktail shaker, with ice. Shake well and strain into a chilled cocktail glass.

WINE

KIR

One of the most sophisticated and attractive wine-based drinks is also one of the simplest. Go easy on the cassis, lest the drink become syrupy and cloying.

♂ lemon twist
½ teaspoon crème de cassis
chilled dry white wine

Rim a chilled white wine glass with the lemon twist. Pour the cassis into the glass, and top with the wine. Stir briefly, and garnish with the twist. (If you prefer, you may add a few ice cubes to the drink before pouring in the cassis and wine.)

LILLET AND SODA

This concoction—light, delicate, and delectable—is as sensational as it is simple—a definite *Drinkology* favorite.

4 ounces chilled Lillet Blanc
2 ice cubes
splash of soda or seltzer
♂ small orange wedge

Place the ice cubes—no more than two!—in a chilled white wine glass, and pour in the Lillet. Add a splash of soda (or seltzer). Squeeze the orange wedge into the drink, and drop it in.

WINE

POMPIER COCKTAIL

Drinkology's version of this cocktail uses Lillet rather than the dry vermouth recommended by many sources. We consider our substitution a stroke of genius.

♂ lemon twist
2½ ounces Lillet Blanc
½ ounce gin
½ ounce crème de cassis

Rim a chilled cocktail glass with the lemon twist. Combine the other ingredients in a mixing glass, with ice. Stir, and strain into the cocktail glass. Garnish with the twist.

PORT SANGAREE

This sangaree is simpler than most such drinks—just port, sweetened up with a little simple syrup, iced, and dusted with nutmeg.

4 ounces ruby port
1 ounce simple syrup
freshly grated nutmeg

Combine the port and simple syrup in a mixing glass, with ice. Stir, and strain into a large red wine glass filled with ice cubes. Sprinkle nutmeg on top.

WINE

RED WINE COOLER

 Here's a summertime drink for those who like red wine. (Don't use expensive wine in this; a simple, decent, cheap shiraz or merlot will do fine.)

♦ lemon twist
about 4 ounces dry red wine
about 4 ounces lemon-lime soda

Rim a highball glass with the lemon twist, and fill it with ice. Pour in the wine and soda (equal parts), and garnish with the twist.

REVERSE MARTINI

 This cocktail, also called the Upside-Down Martini, may be a Dry Martini lover's nightmare, but it was the favorite drink of the late, great Julia Child. Make sure it's made with a very fresh French dry vermouth.

2 ounces dry vermouth
½ ounce dry gin
♦ lemon twist

Rim a white wine glass with the twist. Put three or four ice cubes in the glass, pour in the vermouth and gin, and stir briefly. Drop the twist into the glass.

WINE

SANGRIA

This simple but yummy sangria recipe comes *Drinkology's* way from our old friend Randy Sonderman. Randy's one of the best cooks we know, so it's not surprising that this brew—a superb complement to a Spanish or Mexican meal—is so good. (And, yes, it does call for a full cup of Cointreau or—if you can't afford that extravagance—triple sec.)

1 lemon, cut into four or five thick slices
1 lime, cut into four or five thick slices
1 orange, cut into four or five thick slices
1 cup Cointreau or triple sec
1 bottle rioja (Spanish red wine)
10 or 12 ice cubes

Place the citrus slices in a large glass or ceramic pitcher, and pour in the Cointreau. Carefully muddle the fruit and liqueur, smashing the fruit slightly. Add the rioja and ice cubes, and stir. Refrigerate for an hour. Serve in red wine glasses. Makes about 6 six-ounce servings.

SHERRY COCKTAIL

This is a pleasant variation on straight cream sherry. Don't neglect the orange peel; its aroma adds a hint of complexity to this otherwise very straightforward drink.

↻ orange peel
2½ ounces cream sherry
2 dashes Angostura or Peychaud's bitters

Rim a chilled cocktail glass with the orange peel. Combine the sherry and bitters in a mixing glass, with ice. Stir, and strain into the glass. Garnish with the peel.

SHERRY SANGAREE

The term *sangaree* comes from a root word meaning "bloody"; this simple Sherry Sangaree is bloody good.

↻ lemon twist
4 ounces dry sherry
¾ ounce Cointreau or triple sec
1 ounce simple syrup

Rim a large red wine glass with the lemon twist, and fill it with ice cubes. Combine the sherry, Cointreau, and simple syrup in a mixing glass, with ice. Stir, and strain into the glass. Garnish with the twist.

WINE

VERMOUTH CASSIS

Cassis blends terrifically well with light, dry wines of every sort—aromatic, sparkling, and still. Here's a classic highball.

☌ lemon twist
2½ ounces dry vermouth
½ ounce crème de cassis
club soda or seltzer

Rim a collins or highball glass with the lemon twist, and fill it with ice cubes. Pour in the vermouth and cassis, and top with soda (or seltzer). Stir briefly, and garnish with the twist.

WASHINGTON COCKTAIL

If all those Moscow Mules, London Fogs, and Singapore Slings are making you feel xenophobic, come on home to a Washington Cocktail.

1½ ounces dry vermouth
½ ounce brandy
½ teaspoon powdered sugar
2 dashes Peychaud's or Angostura bitters

Combine ingredients in a cocktail shaker, with ice. Shake well, and strain into a chilled cocktail glass.

WHITE WINE SPRITZER

The Spritzer is endlessly popular among those who claim to be watching their weight. Coincidentally, it's also a refreshing way to enjoy white wine. The drink is especially successful with light, inexpensive Italian whites like Pinot Grigio and San Gimignano.

♂ lemon twist
about 6 ounces dry white wine
club soda or seltzer

Rim a highball glass with the lemon twist, and fill it with ice cubes. Pour in the wine, stopping when the glass is about two-thirds full. Top with soda (or seltzer). Garnish with the twist.

WINE

Frozen and
Blended Drinks

MANY OF THE MIXED DRINKS ENJOYED TODAY ORIGINATED IN the 1800s or even earlier, though it's almost always difficult to pinpoint the moment of their creation. We can date the origin of the frozen drink much more precisely, however. Why? Because frozen drinks' existence depends on the invention of the blender, and the first reliable, commercially viable blender wasn't produced until 1937, when inventor Fred Osius—with the financial backing of a choral-group leader named Fred Waring—presented his newfangled gizmo to a convention of restaurateurs in Chicago. Mr. Waring and his singers—the Pennsylvanians—long ago fell into the dustbin of pop culture history, but the maestro's name lives on in the Waring Blender.

Waring himself was a teetotaling, carrot-and-celery-juice-type guy, but bartenders were among the earliest enthusiasts of the device, and they were soon using their wiles to dream up an enormous variety of ice cream– and crushed ice–based delights. They created some never-before-tasted concoctions, but they also turned their sights toward adapting the recipes of a number of drinks that had begun life as shaken cocktails—the Brandy Alexander, the Daiquiri, the Piña Colada—to the new, frostier regime.

Nearly seven decades after Messrs. Osius and Waring unveiled their "Miracle Mixer," there are thousands of blender-drink recipes. Nearly every bar, it seems, has its own specialty—a Mango Margarita, a Kiwi Fruit Daiquiri, or whatever. (For all we know, there's probably a bartender out there somewhere working to perfect a Green Tea Ice Cream and Sake Frappé.) Our space is limited, so *Drinkology* must settle for presenting a representative sampling of frozen and blended drinks selected to appeal to a wide range of tastes. One (the Vanilla Thrilla) we created ourselves. It's easy to do, once you have the basic principles down.

BREAKING THE ICE

In making frozen and blended drinks, it's essential to have the right equipment. The "right equipment" means a sturdy, professional-caliber blender capable of grinding ice. If your kitchen blender isn't that powerful, you can still create frozen drinks, but you *must* crush the ice before adding it to the mix. To do so, you can either employ an ice crusher—there are numerous such electric and manually operated machines on the market—*or* you can pulverize the ice the old-fashioned way by spreading out a kitchen towel, emptying a tray of ice cubes onto it, folding the towel over the ice, and hammering the package with a mallet until the ice is evenly crushed. That's a lot of work, though; it's hard on the wrist, the ear drums, the towel, and—perhaps—the countertop. (It's also a pain to transfer the crushed ice

FROZEN

into the blender.) So if you're intending to create frozen drinks more often than once in a Blue Margarita moon, you'll be wise to invest in a professional bar blender or, at the least, a mechanical ice crusher.

The principles of creating frozen drinks are simple, but success demands that they be followed to the letter. Here they are:

- Use fresh, clean-tasting ice. If the ice you're using has been loitering for weeks in your not-recently-cleaned freezer, your Banana Daiquiri is likely to taste a bit "off."

- Speaking of "off," do make sure the blender is *turned* off when you begin.

- Place the other ingredients (liquor, other liquid ingredients, fruit, ice cream, whatever) in the blender before adding the ice. If the drink calls for fruit or ice cream, purée this mixture briefly, turn the blender off, *then* add the ice. (And do make sure that the lid is on the blender whenever it's in operation.)

- After you've added the ice, turn the blender onto the lowest speed first; after two or three seconds, increase the speed to medium, then high. About ten or, at the most, fifteen seconds total should be sufficient to thoroughly blend the drink.

- Turn the blender off before removing the carafe from the pedestal and pouring the drink.

Do note that the recipes that follow are necessarily a bit inexact—especially regarding the measurements for ice, which are given in cups or half-cups. These measures are for *crushed* ice; if you're using whole cubes, you'll have to increase the amounts somewhat, since ice cubes can't be tightly packed into a measuring cup. You may need to do a couple of test runs to ensure that the drinks you produce are full-flavored, cold enough, and free of ice chunks but not too soupy. Also, most of these recipes (the exceptions are noted) were designed to fill a large cocktail glass or a margarita glass. Frozen drinks, by the way, are often best drunk through a straw; a few of the ice cream–based concoctions may require a spoon, as well. (For additional blended drinks, see the recipes for batidas, pages 224–225.)

Anna Banana

This rates among the best banana-flavored frozen drinks.

1½ ounces vodka
½ ripe banana, cut into chunks
½ ounce fresh lime juice
½ ounce simple syrup
1 teaspoon orgeat syrup or almond syrup
½ cup crushed ice
⚶ lime slice

Combine vodka, banana, lime juice, and syrups in a blender. Purée briefly. Add the ice and blend until smooth. Pour into a chilled cocktail glass, and garnish with the lime slice.

FROZEN

BANANA DAIQUIRI

The invention of the blender permitted Daiquiri lovers to go bananas.

1½ ounces light rum
½ ounce Cointreau or triple sec
1 ripe banana, cut into chunks
¾ ounce fresh lime juice
1 teaspoon simple syrup
½ cup crushed ice
⚘ lime slice

Combine rum, Cointreau, banana, lime juice, and simple syrup in a blender. Purée briefly. Add the ice and blend until smooth. Pour into a chilled cocktail glass, and garnish with the lime slice.

BLUE HAWAIIAN

Elvis, if he's alive somewhere, is probably slurping one of these.

1 ounce light rum
1 ounce blue curaçao
2 ounces pineapple juice
1 ounce cream of coconut
1 cup crushed ice
⚘ pineapple chunks

Combine all ingredients except pineapple chunks in a blender, and blend until smooth. Pour into a chilled margarita glass, and garnish with the pineapple chunks.

BLUE MARGARITA (FROZEN)

If wasting away in Margaritaville gets you to feelin' kinda blue, this is your cocktail.

1½ ounces white tequila
½ ounce blue curaçao
¾ ounce fresh lime juice
¼ ounce simple syrup
1 cup crushed ice

Combine ingredients in a blender, and blend until smooth. Pour into a chilled margarita glass.

BUSHWHACKER

This café-au-lait-colored concoction is like a coconutty Alexander.

1½ ounce coffee liqueur
¾ ounce gold rum
½ ounce dark crème de cacao
2 ounces heavy cream
1 ounce cream of coconut
1 cup crushed ice

Combine ingredients in a blender, and blend until smooth. Pour into a chilled margarita glass.

FROZEN

CARA SPÒSA

The name, in Italian, means "Dear Wife," but this sinful concoction seems more suited to an illicit affair.

1 ounce coffee liqueur
¾ ounce Cointreau or triple sec
½ ounce heavy cream
½ cup crushed ice

Combine ingredients in a blender, and blend until smooth. Pour into a chilled cocktail glass.

CHERRY REPAIR KIT

Repair? This recipe does a Humpty-Dumpty number on the cherries, but you don't have to worry about putting them together again.

¾ ounce amaretto
¾ ounce white crème de cacao
1 scoop vanilla ice cream
6 maraschino cherries, stems removed
½ ounce maraschino cherry syrup (from the jar)
½ cup crushed ice
♼ maraschino cherry

Combine amaretto, crème de cacao, ice cream, de-stemmed cherries, and cherry syrup in a blender. Purée very briefly. Add ice, and blend until smooth. Pour into a chilled cocktail glass, and garnish with the additional cherry.

FROZEN

CHI-CHI

The Chi-Chi (pronounced "shee-shee") is just a frozen Piña Colada that uses vodka instead of rum.

2 ounces vodka
4 ounces pineapple juice
2 ounces cream of coconut
½ cup crushed ice
⚓ pineapple and maraschino cherry "flag"

Combine vodka, pineapple juice, cream of coconut, and ice in a blender, and blend until smooth. Pour into a large, chilled red wine glass, and garnish with the flag (pineapple chunks and maraschino cherries skewered on a cocktail spear or toothpick).

CHOCOLATE BLACK RUSSIAN

If they'd had this in their arsenal, the Soviets would have conquered the world.

1½ ounces vodka
1 ounce coffee liqueur
1 scoop chocolate ice cream
1 scoop vanilla ice cream
½ cup crushed ice

Combine vodka, coffee liqueur, and ice cream in a blender. Purée briefly. Add the ice, and blend until smooth. Pour into a chilled cocktail glass.

FROZEN

CRANBERRY COOLER

Whiskey lovers can enjoy frozen cocktails, too. This one's light and fluffy—and a very pretty pink.

1½ ounces Canadian blended whiskey
1½ ounces cranberry juice
½ ounce lemon juice
1 teaspoon simple syrup
1 cup crushed ice

Combine ingredients in a blender, and blend until smooth. Pour into a chilled cocktail glass.

DAIQUIRI (FROZEN)

Q: Why was it necessary to invent the electric blender?
A: So that the Frozen Daiquiri could be created.

1½ ounces light rum
½ ounce Cointreau or triple sec
¾ ounce fresh lime juice
1 teaspoon simple syrup
1 cup crushed ice
⌁ lime slice

Combine all ingredients except lime slice in a blender, and blend until smooth. Pour into a chilled margarita glass, and garnish with the lime slice.

FROZEN

DEATH BY CHOCOLATE

Just a taste of this *Drinkology* favorite will send you directly to heaven.

1 ounce Bailey's Irish Cream
½ ounce dark crème de cacao
½ ounce vodka
1 scoop chocolate ice cream
1 cup crushed ice
whipped cream
☙ chocolate sprinkles

Combine Bailey's, crème de cacao, vodka, and ice cream in a blender. Purée briefly. Add ice, and blend until smooth. Pour into a chilled margarita glass. Garnish with a dollop of whipped cream and chocolate sprinkles.

FROZEN CAPPUCCINO

This one ain't on Starbucks' menu.

½ ounce Bailey's Irish Cream
½ ounce coffee liqueur
½ ounce Frangelico
1 scoop vanilla ice cream
¼ ounce heavy cream
½ cup crushed ice

Combine Bailey's, coffee liqueur, Frangelico, ice cream, and cream in a blender. Purée briefly. Add the ice, and blend until smooth. Pour into a chilled cocktail glass.

FROZEN

A Nod to Nog

Eggnog tends to make *Drinkology* a little queasy, but we can't ignore the many devotees of this de-rigueur holiday beverage. Two versions are offered: a traditional nog (opposite), and a (to our taste, better) blender version, below.

Ice Cream Eggnog

 This recipe was contributed by *Drinkology* taste-tester Betsy Keller's mom, Betty. Unlike traditional eggnog, it requires no raw eggs.

6 scoops eggnog ice cream
3 ounces bourbon
3 ounces brandy
3 ounces dark rum
6 ounces half-and-half
freshly grated nutmeg

Combine all ingredients except nutmeg in a blender, and blend until smooth. Pour into chilled punch cups (or old-fashioned glasses) and sprinkle a little grated nutmeg into each. The recipe makes about eight 4-ounce servings. (If you wish, you may refrigerate the eggnog, in the blender carafe, for a few hours before serving.)

FROZEN

TRADITIONAL EGGNOG

 Here's a serviceable traditional recipe.

6 egg yolks
½ cup sugar
1 quart milk
2 cups heavy cream
6 ounces bourbon, chilled
6 ounces dark rum, chilled
6 egg whites
an additional ¼ cup sugar
freshly grated nutmeg

In a large bowl, beat the egg yolks, gradually adding the half-cup of sugar as you beat. When the yolks are light in color and the sugar has been thoroughly dissolved, add the milk, cream, bourbon, and rum, and mix. In a separate bowl, beat the egg whites together with the quarter-cup of sugar until stiff peaks form. Fold the beaten whites into the egg-yolk mixture, continuing to gently fold until the texture is even. Ladle into punch cups, garnishing each with a sprinkle of grated nutmeg. Makes about sixteen 4-ounce servings. (If you wish, you may refrigerate the eggnog for a few hours before serving.)

FROZEN

FROZEN FUZZY

This frozen variation on the Fuzzy Navel (see page 264) looks sensational in a champagne flute.

1 ounce peach schnapps
½ ounce Cointreau or triple sec
½ ounce orange juice
¼ ounce grenadine
splash of lemon-lime soda
crushed ice

Combine ingredients in a blender, adding just enough ice to reach the level of the liquid. Blend until smooth, and pour into a chilled champagne flute.

ICE CREAM ALEXANDER

This recipe comes *Drinkology*'s way from our old pal (and redoubtable mixologist) Betsy Keller; it's her personal take on a classic blender concoction.

1½ ounces brandy
¼ ounce dark crème de cacao
2 scoops vanilla ice cream
½ cup crushed ice
freshly grated nutmeg

Combine brandy, crème de cacao, and ice cream in a blender. Purée briefly. Add the ice, and blend until smooth. Pour into a chilled cocktail glass, and sprinkle nutmeg on top.

FROZEN

MARGARITA (FROZEN)

 This fabulous recipe for making a batch of frozen Magaritas comes *Drinkology*'s way from Joseph Ligammari and Frank Verlizzo, via our mutual friend Ramona Ponce. Use whole ice cubes only if you have a commercial-grade blender capable of crushing ice; otherwise, you must crush the ice before adding it to the blender carafe. The recipe makes enough to fill four to six margarita glasses, depending on their size.

♣ 4 to 6 lime wedges
salt (optional)
1 12-ounce container frozen limeade concentrate (do not thaw)
about 8 ounces white tequila
about 4 ounces Cointreau
2 standard trays of ice cubes

Rim each margarita glass with a lime wedge and, if desired, salt. (Reserve the lime wedges.) Spoon the frozen limeade in the carafe of a commercial-grade blender. Fill the limeade container about two-thirds full with tequila, add Cointreau to fill the container completely, then pour the liquor into the carafe. Add the ice cubes and blend until smooth. Pour into the prepared glasses, and garnish each with a lime wedge.

FROZEN

MINT DAIQUIRI

Mint's not just a flavor; mint oil actually produces a sensation that the tongue "interprets" as cooling. This cocktail's combination of mint and ice makes for a very chilly refresher on a hot summer evening.

2 ounces light rum
¼ ounce green crème de menthe
4 medium-size fresh mint leaves
½ ounce fresh lime juice
1 teaspoon simple syrup
1 cup crushed ice
♣ sprig of fresh mint

Combine rum, crème de menthe, mint leaves, lime juice, and simple syrup in a blender. Purée briefly. Add the ice, and blend until smooth. Pour into a chilled margarita glass, and garnish with the mint sprig.

FROZEN

MISSISSIPPI MUD

The sweet, inimitable flavor of Southern Comfort dominates this ice cream–based confection.

1½ ounces coffee liqueur
1½ ounces Southern Comfort
2 scoops vanilla ice cream
½ cup crushed ice
♣ chocolate sprinkles or shaved chocolate

Combine coffee liqueur, Southern Comfort, and ice cream in a blender. Purée briefly. Add the ice, and blend until smooth. Pour (or, if necessary, spoon) into a chilled cocktail glass. Garnish with chocolate.

PEACH DAQUIRI

Frozen Daiquiris can be made with virtually any kind of soft, blendable fruit. Here's a peach-based variation. Use a ripe, fresh peach if possible—but note that a canned peach is better than an unripe, pithy, tasteless fresh one. Substituting tequila for the rum makes this drink a Peach Margarita.

1½ ounces light rum
½ ounce peach schnapps
¾ ounce fresh lime juice
½ fresh peach, peeled, pitted and cut into a few slices
    (or ½ canned peach)
1 teaspoon simple syrup
1 cup crushed ice

Combine rum, schnapps, lime juice, peach, and simple syrup in a blender. Purée briefly. Add the ice, and blend until smooth. Pour into a chilled margarita glass.

FROZEN

PEPPERMINT TWIST

This fabulous concoction is a *Drinkology* favorite. If you have the energy, you might consider rimming the glass by moistening the lip with some crème de cacao and then upending the glass onto a small plate on which you've spread ground-up peppermint candies. (Grind them in a clean coffee grinder.)

1½ ounces peppermint schnapps
½ ounce white crème de cacao
2 scoops vanilla ice cream
½ cup crushed ice
♪ peppermint stick

Combine the schnapps, crème de cacao, and ice cream in a blender. Purée briefly. Add the ice, and blend until smooth. Pour into a large, chilled red wine glass. Garnish with the peppermint stick.

FROZEN

PIÑA COLADA (FROZEN)

It's doubtless true that most of the Piña Coladas served up in today's bars are of the frozen ilk. *Drinkology* prefers the original, more robustly flavored, shaken version of this quintessential tropical cooler (see page 209), though we grudgingly admit that a frozen Colada is awfully good when you're doing some poolside lounging.

2 ounces light or gold rum
4 ounces pineapple juice
2 ounces cream of coconut
½ cup crushed ice
⚘ pineapple and maraschino cherry "flag"

Combine rum, pineapple juice, cream of coconut, and ice in a blender, and blend until smooth. Pour into a large, chilled red wine glass, and garnish with the flag (pineapple chunks and maraschino cherries skewered on a cocktail spear or toothpick).

STRAWBERRY ALEXANDRA

 God, is this thing good. Please, please, *please* use fresh strawberries in this dreamy confection. (If you *must* have one of these but can only find frozen berries, increase the number to six or eight.)

1 ounce brandy
1 ounce white crème de cacao
4 medium-size fresh ripe strawberries, hulled
1 scoop vanilla ice cream
½ cup crushed ice
♦ strawberry

Combine brandy, crème de cacao, strawberries, and ice cream in a blender. Purée briefly. Add the ice, and blend until smooth. Garnish with the additional strawberry.

FROZEN

STRAWBERRY DAIQUIRI

And here's a frozen Daiquiri that uses strawberries. If you have no option but frozen strawberries, increase the number of berries to six or eight (frozen strawberries are not only less flavorful than fresh, they're also generally smaller). Substituting tequila for the rum makes this a Strawberry Margarita.

1½ ounces light rum
½ ounce Cointreau or strawberry liqueur
¾ ounce fresh lime juice
4 medium-size fresh strawberries, hulled
1 teaspoon simple syrup
1 cup crushed ice
⚘ strawberry

Combine the rum, Cointreau (or strawberry liqueur), lime juice, strawberries, and simple syrup in a blender. Purée briefly. Add the ice, and blend until smooth. Pour into a chilled margarita glass. Garnish with the additional strawberry.

FROZEN

VANILLA THRILLA

Chocolate lovers have lots of frozen drinks to choose from. *Drinkology* thought vanilla fans ought to have one to call their own, so we invented this concoction.

1 ounce vanilla-flavored vodka
½ ounce brandy
½ ounce light rum
1 scoop vanilla ice cream
½ cup crushed ice

Combine vodka, brandy, rum, and ice cream in a blender. Purée briefly. Add the ice, and blend until smooth. Pour into a chilled cocktail glass.

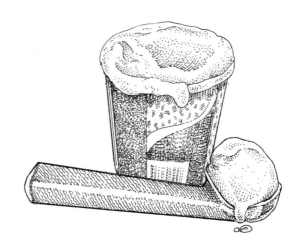

FROZEN

Hot Drinks

H OT ALCOHOLIC BEVERAGES HAVE A TWOFOLD PURPOSE: TO warm you in the body *and* the soul simultaneously (or, in the case of coffee-based drinks, to keep you wide awake while snookering you).

They've been around for a long time. Toddies—drinks in which liquor and other ingredients are added to hot water (or, sometimes, tea)—were being quaffed in Great Britain and in England's North American colonies at least as early as the eighteenth century. *Toddy*, in case you're interested, has one of the strangest etymologies *Drinkology* has come across. Originally, the word—from a South Asian root—stood for booze made from fermented palm-tree sap. It's vastly unclear how the term got transmuted to mean the kind of drink—whiskey and hot water, say—that some old India hand might have sipped while mulling over his memories in front of the fire on a drizzly night in Edinburgh. But it did.

Toddies weren't the only hot drinks being imbibed back in those days of auld lang syne. On both sides of the Atlantic, innkeepers were in the habit of whipping up steaming, frothy concoctions called *flips* for their road-weary, bone-chilled clientele. These drinks consisted of a sugar, egg, and cream batter into which a hot poker, straight from the hearth, was thrust. A shot of brandy, rum, or whiskey was then added to the sizzling brew. To the contemporary ear, this sounds about as appetizing as having a wound cauterized. The flip does survive in two modern forms: a series of cold cocktails—generally disdained by *Drinkology*'s taste-testers—to which a whole raw egg is added before shaking, as well as the well-known hot eggnog–type drink called the Tom and Jerry (page 359).

It seems that hot alcoholic beverages utilizing coffee have a briefer heritage. The best-known coffee-based drink—Irish Coffee (page 355)—was created in the early 1940s by a fellow named Joe Sheridan, a chef at the airport in Foynes, Ireland. Back in those pre-747 days, transatlantic air travel was rough going. You boarded a seaplane (called a flying boat) in New York, and some eighteen hours later were deposited at Foynes, on the west coast of Ireland near Limerick. By that time, having spent the better part of a day cooped up in a tiny, unpressurized cabin, you were *stiff* with cold. Sheridan came to the rescue, presenting arriving passengers with glass mugs filled with hot, sugar-sweetened coffee laced with Irish whiskey and topped with heavy cream. They were very grateful. *Drinkology* remains grateful.

One caution: if you're using glass mugs for your hot drinks, warm the glasses before pouring in the hot liquid so they won't crack.

AMARETTO TEA

Mild-flavored teas like orange pekoe and Earl Grey are best for tea-based libations. This simple concoction is very pleasant.

hot tea
2 ounces amaretto
whipped cream

Pour hot tea into a warmed Irish coffee glass or ceramic mug, leaving room at the top for the additional liquid and the cream. Add the amaretto; do not stir. Top with a dollop of whipped cream.

B&B&B

Drinkology's pal Betsy Keller—who tested and adjusted all the recipes in this chapter—needed a pick-me-up at the end of one long day's work, and invented this tasty brew.

¾ ounce Bailey's Irish Cream
¾ ounce B&B
hot coffee
whipped cream

Pour the Bailey's and B&B into a warmed Irish coffee glass or ceramic mug. Add the coffee (almost to the brim), and stir. Top with a dollop of whipped cream.

CAFÉ AMARETTO

Amaretto's almond flavor nicely complements coffee. Adding a small amount of brandy makes the brew more interesting.

1 ounce amaretto
½ ounce brandy
hot coffee
whipped cream

Pour the amaretto and brandy into a warmed Irish coffee glass or ceramic mug. Add the coffee (almost to the brim), and stir. Top with a dollop of whipped cream.

GROG (HOT)

Simple, rum-based grog is the perfect antidote to a depressing winter afternoon. For best results, use Myers's Rum or another robust, full-bodied rum.

¾ ounce honey
¾ ounce fresh lemon juice
1½ ounces Myers's Rum or other dark rum
hot water
⚘ cinnamon stick

Pour the honey into a warmed Irish coffee glass or ceramic mug. Add a splash of hot water and stir, to thin the honey. Pour in the lemon juice and rum, and fill the glass or mug with hot water. Stir, and garnish with the cinnamon stick.

HANDICAPPER

The trifecta of amaretto, Irish whiskey, and coffee makes for a winning combination.

1 ounce amaretto
1 ounce Irish whiskey
hot coffee
whipped cream

Pour the amaretto and whiskey into a warmed Irish coffee glass or ceramic mug. Add the coffee (almost to the brim), and stir. Top with a dollop of whipped cream.

HOT BRANDY ALEXANDER

Try this steaming variation on the classic Brandy Alexander (page 71) just before settling down for a long winter's nap.

1 ounce brandy
1 ounce dark crème de cacao
hot whole milk
whipped cream
freshly grated nutmeg

Pour the brandy and crème de cacao into a warmed Irish coffee glass or ceramic mug. Add the hot milk (almost to the brim), and stir. Top with a dollop of whipped cream, and sprinkle the nutmeg on the cream.

HOT BUTTERED RUM

Traditionally, Hot Buttered Rum is made with rum, sugar, and plain old hot water (with, of course, a pat of butter floated on top). If you find that recipe a tad . . . well . . . boring, feel free to substitute hot milk for the H$_2$O.

1 teaspoon brown sugar
2 ounces dark rum
hot water
1 teaspoon butter
freshly grated nutmeg

Place the brown sugar in the bottom of a warmed Irish coffee glass or ceramic mug, and add a splash of hot water, stirring until the sugar has dissolved. Pour in the rum, and fill the glass or mug with hot water. Float the butter on top, and sprinkle with nutmeg.

HOT NUTTY IRISHMAN

This recipe—a steamy variation on the well-known liqueurs-based cocktail (page 174)—goes out to all the hot, nutty Irishmen we know.

¾ ounce Bailey's Irish cream
¾ ounce Frangelico
hot coffee
whipped cream

Pour the Bailey's and Frangelico into a warmed Irish coffee glass or ceramic mug. Add the coffee (almost to the brim), and stir. Top with a dollop of whipped cream.

HOT SPIKED CHOCOLATE

Reading this recipe, you might find yourself thinking, Gee, how could this be bad? You'd be right.

1 ounce brandy
½ ounce dark crème de cacao
prepared hot chocolate
whipped cream
freshly grated nutmeg

Pour the brandy and crème de cacao into a warmed Irish coffee glass or ceramic mug. Add the hot chocolate (almost to the brim), and stir. Top with a dollop of whipped cream, and sprinkle the nutmeg on the cream.

IRISH COFFEE

This classic hot beverage still ranks as one of the best. It's well worth whipping up your own whipped cream (rather than using the canned variety) for this superb drink.

1 teaspoon brown sugar
1½ ounces Irish whiskey
hot coffee
whipped cream

Place the brown sugar in a warmed Irish coffee glass or ceramic mug, and add a splash of hot coffee, stirring until the sugar has dissolved. Add the Irish whiskey, and pour in more coffee, stopping when the glass or mug is about three-quarters full. Spoon the whipped cream on top.

JAMAICAN COFFEE

Jamaica's as famous for its coffee as for its rum. The only thing that's missing from this recipe is a reggae backbeat, so you'll have to have some Bob Marley on the iPod to complete the experience.

1 ounce Jamaican rum
1 ounce coffee liqueur
hot coffee
whipped cream

Pour the rum and coffee liqueur into a warmed Irish coffee glass or ceramic mug. Add the coffee (almost to the brim), and stir. Top with a dollop of whipped cream.

JAMES'S HOT TODDY

Here's a toddy that *Drinkology*'s author makes for himself whenever he has a bad cold. It's not a cure, but it will dress your suffering in a gauze of soothing incapacitation.

½ lemon
1½ ounces bourbon
hot tea
1 tablespoon honey

Squeeze the half-lemon into a large ceramic mug, and drop in the hull. Pour in the bourbon, followed by the hot tea, filling the mug almost to the brim. Add the honey, and stir.

MEXICAN COFFEE

The small amount of tequila adds a pleasantly sharp note to this concoction.

1 ounce coffee liqueur
½ ounce tequila
hot coffee
whipped cream

Pour the coffee liqueur and tequila into a warmed Irish coffee glass or ceramic mug. Add the coffee (almost to the brim), and stir. Top with a dollop of whipped cream.

MULLED WINE

 This classic hot punch is traditionally served at holiday time, though it will brighten up any winter gathering. When selecting a red wine, choose a "softer" (less tannic) red—most merlots will do just fine.

2 bottles dry red wine
½ cup dark brown sugar
12 whole cloves
4 cinnamon sticks
peel of 1 orange, cut into a long, spiraling strip
peel of 1 lemon, cut into a long, spiraling strip
2 cups ruby port
2 cups brandy

Combine the wine, sugar, cloves, cinnamon sticks, and citrus peels in a large, nonreactive cooking pot. (Do not use an aluminum pot for this recipe.) Heat on a burner set to medium high, reducing the setting to low the moment that the liquid begins to boil. Simmer for ten minutes, stirring occasionally. Add the port and brandy, and heat until the liquid begins to steam (do not allow it to boil). Ladle into heatproof mugs. Makes twelve to fourteen 6-ounce servings. (If you wish, you may transfer the mulled wine—pouring very carefully, into a large, warmed, heatproof bowl before serving.)

PEPPERMINT PATTY CAFÉ

Mint, chocolate, and coffee make a delectable *ménage*.

1 ounce peppermint schnapps
½ ounce dark crème de cacao
hot coffee
whipped cream
dash of green crème de menthe

Pour the schnapps and crème de cacao into a warmed Irish coffee glass or ceramic mug. Add the coffee (almost to the brim), and stir. Top with a dollop of whipped cream, and drizzle the crème de menthe on the cream.

RUSSIAN MONK

This unorthodox, though delicious, concoction comes *Drinkology*'s way via mixological wiz Betsy Keller.

¾ ounce Bénédictine
¾ ounce vanilla-flavored vodka
hot coffee
whipped cream
ground cinnamon

Pour the Bénédictine and vodka into a warmed Irish coffee glass or ceramic mug. Add the coffee (almost to the brim), and stir. Top with a dollop of whipped cream, and dust with the cinnamon.

SNOW BUNNY

Cointreau and hot chocolate make affable companions. Take them along on your next skiing trip (but wait till you're off the slopes to enjoy their company).

1½ ounces Cointreau
prepared hot chocolate

Pour the Cointreau into a warmed Irish coffee glass or ceramic mug. Add the coffee (almost to the brim), and stir.

TOM AND JERRY

The invention of this hot eggnog–like drink is widely credited to Jerry Thomas, a nineteenth-century mixologist who was probably the most famous bartender who ever lived.

1 egg
1 ounce brandy
1 ounce dark rum
1 teaspoon sugar
hot milk
freshly grated nutmeg

Separate the egg into two small bowls. Add the brandy and rum to the yolk and whisk until frothy. Beat the white until soft peaks form, then add the sugar and continue beating until the peaks are stiff. Gently fold the beaten egg white into the yolk-and-liquor mixture, and transfer this batter into a warmed Irish coffee glass or ceramic mug. Pour in the hot milk (almost to the brim), and sprinkle the nutmeg on top.

Glossary

The following glossary gives the meanings of a few common bartending terms that, for the most part, go undefined in the text of this book. Names of various glasses and kinds of bartending equipment are given in *Drinkology*'s first chapter (see pages 5–10 and 10–14). For more information on specific liquors, consult the chapter intros.

Alcoholic beverage: A catchall term for hooch of all kinds, including fermented beverages (beer and wine), distilled spirits (gin, vodka, whiskey, et al.), and compounded spirits (liqueurs). In the U.S., anything containing between 0.5 and 80 percent alcohol is considered an *alcoholic beverage*.

Aperitif: Derived from a Latin verb meaning "to open" (as in your palate), *aperitif* refers to any alcoholic drink taken before a meal. AROMATIZED WINES and COCKTAILS made from them are popular aperitifs.

Aromatized wines: FORTIFIED WINES to which any number of herbal flavorings have been added. All vermouths, as well as Dubonnet, Lillet, Campari, and other bottled aperitifs, are *aromatized wines*. Alcohol content ranges between 15 and 20 percent.

Bitters: A group of highly alcoholic elixirs distilled from various herbal ingredients combined with liquor. (See pages 21–23 for more information.)

Blended whiskey: In the U.S., a *blended whiskey* is legally defined as one that combines whiskeys distilled from several different grains but in which none of the component whiskeys represents more than 51 percent of the total. (Compare STRAIGHT WHISKEY.) A *blended scotch whiskey* combines the products of several (or many) SINGLE-MALT distilleries with whiskey distilled from unmalted grain. All Canadian whiskey is blended whiskey, as are most Japanese whiskeys.

Chaser: When you guzzle something immediately after downing something alcoholic, you're *chasing* it. Beer and club soda are popular chasers.

Cocktail: Though the word is often used loosely to refer to any MIXED DRINK, a *cocktail*, technically speaking, is a drink that is either shaken or stirred and is served UP, in a cocktail glass.

Condiment: Any of the ingredients used, generally in small amounts, to "season" a mixed drink. BITTERS, grenadine, simple syrup, and Tabasco sauce are examples of *condiments*.

Dash: The equivalent of $1/16$ of a teaspoon. But you're mixing drinks, not pharmaceuticals, so don't make yourself crazy.

Dry: When discussing wine, *dry* is the opposite of sweet, and indicates that the yeast consumed nearly all of the sugar in the mash during fermentation. In cocktail-speak, "dry" often refers to drinks incorporating a small amount of dry vermouth.

Flag: Pieces of fruit (often pineapple chunks and maraschino cherries) skewered on a cocktail spear or toothpick and used to garnish a drink. Do not hang this flag out the window on July 4.

Fortified wines: Wines sweetened with brandy, sometimes called *dessert wines*. Sherry, port, and Madeira are all *fortified wines*. Alcohol content ranges between 14 and 24 percent.

Garnish: A mixed drink's "decoration." Fruit and spice garnishes subtly influence the drink's flavor.

Highball: Any iced drink served in a tall (highball) glass. The term is sometimes used to mean a tall, iced drink combining whiskey and club soda or other soft drink (e.g., ginger ale).

Lowball: You guessed it—any drink served with ice in a short glass.

Mixed drink: Though it can refer to any drink combining two or more beverages, *mixed drink* usually means an alcoholic drink containing two or more kinds of liquor, or one or more kinds of liquor as well as CONDIMENTS and/or MIXERS.

Mixer: Any nonalcoholic beverage—juice, soda, or just plain water—combined with liquor to make a MIXED DRINK.

Neat: Liquor served in a glass all by its lonesome. No ice, no mixers, no other liquors, no nothin'.

Perfect: You may be a perfect cocktail-party host, but your Manhattans and Rob Roys are not *perfect* unless they contain equal parts dry and sweet vermouth.

Proof: A legal term denoting a liquor's alcohol content by volume. In the U.S., a liquor's *proof* is equal to the percentage of the alcohol multiplied by two (90-proof whiskey contains 45 percent alcohol by volume).

Rocks; on the rocks: *Rocks* are ice cubes. Drinks *on the rocks* are served over ice. But you knew this already.

Shooter: Shots or shot-size MIXED DRINKS that are downed in a single gulp, *shooters* are popular with the get-drunk-quick crowd.

Single-barrel bourbon: Bourbon is aged in barrels, and then the contents of the individual barrels are blended. *Single-barrel bourbon* is unblended, but, alas, fairly rare. The term is often misapplied to what are actually SMALL-BATCH BOURBONS. (The term *single barrel* is also applied to certain premium rye whiskeys.)

Single-malt scotch: The product of a single scotch distillery, made only from the malt of one type of grain. Prized by connoisseurs, highly distinctive single malts are inappropriate for mixed drinks.

Small-batch bourbon: Premium bourbon distilled in small quantities (generally fewer than 20 barrels); *small-batch bourbons* are the bourbon world's equivalent to SINGLE-MALT SCOTCHES. (The term *small batch* is also applied to certain premium rye whiskeys.).

Sparkling wine: Effervescent wine whose bubbles result from a second fermentation or carbonation. Champagne is the best-known *sparkling wine*; *cava, Sekt,* and *spumante* are the sparklers of Spain, Germany, and Italy, respectively.

Spirit: Synonymous with liquor, a *spirit* is any alcoholic beverage produced by distillation. Vodka and rum are spirits; beer and wine, which are fermented but not distilled, are not.

Splash: More than a DASH but less than an ounce. Use your judgment.

Still wine: Everything but the bubbly stuff.

Straight: A liquor served *straight* is undiluted by any condiment or mixer; more loosely, the term is used for ON-THE-ROCKS drinks that contain only ice, one kind of liquor, and perhaps a SPLASH of soda or water.

Straight whiskey: In the U.S., at least 51 percent of the spirits in any bottle labeled *straight whiskey* must have been distilled from a single grain. Bourbons, ryes, Tennessee whiskeys, and sour mash whiskeys are all straight whiskeys.

Up; up glass: A drink that's served *up* is one that's poured into a stemmed cocktail glass, or *up glass,* without ice. (Some mixed drinks—e.g., Manhattans, White Russians—can be served up or ON THE ROCKS.)

Zest: The peel of a citrus fruit.

Drinkology Favorites

Drinkology's taste-testers are pleased with each and every one of the recipes presented in the book, but there are certain concoctions that just set our hearts on fire. Here's the list of our absolute favorites.

FAVORITES

Index

INDEX

ABOUT THE AUTHOR

James Waller is the author of the Drinkology series of books, which also includes *Drinkology Wine* and *Drinkology Beer*. He has been known to have a cocktail or two in the evening.